Our Stories

Black Families in Early Dallas

Edited by George Keaton Jr.
and Judith Garrett Segura

Number 7 in the Texas Local Series

University of North Texas Press
Denton, Texas

Remembering Black Dallas, founded in 2015 by George Keaton Jr., PhD, acquired all assets of Black Dallas Remembered, publisher of the two books from which this book is edited, becoming the formal successor of the original organization. The original titles and dates follow:

First African American Families of Dallas:
Creative Survival
Volume I
Dr. Mamie L. McKnight, editor
(Black Dallas Remembered, 1987)
and
African American Families and Settlements of Dallas:
On the Inside Looking Out
Volume II
Dr. Mamie L. McKnight, editor
(Black Dallas Remembered, 1990)

Permissions:
University of North Texas Press
1155 Union Circle #311336
Denton, TX 76203-5017

The paper used in this book meets the minimum requirements of the American National Standard for Permanence of Paper for Printed Library Materials, z39.48.1984. Binding materials have been chosen for durability.

Library of Congress Cataloging-in-Publication Data

Keaton, George, Jr., 1956– editor. | Segura, Judith Garrett, 1944– editor.
  Our stories : black families in early Dallas / edited by George Keaton Jr. and Judith Garrett Segura.
      pages cm
  Includes bibliographical references and index.
  ISBN-13 978-1-57441-882-8 (cloth)
  ISBN-13 978-1-57441-888-0 (ebook)
  1. African American families—Texas—Dallas—History. 2. Free African Americans—Texas—Dallas—History. 3. African American leadership—Texas—Dallas—History. 4. Dallas (Tex—Ethnic relations—History. 5. LCGFT: Oral histories.

  F394.D219 N457 2022
  306.85/08996073077642812--dc23
                            2022013417

Number 7 in the Texas Local Series

The electronic edition of this book was made possible by the support of the Vick Family Foundation. Typeset by vPrompt eServices.

"With the ending of the slave institution and the passage of many decades of Black ownership of the land, Black pride developed to the highest level. The ex-slaves purchased land, built homes, raised their children, erected their educational and religious facilities, educated their children, and profited from their labor. They walked proudly and taught the new generations to strive to become whatever they wished to be. Some continued as farmers, while others sought careers in education, medicine, law, engineering, and other sciences. The ex-slaves and their descendants made great strides during this period and laid a firm foundation for those who will follow in their ancestral footsteps."

Eva Partee McMillan, 1921–2021, the great-granddaughter of Moriah, who was enslaved in the James K. Polk household. The community celebrated with her on her 100th birthday in May 2021 before her passing in September 2021.

Contents

Illustrations

Editors' Preface

"Rather than emulating the oppressor, whose role in society is
inevitably one of self-destruction, let all who dare to dream of
a better world consider the survivalist perspective reflected in
the lives of these pioneer families. The writers' views do not
deny the horrors of slavery and a segregated society here in
Dallas, but they reveal a celebration of triumph over adversity in a hostile environment and the maintenance of a proud
African American heritage."

Mamie L. McKnight, PhD (1929–2018), educator,
counselor, preservationist, community historian

Our Stories: Black Families in Early Dallas is a republication of the
timeless content of two cherished books produced by Black Dallas
Remembered under the direction of Dr. Mamie L. McKnight.
Volume I, *First African American Families of Dallas: Creative
Survival*, was produced in 1987. Volume II, *African American
Families and Settlements of Dallas: On the Inside Looking Out*,
was produced in 1990, and both have been out of print for more
than thirty years and difficult to find.

Those two publications were originally exhibition catalogs
produced to accompany events at the time of their publication,
however they contain much valuable information of timeless interest.
Together the two books contain the memoirs of many of Dallas's earliest African American families, written by their descendants. Additionally, along with the family stories the family members provided
descriptions of many of the earliest African American communities, in
which their families lived. The second volume contains transcripts of
a few oral histories recorded in 1988 with descendants of the earliest
families, which enrich the unique perspective of this history.

This new publication, *Our Stories: Black Families in Early
Dallas*, presents the stories with little alteration, except in organization of the material and in clarifying a writer's meaning where

helpful. Additionally, *Our Stories* includes editorial notes, providing information from more recent research, if available, regarding the original subjects.

Keep in mind as you read the stories that references to events current at the time of writing the original text refer to the late 1980s, when these materials were collected for publication. Furthermore, references to living individuals similarly refer to the time the entries were written. Similarly, you will find use of the terms "pioneer" and "settler" throughout the text, which was written years before the current conversation emerged about respecting Indigenous/Native American experience by avoiding these terms. Additionally, those terms today might be considered inappropriate when used for people who had little or no say in the circumstances of their lives.

The stories in this book are, in many cases, based entirely on the family historian's memories of the stories told by parents and grandparents, most of which were based on their memories of earlier stories. Many of the stories had not been written down until the call went out in 1984 for contributions to the original books. Many of the contributors to the books were elderly in 1988.

The publisher of this new volume, Remembering Black Dallas, Inc., was founded by Dr. George Keaton Jr. in 2015 as a nonprofit organization to be the successor of Black Dallas Remembered, which was founded in 1984 by the Dallas Historical Society and the late Dr. Mamie L. McKnight but had been inactive for more than ten years.

The mission of Remembering Black Dallas is the same as its predecessor organization: to research, preserve, document, and promote the history of African American life and culture in Dallas and the surrounding cities, from the earliest days.

After Remembering Black Dallas, Inc. applied successfully to the State of Texas for the intellectual and other properties of Black Dallas Remembered, it undertook to publish this volume. *Our Stories: Black Families in Early Dallas* presents to new generations the intimate stories passed down over time in oral traditions and captured in writing within the two original publications.

It has been our great honor to produce this manuscript for readers of today. Our intent throughout has been to further the hopes of Dr. Mamie McKnight and her many volunteers to "piece together a great uncontaminated mosaic that would right, and write, the saga of their heritage from a fresh perspective."

As educational materials are developed over time to teach the more complex and complete history of our country and our state, *Our Stories* will help fill some of the gaps in our quests to know and understand what it was like when our forebears were growing up. Our aim is to cultivate understanding.

George Keaton Jr., PhD
Judith Garrett Segura
2022

Acknowledgments

First, we must gratefully acknowledge the wisdom and commitment of the members of Black Dallas Remembered, who collected these remarkable, inspiring stories more than thirty years ago, preserving in them the history of Dallas. Their efforts were the foundation for this memorial to dignity and courage, which otherwise would not have been possible.

Next, we must thank Ron Chrisman, Director of the University of North Texas Press, who responded to our manuscript with encouragement and shepherded us through the initial stages of approvals with great kindness. Carolyn Elerding, Managing Editor, then patiently guided and coached us through the complexities of polishing the manuscript for ultimate publication.

We thank Dr. David Grear for his expertise in creating the map locating the early communities, and lastly, we thank our friends and family members for their advice, encouragement, and for reading drafts throughout the project.

George Keaton Jr. &
Judith Garrett Segura

Introduction: Early Settlements and First African American Families of Dallas

By Dr. Mamie L. McKnight

1987 Black Dallas Remembered Steering Committee

Black Dallas Remembered was conceived in 1984 by several life-long residents to examine and systematically document the history of African American life and culture in Dallas. Founding members were L. A. Bedford, Phillipa Butler, Mamie McKnight, Donald Payton, and Peggy Riddle.

The rewarding experience by the Steering Committee and other volunteers during the past year ballooned from an idea into a full-blown community-wide project. Many excited African American Dallas residents were involved. The project focused on families whose ancestors settled at least sixty years earlier. This roughly covered the period from the 1850s through the mid-1920s.

The response to the appeal for family histories, pictures, artifacts, and documents was overwhelming. More than sixty families brought boxes of scrapbooks, pictures, books, and other family treasures for inclusion.[1]

---

1. The archives of Black Dallas Remembered were donated to the African American Museum of Dallas in 2020 by Dr. McKnight's daughter, Ginger McKnight Chavers.—Eds.

It must be understood that the information presented here barely touches the surface in documenting the many, many outstanding contributions and experiences of African Americans since Dallas was chartered in 1846. However, we commend the family members who stepped forward and made this effort a tremendously successful contribution to history.

The role of the African American in the development of America has been either ignored or negatively portrayed in history. More often than not, missing from the writings about African American experiences are the positive adaptations and contributions that African Americans made and continue to make to society. More specifically, many studies continue to stereotype African American family life as poor, problem-centered, and "irrevocably inferior."

As the following stories about pioneer African American families and the communities they created in Dallas County are read, one must acknowledge and accept the fact that their moment-by-moment experiences included a struggle against racism and denied opportunity. One hopes that a deep and sensitive understanding of this fact raises readers to a level at which they can only marvel at the undiminished pursuit by African Americans for dignity and justice.

A thread running through all of the writings is a strong message that the yardstick for measuring the worth of an individual is not based on material or social success but on whether that individual is good or bad to the "family," to "kinfolk," to "humankind," and to the "community."

This collection of histories of pioneer African American families and neighborhoods of Dallas provides a unique voice from the "inside looking out." [It is the voice of] the family historians who carefully guard and cherish the memoirs of their elders and the family archives of photographs, news clippings, and deeds.

These stories represent the beginning of a movement by the descendants of pioneer Dallas families to erect permanent, historically accurate monuments to their courageous, freedom-seeking African

American ancestors who migrated to the shores of the Trinity River from the late 1840s to the mid-1920s.

They substantiate a unique sensibility possessed by those who dared, dreamed, delivered, and died together for a better way of life for their families. More importantly, they establish a pattern of action for making dreams come true—the hard, grueling work required to fulfill dreams and aspirations for present and future generations.

When the first government of Dallas was established in 1856, the city contained little more than one square mile of territory. [Many early settlers had come from Southern states, bringing along enslaved people.]

African American settlements emerged after the Civil War. Some of those early settlements became well-established cities within a city. Some of those remained and grew, while others vanished due to shifting populations and sources of livelihood.

Many of the early settlements were outside the small city of Dallas. They developed near the large farms and plantations throughout Dallas County. They grew up along the northern boundaries of White Rock Creek; in areas such as Hord's Ridge, later renamed Oak Cliff; and areas west of the Trinity. They were in what became Farmers Branch, Carrollton, Addison, Richardson, Grand Prairie, and Irving, among others.

The more centralized enclaves during this era were located primarily along the railroads and creeks and became firmly established before the turn of the [twentieth] century. One of the factors which contributed to the growth of the settlements was their geographic proximity to sources of employment. Opportunities for professional, agricultural, day labor, domestic work, and blue-collar work were available near the enclaves.

Freedman's Town, Deep Ellum, and Stringtown developed into one large mass of Black residential areas, businesses, and other well-established institutions. [The area was referred to collectively as North Dallas, and now those neighborhoods are known as Uptown,

Deep Ellum, and The Arts District, respectively]. Along the MK&T [Missouri-Kansas-Texas] Railroad line and Rock Island Railroad line was Frogtown, just north of downtown; Booker T. Washington Addition, northeast of downtown Dallas, was in the triangular wedge formed by the intersection of the H&TC [Houston & Texas Central] and MK&T Railroads; and Boggy Bayou along the Santa Fe Railroad was south of downtown and west of Lamar Street.

The communities in the northern corridor of Dallas County developed along White Rock Creek, crossing the county from the north to the southeast. The southern settlements were primarily by the Trinity River, along Five Mile Creek, and the railroads. In West Dallas and Eagle Ford, the communities grew as the railroad moved westward.

The task of Black Dallas Remembered was to identify the settlements by name. The list contains approximately thirty enclaves and is not complete. Some names represent the same area or portions thereof. To date they are Arlington Park; Bermuda Lawn; Boggy Bayou; Bonton (South Dallas); Booker T. Washington Addition; Cedar Crest; Colonial Heights; Cotton Mills Addition; Deep Ellum; Eagle Ford; Elm Thicket; Fields Addition; Five Mile Addition; Freedman's Town; Frog Town; Hamilton Park; Joppa (Joppee); Lincoln Manor; Lincoln Place; Little Egypt; Lower and Upper East Dallas; McShann Road; Mill City; North Dallas (Thomas Avenue and Hall Street); Queen City; Roosevelt Addition; Stringtown; The Bog; The Bottom; The Prairie; The Sand; Thomas Hill Community; Trinity Heights (The Heights); Trinity Valley (Cedar Valley); Upper and Lower White Rock; Vickery Addition; Wahoo Addition; Wheatley Place; and West Dallas.

According to the records that currently exist, the first African American families, without exception, followed the trails westward in search of a better way of life for themselves and others. Some of the early settlers came with the "masters" as slaves. Others came as freedmen prior to and after the Civil War. Most however, came after the war fleeing the cruel and dehumanizing vestiges of slavery throughout the South. They came by foot, by mule, by wagon, and eventually by train. They came from plantations, and they came to build new plantations.

Included among those who came westward were skilled craftsmen, farmers, entrepreneurs, educators, professionals, laborers, domestics, and railroad workers. Their unique talents were very quickly recognized and utilized throughout the community. Though relegated to restricted areas, they built highly productive and self-sustaining enclaves throughout the city. Pride in the ownership of "real" property—land—educational attainment, exceptional talents, and family security were the unmistakable barometers of success. Using their talents to serve the community comes through loud and clear as a strong value held by the early residents of the totally segregated Black communities.

Still plagued by an inability to secure full rights as citizens throughout this period, the abiding strength of the pioneers appeared to be in their unity of purpose—freedom and dignity—as descendants of a proud people. Through constant nurturance and support in their segregated and often oppressive environs, they were able to creatively pool their resources and develop thriving businesses, educational institutions, churches, homes, farms, and other entities that were necessary for group survival. As a result of their focused and united efforts, both in and outside their own communities, they made significant contributions toward the overall growth and development of the city.

Many of the players will remain anonymous and unsung. Nonetheless, each individual did his or her share toward making Dallas possible. The commonly accepted values of education, family unity, work, ownership of land, and reverence to God were the glue ingredients that bound them together and enriched the quality of their lives.

During the Texas Sesquicentennial Year, many of the descendants of these creative survivors of African American heritage made a commitment to begin the process of piecing together a great uncontaminated mosaic that would right, and write, the saga of their heritage from a fresh perspective. Their children could then learn and pass on to their own children the great survival messages of family that were passed on to them.

Rather than emulating the oppressor, whose role in society is inevitably one of self-destruction, let all who dare to dream of a better world consider the survivalist perspective reflected in the lives of these pioneer families. The writers' views do not deny the horrors of slavery and a segregated society here in Dallas, but they reveal a celebration of triumph over adversity in a hostile environment and the maintenance of a proud African American heritage.[2]

---

2. The following descriptions of early settlements and freedmen's towns represent the complete text as it appeared in *African American Families and Settlements of Dallas: On the Inside Looking Out*, published by Black Dallas Remembered in 1990. Although the introductory text names at least thirty-nine communities, only about sixteen of them were presented, and some of those were not named in the list. That volume was the last one produced in the series.—Eds.

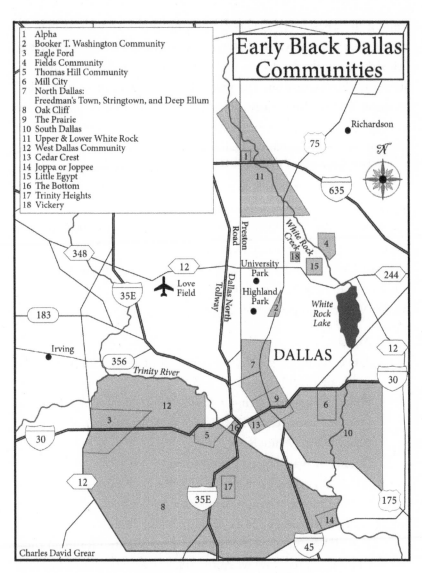

The communities identified within the text of *Our Stories* are shown here on a single map, identified by number corresponding to the list of communities on the following pages. *Map by Charles David Grear.*

Among the early Black Dallas Communities shown on this map are several that were freedman's towns, meaning that they were established by recently freed men and women during the years immediately after Emancipation. The years of their formation spanned 1865 to about 1873. Other early Black Dallas communities on this map were established later by succeeding generations over the next twenty years or so. The research on Dallas area freedman's towns is ongoing, and a definitive list is illusive.

The current recognized freedman's towns on this list are Alpha; Joppa; Little Egypt; North Dallas, including what was formally called Freedman's Town (the State-Thomas District), Stringtown, and Deep Ellum; and the Tenth Street District. Another known freedman's town was Bear Creek in today's Irving. It was not covered in these texts, but it is known to have been established in the late 1850s by a mix of freed Blacks, Whites, and people still enslaved.

1. **Alpha**

   The community of Alpha was established as a freedman's town north of today's Interstate 635, between Montfort Drive and Hillcrest Road, centering on the intersection of Alpha Road and Preston Road, near White Rock Creek. It was part of what was called Upper White Rock.

2. **Booker T. Washington Community**

   Originally called "Armstrong Addition for Negroes," the Booker T. Washington Community was a ten-acre triangle left undeveloped between the Missouri Kansas and Texas Railroad (today's Katy Trail) and the Houston and Texas Central Railroad (now Central Expressway) when the tracks were completed in 1874. The community extended from the end of today's Katy Trail at Central Expressway, at about Beverly Drive on the north, to about Fitzhugh on the south.

3. **Eagle Ford**

   The Eagle Ford Community of small farms was located on the west side of the large area called West Dallas. Eagle Ford

Community was located on both sides of today's Interstate 30, east of today's Loop 12.

4. **Fields Community**

   The Fields Community was established by a family whose parents and grandparents had been brought to Dallas in 1858 by their slave master. It was located northeast of early Dallas in a fertile farming area east of White Rock Creek. It was bounded by today's Church Road on the north, Skillman Road on the East, Merriman Parkway on the south, and Abrams Road on the west. It was part of what was known as Lower White Rock.

5. **Thomas Hill Community**

   The Thomas Hill Community was located within Oak Cliff, in the area around today's Colorado Boulevard and Sylvan Avenue on land inherited from Thomas Hill's former slave master.

6. **Mill City**

   Mill City was also known as the Wahoo District, and it was located around today's Wahoo Park and Community Center, east of Fair Park between today's Military Parkway on the north and Hatcher Street on the south.

7. **North Dallas: Freedman's Town, Stringtown, and Deep Ellum**

   The large area known as North Dallas during the 1920s and 1930s was made up of three distinct communities formed as freedman's towns. The largest of the three was known as Freedman's Town, and later it was called the State Thomas District. It stretched from today's Lemmon Avenue on the north, along either side of today's Central Expressway, south to Elm Street, encompassing what is now called the Arts District. Deep Ellum encompassed the eastern stretches of Elm and Main Streets, extending west to McKinney Avenue. Stringtown was the area connecting Freedman's Town to Deep Ellum. All three areas are recognized as historical freedman's towns.

8. **Oak Cliff**

   Oak Cliff was and still is located south of today's Interstate 30, with the Trinity River as the eastern boundary. Today's Loop 12 corresponds roughly to the western and southern boundaries. The large area encompasses several historical Black communities, including the Tenth Street District, which was established as a freedman's town.

9. **The Prairie**

The Prairie developed southeast of early downtown Dallas, bounded roughly by Canton on the north, Second Avenue, Hickory Street, and Harwood Street, with the present-day Farmers Market centrally located within these boundaries. Interstate 30 and Interstate 45 intersect above the center of this former early Black community. The origin of this community is currently unknown and believed to have been established during reconstruction in 1865. This community was demolished by the mid to late 1930s due to the lack of City funding and dire living conditions, leaving little evidence of the community's beginning.

10. **South Dallas**

South Dallas was a large region that encompassed several early Black communities, including Mill City and Wheatley Place, as well as Queen City, Lincoln Manor, Bonton, and the Roosevelt Addition. Although it is difficult to be precise about the early boundaries of South Dallas, generally, it was located south of Interstate 30, between the Trinity River on the west and today's Jim Miller Road on the east, and it extended south to about today's Highway 175.

11. **Upper and Lower White Rock**

The communities known as Upper White Rock and Lower White Rock stretched for miles along either side of White Rock Creek from around today's Frankford Road Southeast on the north to today's Forest Lane on the south. The area encompassed large farms owned by individual families of freed men and women and their descendants.

12. **West Dallas Community**

The early West Dallas Community was bounded on the north by the Trinity River, on the northeast by today's Beckley Avenue, on the south by today's Interstate 30, and on the west by today's Dallas city limits.

13. **Cedar Crest**

The Cedar Crest community was located in the area of today's Cedars District south of downtown Dallas.

14. **Joppa or Joppee**

Joppa, an early freedman's town, is today recognized as a historic district located between Interstate 45 on the west and the Trinity River on the east. It is bounded on the north by Linfield Road and on the south by Loop 12.

15. **Little Egypt**

Little Egypt was established as a freedman's town, located north of today's Northwest Highway and east of today's Central Expressway.

16. **The Bottom**

The Bottom was located in Oak Cliff along the Trinity River levee, west of where the Trinity Heights streetcar line crossed the river (roughly parallel to today's Jefferson Viaduct).

17. **Trinity Heights**

The Trinity Heights community was located southeast of today's Dallas Zoo, between Marsalis Avenue and East Kiest Boulevard.

18. **Vickery**

The Vickery neighborhood was located east of today's Highway 75 and near the intersection of Park Lane and Greenville Avenue.

Part I
Early Settlements

Booker T. Washington Addition
By Floyd Wilkerson

About twenty years after the Missouri Kansas and Texas Railroad and the Houston and Texas Central Railroad tracks were completed in Dallas in 1874, a large landowner named Colonel [John S.] Armstrong was left with a triangular ten-acre spot between the two railroad rights of way. He subdivided the plot and began selling lots to his Black employees. [The ten-acre triangle extended south from the crossing of today's Katy Trail and Central Expressway at Beverly Drive to about Fitzhugh.]

Col. Armstrong owned and operated a packing house in the Lamar Street and the present Corinth Street area. At the packing house, cows, hogs, and sheep were slaughtered and meat and shortening were packed. Col. Armstrong hired more than thirty Black men. These employees had migrated from farms close by.

He chose killing gang [animal slaughter] leader John Wesley as his agent to sell the lots. John reported his collections [of payments] to Armstrong's son-in-law, Edgar L. Flippen, who lived in a mansion in [what later became] Highland Park. Each lot, regardless of its location, was sold for $500.00. The cost could be paid out interest-free over a period of three or four years. The agent was paid $25.00 for each lot he sold.

Word of the new "Armstrong Addition for Negroes" spread in crowded Freedman's Town, four miles to the south, and to John Wesley's relatives on the White Rock farms to the north. Other purchasers came from as far away as Mississippi. Some of the early settlers were:

- Mr. and Mrs. Harrison Adams;
- Malete Adams (Annie);
- Dave, Bessie Bobo, and children—Birdie, Earl, Thelma, and Mae Tobie;
- Bud and Mary Bogan;
- Joe, Lizzie Coit, and children—Charlie and Sammy;
- Amos and Candus Daniels and children—Willie Mae, David, Amos, "Sumps," and Murphy;
- Eddie Daugherty (Robert Howard);
- Charlie and Josie Davis and children—Josie Mae and Dillie;
- Frank and Elzetta Euless and children—Esther, Frank Jr., and Ida Mae;
- Sam and Emmie Hudson and children—Sam Jr., Alice Mae, Dorothy, Emmie Jean, Joe, Jacob, and Elsie;
- Jake and Rena Hunt;
- Sam and Mae Alice Johnson;
- Mrs. Kimbrough;
- Nelson and Havana Lacy;
- Mr. and Mrs. McBay;
- Mitchell family—Theodore, Seraptha, Tera Lloyd;
- Mr. and Mrs. A. L. Rose;
- Mrs. Rosenborough and children—Nancy, Jim, Queen Esther, and Steve;
- John and Beryl Skeins and children—Geraldine, Mary, and Judith;
- Mr. and Mrs. Smith;
- Paul and Sally Smith and children—Joe Ambrose and Adrick Paul;
- Mr. Watts;

- John and Sarah Wesley and foster son John, who later changed his name to Juan Bastanes;
- Calvin and Lula Wilkerson and children—George, Floyd, Eugene, Josephine, and Mabel;
- Houston Williams;
- Jamie Wilson.

With these first settlers and others, social settings were begun in John Wesley's home. At first, he was moderator or speaker for about three Sundays. Thereafter, a Methodist and later a Baptist Church were begun. Reverend Childs pastored the Methodist Church and Greater Mt. Zion, which had several effective pastors—Reverend Peter Donnell, E. G. Gibbs, B. M. Moss, A. V. Voice, and J. Whitlow Washington.

A school was set up in the Methodist church about 1909. [It was] a wooden structure then, with one teacher, where seven grades were taught under one roof. The teacher, Mrs. Beryl White, taught reading, math, spelling, geography, and writing. Children were not taught science, art, music, or physical education.

About 1915, Col. Armstrong changed the name of the Black settlement to the Booker T. Washington Addition. Still a country enclave, the name change did not help much, since there still was no electricity, gas, water, sewage, or home mail delivery. There were telephones, however, because lines had been extended to the more remote homes.

About 1925, the area was annexed to the City of Dallas. A few years later, residents had access to utilities and streets were paved. Rural mail delivery was stopped, and house-to-house mail delivery began. In 1950, Central Expressway was begun, taking the place of the Houston and Texas Central Railroad tracks. The land became more valuable, attracting many residents to sell their property during the late '60s. At present, Booker T. Washington Addition is highly commercialized.

———————

Eagle Ford

By Chloe Baker

Eagle Ford, Texas, a vast farming community six miles west of Dallas, was organized in the 1830s and early 1840s. Most of the inhabitants were farmers who grew small amounts of cotton for domestic use. Wheat soon became the dominant crop, so much so that in the 1850s Dallas County became known as the great wheat region of Texas. It was not until the 1870s that cotton became the major crop.

Eagle Ford was a triracial community whose inhabitants were Anglo, African American, and Mexican American. Each group made worthwhile contributions to the development of this area.

One prominent White pioneer of this Dallas County community was James Horton Sr., a native of Virginia. He settled on a 320-acre tract in mid-November 1844. The tract has since become known as the James Horton Headright. Mr. Horton made improvements on this tract, acquired other properties and, at the time of his death, owned a 4,000- or more acre estate.

He gave the land for the Horton Cemetery for Whites and Crestview Memorial for Blacks. The site is located east of Loop 12 (Walton Walker Boulevard) and South of Dallas/Fort Worth Turnpike (I-30) in what is now Arcadia Park.

Around 1857, James Horton Sr. built the Eagle Ford Grain Mill. Horton and his sister, Sarah Horton Cockrell, made the mill their lifelong interest. She and her son, Frank, built the Dallas (grain) Elevator Co., circa 1885. Mr. Horton also donated land at Eagle Ford for the train depot and in September 1907 sold some two hundred acres of the homestead to the cement company, which is still in operation. There have been three or more changes in ownership since the original purchase.

One of the oldest African American pioneers of Eagle Ford was Mrs. Alzie Caldwell. She, her husband, and eighteen children were among the oldest and largest families during the early 1900s.

There were some twenty-five or more families living in Eagle Ford. Ten or more of these families were original Eagle Fordites, and the others were latecomers to the community.

The Reverend Bernard Byrd grew up for a time in Eagle Ford. He became a very prominent minister in Dallas. He built and pastored Munger Avenue Baptist Church for a number of years. Records indicate that Rev. Byrd led a protest movement to prevent the government from displacing Black homeowners to build Roseland Homes in North Dallas. He made a gallant attempt to save one of the nicest Black-owned and Black-built neighborhoods in the city at the time.

Another prominent pioneer of the Eagle Ford area was Mr. Thomas E. Crump. Mr. Crump was a native Dallasite who grew up in South Dallas. His parents established residence in the area of Dallas called The Prairie. He was reared by Christian parents. According to the late Mr. T. E. Crump, Salem Baptist Church was organized in the family living room.

Mr. Crump was educated in the Dallas schools and was a cobbler by trade for years. He migrated to Eagle Ford in search of work and found work with the cement company. Mr. and Mrs. T. E. Crump were the proud parents of their children—Erma L., James, and Margaret. All the children were educated in the Dallas schools, graduated from Booker T. Washington High School, and spent time at Texas College, Tyler, Texas. Margaret, the youngest was married to the late Nathan Gilbert, and together they built a grocery store serving the West Dallas Community and acquired other profitable businesses with the Gilbert Enterprises.

The story presented of Mrs. Nathan (Margaret) Gilbert, a former Eagle Fordite, is truly a marvelous testimony of a Christian woman. She was reared by a Christian father, touched by the hand of God to give of herself, and served humanity as a servant of God.

Mr. Crump was a loyal, devoted father to his children. He fulfilled the responsibilities of both mother and father after the passing of his wife, Mrs. Eura Crump. Mr. Thomas E. Crump was a proud, faithful, loving parent and prominent pioneer of the Eagle Ford community.

Two other prominent pioneers of Eagle Ford, Mr. Henry Drake and Ms. Hallie Walker, are credited with providing entertainment for Eagle Ford, Dallas, and other cities. Drake and Walker's Traveling Show was famous and appeared often at Ella B. Moore's Theater, Dallas's first theater for African Americans during the early 1900s.

The Eagle Ford families included:

- Mr. and Mrs. Henry Anderson;
- Mr. and Mrs. Tom Brown—a family of twenty-five;
- Mrs. Alzie Caldwell and her eighteen children;
- Mr. and Mrs. Rueben Cook and three children;
- Mr. and Mrs. Rueben Gadberry and six children;
- Mr. Allen Gillespie;
- Mr. and Mrs. Ben Franklin Heights and eleven children;
- Mr. and Mrs. Preston Johnson and four children;
- Mr. and Mrs. Saul Kennedy and son;
- Mr. and Mrs. Willie Knowles and four children;
- Mr. Randle Lester, son of Mrs. Pearl Lester;
- Mr. Randle's son Willie Randle;
- Mr. and Mrs. Jessie McCloudy and two sons;
- Mr. and Mrs. Carl McCoy and their sixteen children;
- Mr. and Mrs. Clarence McCoy;
- Mr. and Mrs. Fred McCoy and their fourteen children;
- Mr. and Mrs. John McCoy;
- Mr. and Mrs. Quilmer McCoy and their three children;
- Mr. and Mrs. Columbus Moore and nine children;
- Mr. and Mrs. Will Moore and son;
- Mr. Wesley Patterson;
- Mr. and Mrs. Albert Powell—latecomers to Eagle Ford;
- Mr. and Mrs. Charlie Randall and their six children;
- Mr. and Mrs. John Sheppard and their eight children;
- Mr. and Mrs. Buck Standmore and four children.

The Fields Community

By Ora L. Giddings Clayton

The Fields Community, a settlement located northeast of Dallas, was bounded by [today's] Skillman [Street], Church Road, Abrams Road, and Merriman [Parkway]. It was named for two brothers—Anderson and Lewis Fields. Anderson Fields was named for his mother's brother, Anderson Bonner.

These two brothers came from Kentucky with their mother (Caroline Bonner Fields) and father (Edward Fields), sisters, brothers, and the [John Caruth family in 1858].[3]

I am trying to tell this as I remember my mother telling us. My mom, the daughter of Anderson Fields (Mrs. Estella Fields Giddings, who died July 30, 1988), was the last survivor of the Fields brothers. Anderson, the older brother, lived longer than Lewis. Anderson and Lewis bought more than two hundred acres of land from Mattie Caruth in the late 1870s or early 1880s. They each paid $775.00 for the land.

Anderson met Martha Anne Jones, who came to Texas from Mississippi as a slave with her three sisters and mother. They left behind in Mississippi two half-brothers, Percy and Lucious. Percy

---

3. The original text says the Fields family moved with "the W. W. and Mattie Caruth family." However, that was incorrect, reflecting a confusion of several generations of the Caruth family. Recent research found that, in fact, the Fields family moved from Kentucky with John Caruth and his second wife Emily in 1858.

John Caruth was a successful merchant and man of influence in Kentucky. He owned a cotton plantation operated by enslaved men, women, and children, and he served as County Judge of Bowling Green, Kentucky, a position he resigned when he left for Texas.

He moved to Dallas, Texas, in 1858, fleeing the growing abolitionist movement. There he joined his two sons, William Barr Caruth and Walter Caruth, who had moved to Dallas ten years earlier, in 1848 and 1849, respectively, establishing themselves as proprietors of a general store and acquiring land. William Barr Caruth and his wife, Mattie Worthington Caruth, were the owners of the Caruth Farm, which he had begun to build soon after his arrival in 1848. (Sources: US Census records; Caruth family archives, Dallas Historical Society; and *The Caruths, Dallas' Landed Gentry*, 1988, and *Dallas, Her Golden Years*, 1989, both self-published by family historian Barrot Sanders.)—Eds.

said he never forgave his mother for leaving them. Naturally, she did not want to leave them, but she had no alternative. In later years, both brothers came to Texas, where they lived the remainder of their lives.

Anderson and Martha married later. To this couple eleven children were born. One daughter died in infancy, and a son died when he was twelve years old. The other three girls and six boys lived through adulthood.

When the boys of the Fields brothers married, they would build a house on their parents' property. There they would rear their families. Most of them had from two to ten children. These families made up the Fields Community. However, people who lived on other nearby farms—mostly sharecroppers—were also a part of the Fields Community.

The Rodgers School, then known as the Colored School, was moved from Little Egypt [north of Northwest Highway and east of what is now Central Expressway] to the Fields Community. Its name was changed to Fields School. This happened in the early 1920s. Prof. J. S. Giddings was the teacher for more than thirty years at that school. He ended his teaching career there. The Black children would walk for miles—passing the White school—in order to go to school. A school term then was from five to seven months a year.

The Home Demonstration Club was a very active organization in the Fields Community in the later years. Mrs. I. Hodge was the demonstrator. Many helpful things were taught. Before that time, canning was a very necessary way of preserving foods. They also cured meats—beef, pork, lamb, chicken, etc.

Farming was the chief industry, which kept the family happy and healthy. Corn, cotton, cane, oats, wheat, barley, etc., were the major crops. Peaches, plums, figs, peas, and berries were a part of the family orchards, as well as gardens with all kinds of vegetables.

Anderson had a sorghum mill where syrup was made from cane. He also had a thrasher, a machine that separated the grain from the hay.

Three brothers of the large Fields family are shown in an undated portrait. Left to right, they are Edward Fields, Alonzo Fields, and George Fields. *Courtesy of George Keaton Jr.*

Birdie Turner and George Fields are shown with their children, James, Audrey, and Agusto. *Courtesy of George Keaton Jr.*

He used this machine for many farmers—White and Black. Anderson was also a carpenter; therefore, their home was considered very nice. He could fix almost anything. Anderson was a very talented and versatile man.

Water was supplied by wells, drawn with a rope or chain with a bucket on the end. Each family would dig a well on its premises. In order to dig a well, it would be witched by someone who had the talent to know where water streams were located. Sometimes when there was a drought, wells would go dry and neighbors would share their water.

Dry toilets were the only means to dispose of body waste. The toilets would be kept clean by scrubbing them with lye water and lye soap made by family members. They used ashes to deodorize them. These ashes were obtained from the burning of wood when cooking and heating the home.

There were neighborhood stores and selling areas. One store was about five miles away in Little Egypt.

There is also a family–cemetery on what was the Fields' farm. Many family members and a few friends are buried there. The Fields Community no longer exists—only the cemetery. People will soon forget what they did there, but they can never forget the people who once lived there. Let the records show.[4]

An article by Ann C. Herring in 1984, entitled "Dallas and Its Peoples in History," gives the history of The Fields Cemetery located on Skillman Street in North Dallas. According to Herring, "The burial plot known as the Fields Cemetery was set aside for the family though it also includes the graves of friends and neighbors. There are a total of about seventy-two graves. Anderson (1858–1920) and Louis [Lewis] (1862–1926) are buried here. The oldest grave

---

4. When the Fields brothers established their community on land purchased from William Bar and Mattie Caruth, the Caruths donated a parcel of their land for the Fields Community Cemetery. (Source: Barrot Sanders's self-published story of the family, *The Caruths, Dallas' Landed Gentry*, 1988.)—Eds.

is that of James R. Fields (1898–1910), a son of Anderson and Ann Fields. At least eight veterans of World War II are buried here, also."

Because a lodge was also located on the Fields Farm, graves of a number of Masons and Eastern Star members are also recorded.

The Fields were prosperous for the times. They were highly regarded by friends and neighbors.

The Thomas Hill Community
By W. B. Anderson

Few Dallasites know about an all-Black community whose recorded history dates back to 1875. It was situated in a sylvan setting of pecan trees and cliffs, bubbling brooks and cool springs. Standing in this locality today are mansions of breathtaking architectural beauty [built] by Anglo Americans.

The community was so named for the large Black family of Thomases. However, one will find such other family names as Coit, Jones, Scott, Haynes, and Wilson.

If one should go looking for this community, one would take West Commerce to Sylvan Street and left to Colorado Boulevard. There in its place is a totally new community of Anglo Americans.

Most of the people worshipped at the Jackson Temple CME Church located in West Dallas. They remain faithful to this day.

The community was situated on ten acres of land owned by the patriarch of the family, who was one of the descendants of the slave family brought to the area by Judge William Hord, the first known settler south of the Trinity River. The area was called Hord's Ridge and later named Oak Cliff.

Mill City

Contributors: Jere Blanton and Rosa Elston

Better known as the Wahoo District, Mill City extended from Second Avenue to South Haskell around Wahoo Lake. Immediately after World War II, C. J. Jackson reported that "the heart and center of Southeast Dallas' cultural, social, and political life might well be said to center about the following institutions: Frazier Courts Housing Project, Julia C. Frazier School, and the Wahoo Park and Community Center.

"The religious life of the community is also amply provided for through the efforts of two Churches of God in Christ, three Methodist churches and eight Baptist churches serving a community population of approximately ten thousand persons."

According to Jackson, the original community consisted of a group of Negro, White, and German landowners engaged in the truck farming business. The principal Black landowners about the turn of the century were Andrew Jackson, Sam Skillern, Joe Duckett, Milton Daniel, Boots Wiley (a lawyer-industrialist), and William Porter.

By 1905 there were about fifty Black families in the community and about twenty-five Whites. Under the leadership of Andrew Jackson, Sam Skillern, Joe Duckett, and Milton Daniels, the first one-room rural school was established.

About the same time, Joe E. "Boots" Wiley, an attorney, opened a cotton mill devoted to the manufacture of thread, cloth, string, and other cotton products. This new industrial venture gave rise to an influx of people, who formed the core of a modern urban community.

The real estate boom, occasioned by World War I, saw the Black and White landowners subdividing their estates and selling them out as homesites for city dwellers. The Sam Skillern estate was the only large tract to survive the booms of both World Wars.

The Frazier Courts Project was built on the Boots Wiley millsite and the Andrew Jackson estate. This federal housing project contains two hundred and fifty units. The Julia C. Frazier School is only one-half the Jackson estate.

According to Mrs. Vernetter Calloway Hill, a descendant of one of the early Mill City families, the Calloway family first settled on Collins Street and later owned property on Ensley Street. When the Calloways first settled in the area, it was not in the city. There was a lot of mud and sand, with many vacant lots.

The Mitchells owned property on Jones Street with other members of the family living on Jones Street and Fletcher Street.

In later years, the Skillerns lived farther east, on a street which was known as Skillern Street. Other families included: the Ducketts, Andrew Jacksons, Tysons, Steve Browns, Richard Smiths, Peter Johnsons, Walkers, David and Liza Johnson, Rufus Beel, Littletons, Mangrums, Seatons, R. Madisons, Williams, Henry and Alice West, Marie Prince, Sims, Joe Tipps, Sam Tipps, Pullins, and Waggoners.[5]

North Dallas: Freedman's Town/ Stringtown/Deep Ellum

By Arrie Hughes Jr. and Deborah Fridia

A community that during the 1920s and 1930s was one of the most exciting places to be in the South now lays barren—except for a few homes in or near the State-Thomas Historic District. North Dallas was held in high esteem by African Americans across the country. A victim

---

5. Source: *Applause*, 1946.—Eds.

of bulldozers ordered in the late 1970s when the area was targeted for "renewal," it is no more.[6]

Most of the neighborhood has been leveled, except the State-Thomas Historic District. In 1984, the City of Dallas declared an eight-block section a protected area. It is bounded by Fairmount, Boll, Colby, and McKinney Streets. It comprises Victorian-style homes once owned by more affluent [Black] residents.

Thomas Avenue and Hall in Dallas was as well-known during the Black Renaissance in the 1920s as Harlem in New York, Fifth and Vine in Los Angeles, and other thriving communities in Chicago, New Orleans, and Houston.

"North Dallas" was for many years a mecca for Blacks throughout the Southwest and beyond. From the 1890s through the early 1950s, people would venture to Texas just to savor and experience the excitement, bustle, and prosperity of the area that surrounded Thomas Avenue and Hall Street. In the 1920s, it held the distinction of being the cultural center of Texas and the Southwest. It was a vibrant, pulsating, self-contained community with its own churches, businesses, homes, hospitals, and schools. Yes, all were financed, built, and managed by African Americans in the community.

"North Dallas" was the largest totally segregated African American enclave in Dallas. It became the nexus of what began as three separate settlements: Freedman's Town, Deep Ellum, and Stringtown. Records tend to indicate that Freedman's Town began to develop prior to the Civil War, when a rural cemetery [for African Americans] was established at the intersection of what is now known as Lemmon Avenue

---

6. The area then referred to as North Dallas included three distinct neighborhoods, as named in the heading: Freedman's Town, Stringtown, and Deep Ellum. Today, Freedman's Town and Stringtown are known as Uptown and the Arts District, and Deep Ellum has retained the name that was used by the early African American community. In addition to the disturbances noted in the text, further disruption of the North Dallas neighborhoods was caused by the creation of the Woodall Rodgers Freeway, which resulted in the rerouting of streets, the changing of street names, and the loss of most of the few remaining fine homes built by African American families.—Eds.

and Central Expressway.[7] After the war, more than three hundred former slaves began to settle near the cemetery.

In 1872 when the Houston and Texas Central Railroad reached Dallas going north, the two other communities in this vicinity began to develop—one around Elm Street near the crossing of the two rail lines and one along the tracks, called Stringtown. Stringtown joined the two communities—Freedman's Town on the north and Deep Ellum on the southeast end of downtown Dallas.

The "North Dallas" enclave—including all three major sections, encompassed an area bounded by Elm Street and/or Ross Avenue on the south, McKinney on the north, Haskell on the East, and Leonard on the west.

Some of the early pioneers in the North Dallas area brought a wealth of talent to this and other enclaves throughout Dallas County. The following paragraphs include only a few of them.[8]

Drs. Majors, Benjamin R. Bluitt, and J. W. Anderson were the first medical doctors on record to settle in Dallas. Their clientele was from both the majority and minority communities. Dr. Bluitt built the first clinic for Black patients, the Bluitt Sanitarium, in 1905 on Elm Street. Dr. Bluitt came to Texas in 1888.

Dr. Anderson was a physician, dentist, and pharmacist and owned land throughout the United States. A philanthropist, Dr. Anderson donated to varied causes and was in the forefront of the most positive community endeavors. Early in 1900, he financed the construction of the Anderson Anatomical Building at Meharry Medical and Dental School in Nashville, Tennessee, his alma mater. On June 3, 1892, Dr. Anderson gave the commencement address to Dallas's first Black high school graduating class.

Dr. M. C. Cooper was the first Black dentist in Dallas. Dr. Cooper's office was in the Pythian Temple. He was active in church, business, and fraternal efforts. He was a major participant in the founding of the Penny

---

7. Source: *Applause*, 1946.—Eds.
8. Source: *Applause*.

Savings Bank, Dallas's first Black bank. His daughter, Mrs. Marzelle Cooper Hill, and her daughter, Frances Burns, still live in Dallas.

Attorney Joe E. Wiley was the first Black lawyer to settle in Dallas. He was followed by Attorneys Chase, A. Wells, D. M. Mason, J. L. Turner Sr., and others.

S. W. J. Lowery owned a successful grocery store on the corner of Akard and Commerce Streets, where the Adolphus Hotel now stands. He later served as bailiff of a federal grand jury.

Dr. A. E. Hughes, a dentist, was the first to introduce dental hygiene at B. F. Darrell School and to visit and examine youngsters in the local Black elementary schools.

Peoples Undertaking Establishment is said to be one of the first Black-owned major businesses in Dallas. It was organized by Rev. W. D. West and Rev. Abner Taylor. Peoples was located on Pearl Street, between Elm and Pacific. It was managed by J. P. Starks, a gifted entrepreneur and educator.

The first barber shop owned and operated by a person of color was located on Commerce Street, across from the block now occupied by the Dallas Power and Light Company.

Four early Black settlers were successful tradesmen and land-owners and were among the original stockholders/investors in Sanger Brothers. They were Tobe Watson, Silas Pittman, Thomas Orman, and George Fuqua. Fuqua had a street in Freedman's Town named for him, as did Attorney Mason, Mr. Winn, Mr. Campbell, Mr. Routh, Mr. Towns, and others.

Some of the first organized Black churches in North Dallas were: Bethell AME ("Mother Bethel"), 1869–1872; New Hope Baptist Church, 1873; St. Paul Methodist Church, 1873; and Evening Chapel, 1873.

The Reading Circle is the oldest organization on record founded by Black women [in Dallas], in 1891. The first known club for men is the Mystic Club, founded in the 1880s by S. H. Ewell, J. P. Starks, M. C. Cooper, W. W. Maxwell, S. W. J. Lowery, D. M. Mason, and others.

Charles "Charlie" Brackins was an industrious, affable, and outstanding businessman. He was an insurance executive, bondsman, and property owner/manager.

Harry Boswell and other former slaves settled in Dallas before Texas became a state. He married Mary Fuqua, daughter of George Fuqua, another pioneer. They built one of the first homes in Freedman's Town.

Harold Harden, R. F. Doyle, and M. B. Anderson were also scions of first families. So were B. J. Cook and Tobe Watson.

W. E. King was the first Negro journalist in Dallas. His business was located on Swiss Avenue.

One of Freedman's Town's first grocers was "Doc" Rowen. He was also one of the State Fair's original stockholders. Doc Rowen's granddaughter, Mrs. Marietta Prince, and her two children, Dr. Robert Prince and Dr. Elaine Lockley, still reside in Dallas.

Dr. W. R. McMillan built the McMillan Sanitarium in 1925, on Hall Street at State Street. The two-block, two-story edifice included doctors' offices, insurance offices, and a surgical complex upstairs. Other businesses in the establishment included a druggist, tailor/cleaners, barber shop, cafe, [and more].

In 1927 Dr. L. G. Pinkston founded Pinkston's Clinic. Drs. B. E. Howell (1931), W. K. Flowers Sr. (1927), M. A. Leach (1927), and William Green (1935) all had two-story brick buildings that housed various businesses.

As early as 1891, there was a Black Women's Clubhouse, which later became a YWCA, on the corner of Washington Avenue at State Street. All types of courses for children and adults were offered in this facility.

A golf course, run by Mr. and Mrs. O. Love, was located on Washington Avenue at Central Avenue.

In the early 1920s, Mrs. C. J. Coleman, a fine caterer, began beauty work. She soon owned two shops and later opened Madame Coleman's Beauty College on State and Allen Streets.

Robert Vassel was the owner of Vassel's Jewelry Store and School. It was located in the Flower's Building at 2317 Hall Street.

Brady Hunter owned a Texaco Station on Thomas Avenue at Leonard Street, and Jack Wright owned a service station at 2001 Hall Street.

Citizens of color in North Dallas owned hotels. The Pride of Dallas on Allen Street was a multistory complex with a restaurant, maid service, and a barber shop. The McMillan's first hotel was on Central Avenue near Elm. The Powell Hotel on State Street near Hall had a second-floor ballroom and outside veranda/balcony with lounge furniture. The Powells owned six other hotels in Dallas and Oklahoma City. The Ritz Hotel on Bryan Street at Good was another first-rate hotel.

Clubs, cafes, and taverns were abundant in the North Dallas area. There were also ice cream parlors, drugstores, barber and beauty shops, liquor stores, milliners, ready-to-wear shops, dressmakers, tailors, [and more].

Thursdays were always busy nights for businesses. It was the "maid's night off." The beauty and barber shops, shine parlors, clubs, and "the streets"—Thomas Avenue, Hall Street, Leonard Street, and Washington Avenue—were a veritable rainbow of color and sound. The frenzied pace and mood found in the vast crowds moving pell-mell from one location to the other was electric. The area was considered one of the finest examples of Black life in the country.

Property owned by some early settlers in Freedman's Town[9] was literally taken [by the City] to build Roseland Homes. Pioneer names like Fuqua and others were obliterated as streets. Also, when Central Expressway was laid out, it caused the destruction of businesses and many fine homes (those of Wade, Pinkston, Morgan, Bedford, Tyree, and Watson, to name a few).

---

9. Throughout the two original books, several names were used for Freedman's Town, including Freedmen Town, Freedmantown, and Freedmen's Town. These various names have been used over the course of time.

The Expressway exits (Washington and Ross Streets) made the heart of the Black community difficult to enter. Thomas Avenue and State Streets were blocked, and Hall Street was altered between Thomas and Munger Avenues. Further commercial growth in Freedman's Town was hampered by the second phase of the Central Expressway and Good Latimer Street. Other homes (Starks, Burke, Ewing, Crawford, Doyle, etc.) and long-time churches and businesses were torn down.

Contributors: Mamie McKnight, Excella Dillard, Allison Tucker, Jimmie Mae Moore, and Muriel Penn.

Oak Cliff

By Mamie L. McKnight and Ellen Ruth Larkin, with Lillian Thompson and Simon Pentecost

According to an article by William Allen Ward in *The Dallas Morning News*, October 10, 1948, "Oak Cliff is as old as the Republic of Texas."[10] Ward further stated in his article on the history of Oak Cliff that "as early as 1837 a band of Texas soldiers spent several weeks in a small stockade they built near the site of the present approach to the Corinth Street bridge. The soldiers had chased Indians through northwest Texas and there was a battle with Comanches north of the present Fort Worth. The soldiers withdrew and followed the Trinity to the site they chose for their stockade."

Present-day historians consider Judge William H. Hord the first settler of Oak Cliff, even though records indicate that signs of earlier settlements existed in the area.[11] According to a clipping from a local

---

10. Ward, William A., *Dallas Morning News*, October 10, 1948.
11. *Dallas Times Herald*, January 28, 1955

newspaper printed in the mid-1930s,[12] the first African Americans to come to the area were with Judge Hord and his family. Judge Hord, his wife Mary, his three children, and their slaves—Daddy Bum, Mammy Julliet, and their one child—came to the area by covered wagon from Tennessee in 1845.

The log cabin erected by the Hord pioneers was the first permanent structure on a hill overlooking the west bank of the Trinity River.[13] For many years, the area around the cabin was known as Hord's Ridge.[14] The cabin is still standing and was moved to a tract near the Marsalis Zoo after it was given to the American Legion.

It is interesting to note that the 1962 historical marker on the Hord Log Cabin makes no mention of the three African Americans who came with the Judge from Tennessee. It simply states: "First permanent structure built on the west side of the Trinity River in Dallas, this cabin of hand-hewn logs was erected in 1845 by Judge William H. Hord (d. 1901), Dallas County Judge, 1848–50, who brought his family here by covered wagon."

The two slaves, who without a doubt helped Judge Hord build the cabin, had one child when they came from Tennessee. Nine other children were born on the Hord place. According to family records and the local newspaper article cited earlier, Frank, the last of the children, died in Dallas in the mid-1930s.

The newspaper clipping, by Graydon Heartsill, was titled, "Uncle Frank, Last of 'Slave Chillun' Born on Historic Hord Place 86 Years Ago, Comes to End of Lonesome Road."[15] The article described the funeral of Frank Thomas at the Jackson Temple CME Church and described many of his activities, both as a slave child on the Hord place and as a free, working man in the community.

In 1887 Oak Cliff was officially founded by T. L. Marsalis, a wealthy grocer and developer. During the same year, Marsalis bought all the

---

12. *Dallas Times Herald*, January 28, 1955.
13. *Dallas Morning News*, 1922.
14. *Dallas Morning News*, 1922.
15. *Dallas Gazette*, January 8, 1938.

Hord property, except the ten acres Hord deeded to Frank Thomas and his son, Frank Thomas Jr., descendants of Daddy Bum.

The descendants of Daddy Bum remained in homes on the acreage until after World War II. According to Mrs. Lula Thomas Wilson, some of the longtime family members who remained on the estate were Henry Thomas, Mrs. Caldwell, Mrs. Susie Jones, Gilliam White, and Frank Thomas. They lived in five or six homes on Sylvan, overlooking Kessler Lake. She also indicated that a very prominent Oak Cliff businessman attempted on several occasions to get White residents in the area to sign a petition that would force the Thomas family to move out of the area. Many of them refused to do so because they had lived together with the families for many years.

With the exception of a few feet of land sold for the road, the tract was still intact until recent years. Known as the Thomas Hill Community, it was one of the first, if not the first, communities of African Americans in the Oak Cliff area. The small community adjoined what is now referred to as the Kidd Springs Area on Sylvan Street, south of Colorado Boulevard. The family homes were built at the top of a hill overlooking a lake which was a part of the original acreage.

Another early settler in the Oak Cliff area was William Brown Miller, who came to the Dallas area from Alabama in 1847. He was born in Kentucky in 1807 and later owned a plantation in Alabama. He settled on the banks of the Trinity on the easternmost side of what is now known as Oak Cliff. He became one of the largest slave owners in the state.

The plantation house, which was built by slave labor, was moved to the Old City Park area when the property was bought by Good Street Church. The site is on present-day Bonnie View Road, between Kiest Boulevard and Illinois Avenue.

According to Dallas County records,[16] the following slaves and servants were buried in the Miller Family Cemetery: Della Booker,

---

16. *Dallas Gazette*, January 15, 1938.

died 1922; Dick Hines, servant, 1871–1907; Lula Hines Neal, servant, 1874–1940; Arch Miller, slave, 1824–1905; Charlette, Wife of Arch, 1826–1907; Elliott Sheeley, servant, died 1945; Mamie Sheeley, servant, died 1932; and Maybelle Sheeley, nurse, died 1936.

Many of the descendants of the Miller slaves gather each year for a family reunion. One of the descendants, the late Mrs. Historia Jones, recalled living on the old Miller plantation. She lived below the "big house," down near the banks of the river. She had to carry baskets of wet clothes her mother washed, back up the hill to the Miller family [home]. The Miller servants lived below the horse stables, which, for the most part, were still intact until the early 1970s. She also remembered the many former slaves who wandered into the area looking for work, shelter, and food. Many of them rode in by train and camped along the river, where they fished for food.

The largest enclave of African Americans in the Oak Cliff area was bounded by the Trinity River on the north, Fleming Street on the west, Compton Street to the south (Eleventh Street was a boundary on the southeast side), and the Trinity Heights streetcar line on the east. Although there were a few homes outside these boundaries, for the most part the segregated confines of the area were those described above.

T. L. Marsalis filed a map for the Tenth Street Addition on November 18,1890. W. J. Betterton filed a map for the Betterton Circle Addition on February 27, 1904. The section which developed along the Trinity River levee between the streetcar line crossing the river, the Corinth Street bridge, and Eighth Street, was referred to as The Bottom. Until proper drainage was constructed after World War II, flooding was quite frequent in the area.

Another smaller section was the more rural area along the T&P Railroad bounded by Eighth Street, Bonnie View, Eleventh, and Corinth. The Moore Park is in this area. It became a favorite baseball ground and picnic area during the 1930s and 1940s. The park was named for one of the early Black settlers, A. D. Moore.

Some of the structures in the community are still stand-ing. Many of the homes built by the settlers, including several churches and some of the businesses, are still there. Certainly, we do not have all the names of the early African American settlers in this area, but some of the families who resided there before and, in many instances, after World War II, include the following neighborhoods.

Tenth Street: Mrs. Alexander (Novella and Elina); Mr. and Mrs. Smith (Mabel, Lucille, Virgie); Mr. and Mrs. Washington (Shoe Shop owner); Mrs. Sanders; Mr. and Mrs. Welch (Graciels); Mr. and Mrs. R. Gipson (Raymond, Doris); Mr. and Mrs. Black; Dr. and Mrs. R. A. Henderson; Mr. and Mrs. Baker; Mr. and Mrs. R. Simpson; Dr. and Mrs. Haines (Aretta); Mr. and Mrs. Boswell; and the Penn family.

Cliff Street and Hutchins Street: Mr. and Mrs. Cole (Othe, Ethel); Mrs. Marietta Smith (Stone); Mrs. Moore; and Mr. and Mrs. Oscar Glascoe.

Ninth Street: Messrs. and Mesdames Cleveland Swann; Will Smith; Lewis; Turley; Smith; A. D. Moore; George Boswell; N. T. Watts; and the Willie family.

Church Street: Mr. and Mrs. Frank Randall (Cecil); Mr. and Mrs. Martin; Mr. Lott; Mr. and Mrs. C. J. Clark; and Mrs. Jackson (Sadie, Beulah, and Mildred).

Betterton Circle: Messrs. and Mesdames Paul Brigham; Johnson (daughter, Willie Mae); Simon and Estella Hunt; Ed and Historia Jones; Crockett Ferrell; W. P. Vickers; Alf Jordan (Loraine and Birdie Lee Washington); Adams (owner of a vegetable wagon; Walter Scaggs; Stancil; Gus Greer; Jessie Pentecost (Esther); Simon Pentecost (Estella); and Ralue Williams. Also, Rev. and Mrs. Moss; Mrs. Bill Bass; Mrs. Maggie Wright (Bus and Nellie); Mrs. Rita Ellis; Mrs. Bullard (Sugar Foot); Mrs. Moore (Chauncey); Mrs. Ward (Dick); Mrs. Sapp; Mrs. Fleming; Mrs. Brewster; Mrs. Lewis (kinder-garten owner); and Mrs. Meyers.

Eleventh Street: Mr. and Mrs. Thompson, Mr. and Mrs. Raymond Tipps.

East of the Cemetery: the James Abernathys, Fergusons, Turners, Criddells, Eloise Lunday, John L. Sims, the Rileys, Howards, Esther Pentecost, and Mr. and Mrs. Riley. Other families included: the Thompsons, Tipps, Peppers, Wallaces, and Flanagans.

A number of builders and carpenters settled in the area and built many of the homes, some of which are still standing. The Penns, Moores, Swanns, Griggs, and Boswells were among the builders and landlords. A number of streets were named for these pioneers, including Noah, Boswell, Anthony, and Moore.

Among the medical doctors who lived in and served the community were Dr. R. A. Henderson, Dr. W. M. Haines, Dr. Arthur Thompson, and Dr. N. T. Watts Sr. Dr. Henderson's office was on Tenth Street; the Thompson Maternity Clinic (1916) was on the corner of Tenth Street and Cliff Street; and Dr. Watts's office was located on the corner of Cliff and Anthony Streets (late 1920s through 1950s). Dr. Haines had a clinic in the immediate vicinity that burned during the late 1920s.

Ms. Lillian Thompson, sister of Dr. Thompson, recalls her family's move to Oak Cliff from North Dallas in 1919. There were only four houses for African Americans on Eleventh Street when they moved there. It was the boundary street between the Black and White neighborhoods. The Weavers, who owned the grocery store, built the houses. The lots were vacant across the street, and Whites occupied the houses on the west end of Eleventh Street.

In the early 1930s, Mrs. Thompson's brother, Earl, moved his barber shop to Oak Cliff from North Dallas and remained there until he moved to California. Her sister, Celia Mae, opened the Celia Mae Thompson's Beauty shop on Eleventh Street in the early 1930s.

Based on a survey of Oak Cliff, the *Dallas Gazette* carried two stories regarding African Americans, titled "Negro Owned Homes and Business Places Owned by Race Unsurpassed" (January 8, 1938)[17]

---

17. *Dallas Gazette*, January 15, 1938.

and "Oak Cliff Negroes Lead in Business" (January 15, 1938).[18] According to the first article,

> The Oak Cliff Negro section has more commercial business enterprises than any Negro section in Dallas, according to population. The enterprises are there to show for themselves. Sparks and Simpson have grocery stores at either end of the business section on Tenth Street that are not to be equaled anywhere in the city.
>
> Mr. Sparks is twenty years at his present stand and carries only the best in groceries and meats with a service unsurpassed. Mr. Simpson, at the east end of Tenth Street business section, operates a first-class grocery market and ice cream parlor.

The second article listed the following businesses in the Tenth Street Shopping area:

- Barber Shop (Buga Jim);
- Black and Clark Funeral Home;
- Briley's Cafe (opened in 1933);
- Cafe Drug Store (Johnnie Clark);
- Cozy Barbershop (Foy Thompson);
- Crabtree Hall, 1127 E. Tenth Street;
- Economy Bottling Company (James Moore);
- Dr. Haines Clinic (Sanitarium, Tenth and Cliff Streets);
- Dr. R. A. Henderson's Medical Office;
- Jennie Pit Club and Dance Hall;
- Jordan Cafe (opened circa 1922, Mr. and Mrs. Alf Jordan, owners);
- Live and Let Live Barbershop (R. L. Williams);
- Live and Let Live Beauty Salon (Grace Welch);
- Penn Drug Store (Mr. and Mrs. Nathaniel Penn, owners);
- Simpson Grocery and Drug Store;
- Sparks Grocery Store (opened in 1918, Mr. and Mrs. Sparks, owners);

---

18. *Dallas Gazette*, January 8, 1938.

- Superior Barbershop and Beauty Shop (Mrs. Allene Dillard, manager);
- Washington Shoe Hospital (Melvin Washington);
- Wolfe's Stand (G. S. Wolfe, 311 Denley).

According to Simon Pentecost Jr., (son of Simon Pentecost, an early settler in Oak Cliff—1906, and brother of Ellen Ruth Pentecost Larkin):

> Mr. James Moore operated Moore's Bottling Company located behind Black and Clark Funeral Home on Tenth Street.
> This was the only Black bottling company in Dallas. Mr. Moore had one truck and delivered to Black businesses in the city.
> The company made four flavors: Crème Soda, Orange, Strawberry, and his most famous flavor, Barney Google, which tasted like Dr Pepper. His drinks sold for ten cents a bottle.

Simon Pentecost also recalls Mrs. Wolfe, who lived across the street from Ninth Ward School (N. W. Harllee). She and her husband operated a grocery store. Mrs. Wolfe had a lunch stand across from the school and sold chili and beans in a tin cup for five cents. He states, "It was the best chili you could eat."

Lillian Thompson also recalls the Wolfe Cafeteria across the street from the school on the corner of Eighth Street and Denley Drive. She stated: "Ninth Ward Colored School did not have a cafeteria. Mr. and Mrs. Wolfe and their son had a dining room in their home to serve chili, sandwiches, cookies, candy, and soda water during the lunch hour for the Ninth Ward school children."

Three early kindergartens were owned by Mrs. Lewis, 1107 Betterton Circle; Mrs. Garner, 1100 Tenth Street; and Mrs. Eula Montgomery, 100 E. Ninth Street.

The Ninth Ward School and the Dunbar School served the children of the area until the N. W. Harllee School opened in 1928. The Ninth Ward School was on the same site where Harllee was built. Not much is known about the Dunbar School, other than the fact that

Mrs. Wallace, a well-known Oak Cliff teacher, was the principal and Mrs. Ollie Turner was the teacher.

The early churches in the area were Elizabeth Chapel, El Bethel Baptist, Greater El Bethel Baptist, Smith Chapel, and Golden Gate Baptist.

The Prairie (The Prey-Ah)
By Sam Wicks

Back in the latter part of the last [nineteenth] century, a prominent Dallas gentleman peered through a window of one of the city's tallest downtown structures and observed that the area lying just southeast of downtown looked like a prairie; and, thus was named a section of Dallas that later contained a sizeable portion of the city's Black population. An early 1930 local publication, *Guide to History*, reveals: "The first concentration of Negroes in the town, after the Civil War brought freedom, was about the present Elm Street and Central Avenue." From that beginning naturally evolved the congested districts adjacent to 'Deep Ellum' ...

One of those early Black districts that bordered downtown Dallas on the southeast side was designated The Prairie—popularly called The "Prey-ah." Bounded roughly by Elm Street to the north, Harwood to the west, G. S. and S. F. [Gulf, Colorado and Santa Fe?] rail-yard to the south, and Second Avenue to the east, The Prairie as a residential community is now just a memory. Now, that historic area is largely consumed by freeways—East R. L. Thornton, South Central [Expressway], and I-45. Where several hundred residential houses existed, only about twenty remain.

Although some outsiders have tried to paint an inner-city ghetto image on The Prairie, the community has an impressive history.

Dozens of successful former residents belie "the other side of the track" reputation.

At the request of Black Dallas Remembered, several Dallas citizens with Prairie connections agreed to recall some of those experiences.

Mrs. J. D. Hall, Retired Educator

As a preschooler, Lillie Belle Brown Hall moved to The Prairie with her parents, John and Reathy Taswell Brown. They lived there until her family moved to North Dallas during her high school years. Mrs. Hall said that her family's ranch-style home on Williams Street (now Canton) was a popular gathering place for neighborhood kids. Her father would allow the youngsters to make round-trip rides on his horses down to the giant Murry Gin Company, a few blocks away.

The former Lillie Belle Brown has treasured memories of her school days at Colored School No. 4/Fred Douglass on Preston Street, where she entered as a first grader during World War I. She remembers the school being renamed J. P. Starks following the principal's death. C. F. Carr became the principal at Starks in 1923.

Mrs. Hall recalls being one of the three students selected by her music teacher, Fannie Gipson, to dance at various school programs, including those at other elementary schools. According to Mrs. Hall, Fannie Gipson became the first music supervisor for Black Schools in Dallas.

Representing her school in a spelling match competition at the downtown courthouse was another highlight of Lillie Belle Brown's elementary school days. Other memories include "living for Fair Day every year" and the big parades that would move up Preston Street to Elm and east to the Fair Park.

Mrs. Hall recalls two members of the school band, directed by K. B. Polk, going on to outstanding careers in music. Clarinetist Willie Lewis later became a member of a famous jazz band, and vocalist Celestine Cole later went to Europe as a concert artist. And tooting a mean coronet in Mr. Polk's band at Starks was none other than Lillie Belle Brown.

Other schoolteachers during Mrs. Hall's elementary school days included: Lela Wilkins, E. L. Island, Pocahontas Rochon, Minnie Mae Thomas, Lula Mason, Eva Weems, Fannie C. Harris, Edna Ezell, E. T. Hartley, and Mrs. Overton.

Mrs. Hall attended Mt. Rose Baptist Church on the corner of Crowdus and Runnells (later St. Louis) as a girl and remembers living across the street from the church.

Graduation exercises for Lillie Belle Brown and her J. P. Starks classmates were held in the several-story Pythian Temple in Deep Ellum, the northern tip of The Prairie. The Pythian Temple (now an insurance firm) ranks among the largest Black business ventures ever in Dallas.

Mrs. Joe Towery, Cedar Crest Area Senior Citizen

Rosena Turner Towery was born and raised a few blocks from Colored School No. 4/Fred Douglass. During her attendance there, she recalls Principal J. P. Starks standing daily outside the Preston Street School to greet each arriving student.

Following the death of Mr. Starks, C. F. Carr became principal, and the name of the school was changed to J. P. Starks. Rosena Turner's senior class graduation ceremony was held at Salem Baptist Church, which was then located on the corner of Paris and Preston Streets.

Proud of her Prairie community, Mrs. Towery remembers several former Starks students who later gained fame in the music world, including Buddy Floyd, Milton Thomas, and Shorty Clemons.

According to Mrs. Towery, there were some Prairie homeowners whose houses compared favorably with some of the expensive homes in other Black communities. In this regard, she recalls these Prairie homeowners: Mrs. Totten, Mrs. Robert Harden, the Browns, the Beavers, and Mr. Criss, among others.

"A foot-washing service at the Bethlehem Baptist Church was an annual event on the Prairie," Mrs. Towery said. "The participants would march the three blocks from the corner of Bourbon and Eakins Streets to the church located on Bourbon near Louise."

Mrs. Towery said that the old Corner Drugstore, The Prairie's long-time, all-purpose business place, was initially owned by a Black, Henry McMahon. He later sold the business to a White man, "Mr. Earl" (Earl Gaskell). Two Blacks, L. J. Royal and Luther Walton, were long-time countermen at the popular drugstore.

A member of Peoples Baptist Church (then on Eakins Street), Rosena Turner, was baptized in a ceremony at the Hall Street Park swimming pool.

Mrs. Hazel Partee, DISD [Dallas Independent School District] School Administrator

At age four, Hazel Washington Partee came to Dallas from Calvert, Texas, with her parents. The family lived with Hazel's aunt across from J. P. Starks on Preston Street. The Washingtons later moved a few blocks north to Preston and Paris Streets.

As a student at J. P. Starks, Hazel Washington's favorite teachers were Mrs. Minnie Mae Thomas, Mrs. Eva Weems, and Mrs. Monrova, a relative of the principal, J. P. Starks.

Mrs. Partee made the daily walk to Booker T. Washington High School during the early 1930s. Before graduating, she and other Booker T. Washington students were forced to attend school only one-half of a day due to overcrowding at the lone Black high school.

As a young lady growing up on The Prairie, Mrs. Partee recalls seeing Josephine Baker and Ella B. Moore perform at the Palace and Circle Theatres, both on Elm Street and within walking distance from her home.

Mrs. Partee, who took piano lessons from Mrs. Day, recalls living across the street from Mrs. Marie Underwood, a successful seamstress who had both Black and White customers.

Mrs. Annie Bell Washington, Hazel's mother, was the first director of a kindergarten at the Salem Baptist Church, which was located on The Prairie at that time.

Hazel Washington, a 1939 graduate of Bishop College, returned to her former elementary school, J. P. Starks, about 1940 or 1941, seeking a teaching job. In the school office also seeking a job was Cecil James Partee. They met and were married a few years later in 1945.

Volney B. Phillips, Secretary-Treasurer of the Masons of Texas for Twenty Years

As a youngster and the oldest of six siblings—Herman L. Phillips, Carl Phillips, Josie Phillips Galloway, Acie Phillips, and James Phillips—Volney B. moved to The Prairie with his parents, Mr. and Mrs. Volney P. Phillips, in 1925.

Proud of his Prairie background, "Buster" [as he was called] said of his former community, "The Prairie produced some of the more progressive Negroes in Dallas and at one time had teachers in all local schools."

In this regard, Volney B. Phillips talked about outstanding teachers and leaders such as Professor L. R. Lockhart, Professor T. D. Marshall, Dr. Thomas Tolbert, and the Rice family.

One of the progressive Blacks mentioned by Buster was his father, Volney P. Phillips. The senior Phillips was among a group of Blacks who owned one of the largest Black businesses in Dallas history.

Mr. Phillips was president of the West Texas Bottling Works, Inc. This group of Black businessmen financed the construction of the three-story West Texas Building at the corner of Taylor and Duncan (now North Oakland Avenue) more than seventy years ago [circa 1922].

Before demolition sometime during the late 1940s, the West Texas Building housed Reed Funeral Home and Roby Transfer (a trucking firm), both Black-owned, and the Rag House, a waste material company.

Dr. Thomas Tolbert, Esteemed Retired Educator and Orator

Dr. Thomas Tolbert was born on The Prairie. When he was approximately one year old, he began living with an uncle on Spring Avenue in East Dallas. Dr. Tolbert described his uncle's home as a "show place." Dr. Tolbert maintained strong ties with the families on The Prairie and boasts of the many outstanding citizens from that community.

"Because it was such an upcoming neighborhood, the school board brought in J. P. Starks as school principal," states Dr. Tolbert. Some of the many outstanding Prairie residents mentioned by Dr. Tolbert include the following:

- Mrs. Helen Maxwell was one of the first Black caterers in Dallas.
- The Beall family owned a successful grocery store on The Prairie. Later the son owned a grocery store in South Dallas.
- Troy Floyd "lived to become an outstanding musician."
- The Beavers family: Mr. Beavers became successful selling and salvaging clothing. His wife Ann was active in fraternal affairs in the Black community.
- The Pollard sisters, Ruby and Jessie Mae, were both graduates of Wilberforce. Ruby later Married Dr. Holbert Reed. According to Dr. Tolbert, "Jessie Mae married the son of the successor of W. S. Willis, Grand Chancellor of the Knights of Pythias of Texas."

Mrs. Alvernon King Tripp, Retired Teacher, Government Worker, and Musician

A few years into this [twentieth] century, Alvernon King had to walk from her home in South Dallas to attend her "neighborhood school" on The Prairie. Two and four years later, she was joined by her brothers John Robert and Conwallis on the daily three-mile trip from Spence and Cooper Streets to Colored School No. 4/Fred Douglass, Preston and Gano Streets.

Then came high school in 1911, and Alvernon's trek to school grew to five miles when she entered Colored High, Hall and Cochran Streets. Before she graduated in 1915, the school name was changed to Darrell High.

During her attendance at Fred Douglass, Mrs. Tripp remembers money being collected for the hanging of a picture of Douglass in the hall of the frame building. She also recalls the pleasure of having fellow New Hope Baptist Church member Fannie Chase Harris as a teacher at Douglass. Another teaching favorite was Fannie Gipson, an esteemed music teacher.

Although Mrs. Tripp says that "there were some bad fellows on The Prairie," she admits there were some "nice kids" too. Two of the nice kids were Earline Hooper and her half-sister, Lois Smith. Earline and Alvernon were close friends at both Douglass and Darrell.

As a young lady, Alvernon King traveled from her South Dallas home on Sunday afternoons to play the piano in musicals at the Mount Rose Baptist Church. "A good way to get away from home," chuckles Mrs. Tripp.

Albert Nash, Retired Postal Employee

A native of Oak Cliff, Albert Nash was employed on or near The Prairie during the late 1930s and early 1940s. He also developed some close friendships and made frequent visits to the community until he left for World War II.

Nash, who worked at Pollock Paper Company on South Lamar and LaBarba Grocery on The Prairie, says, "People on The Prairie were very nice. Those I knew were very nice people." Nash also said he enjoyed good relations with the sizeable Mexican community on The Prairie.

One of Nash's close friends on The Prairie was Clemmie Love. Nash recalls that Clemmie Love would sometimes give him a ride back to Oak cliff on his bicycle.

Mrs. Mabel White, Businesswoman and Social Activist

Last year, Mrs. Mabel White told Black Dallas Remembered that she was the first member of the Meshack and Blair families to open a business in Dallas. This feat occurred in 1941, when the former Mabel Meshack and her husband William White opened a multi-business venture in The Prairie, called New Way Beauty-Barber and Cleaners. It was located at 2610 St. Louis near Oakland Avenue.

In 1950 the business relocated to Eakins Street next door to the Old Corner Drug Store at Bourbon and Eakins Streets. The Whites later became successful realtors.

Another successful Black-owned business on The Prairie was the popular Carter's Barbecue which opened across from the White's business on St. Louis Street.

"Prai-rie-lous" Journey

In January 1939, Lincoln High School opened in deep South Dallas. Students from The Prairie near downtown were required to attend the new school located on Oakland Avenue, [later renamed Malcolm X. Boulevard], south of Hatcher.

Students from The Prairie made the long, daily trip mainly by walking, sometimes by hitchhiking, and never by bus. The Prairie was the only distant area not served by a special bus to Lincoln. To ride to Lincoln, students from The Prairie had to take a long trolley ride through downtown, then out Lamar Street to Forest Avenue to Myrtle for another long stretch to the end of the line, which was two blocks from the school.

In making the three-mile walk over the G. S. and S. F. railyard overpass and all the way south on Oakland Street, the students sometimes met with peril during the period from 1939 to the mid-1940s. Many of the free rides to or near school were offered by Whites, but many Whites along Oakland would harass and sometimes chase Black students who walked past their property. Students at the nearby all-White Forest Avenue High School would gather in gangs in an effort to harass Black students from The Prairie.

One of The Prairie students of this period was this writer's closest friend at Starks and Lincoln, Marion "Jumbo" Henry. Marion completed a PhD degree and is now a faculty member at Prairie View University.

Prairie Facts and Brags

Prairie-dwellers boasted of the fact that they were more centrally located to important aspects of city living than any other community. They lived closest to downtown, the theatres, Deep Ellum, the circus ground, Pythian Temple, more trolley cars, and buses (on Commerce, Main, and Elm Streets). It was also near East Dallas and the Fair Grounds.

Bus terminals and railroad stations were short distances away from The Prairie. Massive railroad stations were short distances away from The Prairie. Massive railyards near the west and on the south borders, and a stream of water (The Branch) flowing east to west, were physical and natural entities in the several-decades existence of the near-downtown community.

A beloved, gentle veteran teacher of J. P. Starks School was Fred Williams. It is believed he had a photographic memory. He left to work as a train porter before returning to The Prairie school. He became principal of Starks in April 1939, just before the beginning of World War II.

Edmond Anderson joined the faculty at J. P. Starks in 1937 and promptly organized a Boy Scouts troop at the school. He also helped organize a troop at the nearby Salem Baptist Church. One year later, Starks School progressed from having the worst truancy record in the city to the best.

Mrs. J. D. Hall remembers a Black man, Bill Sanford, "owning a lot of property on Williams Street (now Canton) and Commerce Streets" during her childhood days on The Prairie and just after World War I.

A pair of Prairie-ites, quarterback Sam Briscoe and guard Willie D. Lloyd, were key cogs in the 1941 Booker T. Washington High School football team's march to the state championship. Pop Foreman at Booker T. Washington and Bennie Landers of Lincoln were outstanding football players during that period. Charlie Johns (later Brackins), who was probably Dallas's most honored footballer in history, was reared on The Prairie.

Bill Blair, sports historian and former Booker T. Washington athlete, told Black Dallas Remembered of some Prairie athletes of the late 1930s: John Birdwell, track standout and starting football center for Booker T. Washington; Eddie Malone Sr.; Lloyd Sneed, Clarence Martin, and Eddie Collins, baseball standouts; and Joe L. Ellis, football.

Churches in The Prairie

The Prairie had a rich tradition prior to World War II of being the birthplace of more churches than any other Black community in Dallas. A 1930 Directory of Negro Churches and other activities lists the following Prairie churches:

- Church of God in Christ, Runnels and Eakins Streets; Rev. Couch, Pastor
- Greater Sparks Chapel, Bourbon Street; Rev. A. F. Johnson, Pastor
- West Dallas Mission AME, 2624 Eakins Street; Rev. J. E. Finch, Pastor
- Lee Chapel AME, S. Pearl and Runnels Streets; Rev. R. T. Rogers, Pastor
- Union Baptist Church, Bourbon Street and Paris Street; Rev. W. M. Reese, Pastor
- Olivett Baptist Church, 2500 Uvalde Street; Rev. R. W. Shaw, Pastor
- Salem Baptist Church, Preston Road and Paris Street; Rev. M. B. Bilbrew, Pastor
- Peoples Baptist Church, 2932 Eakins Street

- Mt. Rose Baptist Church, Runnells and Crowdus Streets; Rev. W. M. Clark Pastor
- Mt. Olive Baptist Church, Orleans Street; Rev. J. N. Ussery, Pastor
- Bethlehem Baptist Church, Bourbon Street
- Evans Chapel

Salem Baptist Church, one of the city's leading Black churches, was organized in 1888 on The Prairie by Father J. S. Sims. Father Sims headed a mission sent out from the New Hope Baptist Church.

Peoples Baptist Church, another long-time leading Black church, was organized in 1922 on Eakins in the home of Alice Coleman. Rev. A. A. Banks was the founding pastor.

Sparks Chapel, now Porter CME Temple, was organized in 1900, at the home of Mr. and Mrs. Tommie Glaze on Young Street in downtown Dallas, near the fountain at the fork on Young and Commerce Streets. The first name was East Dallas Mission.

South Dallas

In the southern corridor of the city there were several all-Black neighborhoods which were surrounded by Anglo or Jewish neighborhoods. They were Wheatley Place, Queen City, Lincoln Manor, and the Roosevelt Addition. Farther east was the Mills City or Wahoo District. Three members of pioneer South Dallas families, Vallie Jo Smith Estell, Gussie Hoover Montgomery, and Annie Baccus Bell, reflect on two of the South Dallas settlements.

Wheatley Place

Contributor: Vallie Jo Estell

Wheatley Place in South Dallas was described in the *Federal Writers Project* of 1940 as "among the better of the Negro residential areas in Dallas."[19] It was named for Phyllis Wheatley, a Black poet of the eighteenth century. According to the report, it contained a park and a cemetery and the following streets on the east side of Oakland Avenue: Havana, Meyers, Meadow, Coolidge, Roberts, Tuskegee, McDermott, Hampton, and Metropolitan Streets.

There were a number of homes and businesses, including the Rener Store, a mom-and-pop store, and the Blair Store. The Rener Store was the first grocery store in the area.

One of the first families to move into the area from the Booker T. Addition was the Joe and Sereptha Smith family. Their home was at 3710 Meadow, between Metropolitan and McDermott. When they first moved to the area they could look from the corner where they lived to the Oakland Cemetery because there were no houses to block their view. Months later, other houses were built on the same block and encircled the Wheatley Elementary School on Meyers and Havana Streets.

All the shopping done by the families in the area was done at the Rener Store when the community first developed. The Mt. Carmel Baptist Church, then pastored by Rev. A. C. Horton, and the Providence Baptist Church, pastored by Rev. Richardson, were two of the early churches in this middle-income family community.

Miss McMillan's kindergarten is fondly remembered by many of the children who grew up in the neighborhood. It was located in a small Holiness Church next door to the Providence Baptist Church. It was a well-organized kindergarten with a special program for the young ones in the Wheatley community.

Miss McMillan would ring a large bell for the students to begin lunch, for playtime, and to return to the schoolroom. Many of the "graduates" of the kindergarten remember their daily chant that was the height of the day: "Miss McMillan says COME IN, Miss McMillan says COME IN." Each day was such an enjoyable

---

19. The Federal Writers Project was a nationwide program established by the Works Progress Administration in July 1935. Its purpose was to give out-of-work writers meaningful projects to accomplish during the Great Depression.

one for the children that often they would not want to go home at the end of the day.

Queen City

Contributors: Gussie Hoover Montgomery and Annie Baccus Bell

Queen City paralleled Wheatley Place on the West side of Oakland Avenue. The famous Jordan Street is shown in the movie "Juke Joint," which was filmed in Dallas in the late 1940s.

Some of the early settlers between about [blank] and 1930 were the following: Mr. and Mrs. Jackson, their two sons and a daughter, on Atlanta and Metropolitan Streets; Mr. Yancy Britton, principal of the first school in Queen City, located on Romine and Dildock Streets; Oram and Mildred Satterwhite; Professor Davis; John Crouch and family; Mr. and Mrs. J. L. Hayden, store owners; Mr. Edmond Calloway; Mr. Ira Moore, dentist; Mr. James Waldron, barber; Ed McGill; Rev. M. M. McGaughey; John Daniel and son Eddie Daniel, moving business; Elbie Titus, beauty operator; Earl Farris; and the Simmons family.

There were only four Black families on Waldron Street: Williams, Sadler, Baccus, and Patterson. There was one grocery store in the neighborhood and a fire station. Mr. H. Baccus owned the first Black business in the neighborhood. He frequently gave away fruit to kids in Queen City.

[Other families of note included the] Virgil Williams family, principal of Booker T. Washington; A. S. Johnston and wife, music and English teachers at Booker T. Washington; Fred Young and Alice, secretary of the YMCA; J. Mason Brewer, teacher at Booker T. Washington, who later became very famous as a writer, and family; Dr. Key and family; the Kearys; and Elsie Gill and family. Other early settlers in Queen City included Professor Charles Asberry, teacher and lawyer; Jim and Maude Loud; and Rev. Johnny L. Eades. Some of the persons considered to be movers and shakers in the area included Charles Asberry, J. Mason

Brewer, Professor Davis, Fred Young, the Haydens, and Herman Baccus Sr.

The area was very wooded, with deep sand. The homes in the area were primarily sold to professional people. Among the businesses were the Stevens Brothers Drug, Auto [Otto?] and Ezra Stevens on Dildock and Metropolitan Streets. It later became the Classic Drug owned by Mrs. Winn and her daughter, Alam. Hayden Grocery and Market was on Atlanta Street, with a dance hall upstairs. The Will Miller Barber Shop was at 2300 Metropolitan Street. The Candy Store was on Miller. Eades Furniture Store, Britton Ice (1921), and the Century Theatre were also in Queen City.

The churches in existence prior to World War II included Mt. Moriah Baptist Church, St. Paul AME, Sunlight Baptist, Friendship Missionary Baptist Church, Kirkwood Temple, and Romine Christian.

Along with many other organizations, there was a Masonic Lodge and a Reading Circle organized by Mrs. Chase Harris West.

Upper and Lower White Rock

Historian: Eva Partee McMillan with
Luetta Fields and Freddie Keller

Newly freed slaves purchased more land in far North Dallas, including what became known as Upper and Lower White Rock, than any other area in Dallas County. They came from plantations in Carrollton, Farmers Branch, Dallas, and other nearby settlements. Some of their former owners had been of the Coit, Obier, Caruth, Armstrong, Webb, Cochran, Knight, Smith, Bowles, and Scott families.

Some of the freed people had crossed the Collin County line into Dallas because ownership of land by Blacks was forbidden in Collin County. Henry Keller Sr., whose name was given to Keller Springs

Road; George Wells and his wife, Phyllis Jackson Wells; and Phyllis's brother, Mose Jackson, were among those who had left Collin County and settled in Upper White Rock.

Joining them from Wiley, Texas, were Taylor Tarpley and his mother, Ann E. Turner, who settled on Midway Road.[20]

The McShann family from Mississippi settled on Preston Road near Alpha Road. McShann Road, which was once a part of their farm, is named for this family.

From Gibson County in Tennessee had come Isaac Barton, Thomas Jefferson Sowell, and Charles Henry Bryant and his wife, Martha Ann Sowell.

In Lower White Rock, Anderson Bonner and his family arrived from Alabama. They settled in the area that is now Forest Lane and Coit Road. Their neighbors were the Jeff Bush family, whose property occupied land that is now Hillcrest Road and Forest Lane.[21] Settling in the area that is now Abrams Road and Skillman was the Fields family, whose holdings became known as "Fields Settlement" [or Fields Community].

Ex-slave owners entered the area from other states, bringing their former slaves, some of whom were their blood relations. They came in wagons, on horseback, and on foot, lured by rumors that freed people were permitted to acquire the available land. Land was as cheap as two dollars an acre, but the prospective buyers were obliged to work for years as laborers, sharecroppers, and woodcutters in order to earn enough cash to pay for their land.

There was very little opposition to land ownership by ex-slaves, as the Whites already owned more land than they could farm without slave labor. Also, there was a dire need for a cheap labor force, and most of the choice land had been acquired earlier by Whites. When the Republic of Texas [in 1841] commissioned the W. S. Peters Company

---

20. Their stories appear in the family stories section.—Eds.

21. Recent research shows that Jeff Bush was brought to Texas by John Caruth in 1858, along with members of the fields family, including Anderson Bonner's sister, Caroline Bonner Fields.—Eds.

of Louisville, Kentucky, to colonize and settle a vast northern Texas land area—later known as Peters Colony—they advertised extensively for Whites to occupy the wilderness in exchange for free land. White family heads were guaranteed 640 acres, and single men, 320 acres. Settlers hurried in from all the Southern states, England, Scotland, and Ireland.

By 1843, the new Texans had brought in forty-five slaves. The first [known] slave was Allen, who was owned by John Huitt of Farmers Branch. In 1853, the first hanging occurred when a slave woman, Jane Elkins, was convicted of the axe murder of a Mr. Wisdom, who had rented her from her owner to care for his motherless children.

Blacks settled in areas which now have many landmarks and major thoroughfares. Some of the streets are Preston Road, Frankford Road, Keller Springs Road, Midway Road, Alpha Road, Noel Road, Hillcrest Road, Inwood Road, Marsh Lane, Forest Lane, McShann Road, Montfort Road, Coit Road, Dooley Road, Spring Valley Road, Beltline Road, Addison Road, Abrams Road, Skillman Road, and Dallas Parkway. White farm owners and sharecroppers were scattered throughout the area.

White Rock Creek flowed throughout Upper and Lower White Rock, bringing a needed supply of water. It afforded scenic views along the white-rocked banks from which the area derived its name.

For centuries Preston Road had been an Indian trade route, which extended from Texarkana to San Antonio. It was the only north-south route through Texas for many years and was the most important link with the Old Spanish Trail, the east-west route. By 1841, Texas Rangers and the Army of the Republic of Texas routed the Indians from the area, clearing the way for Preston Trail to become the main highway for the new White settlers.

The ex-slaves went about buying land; building homes, churches, and schools; and paving the way for the future of their families.

Taylor Turner arrived in Texas in 1857, along with his slave master, Jesse Turner, who was also his father. Taylor was about twelve years old, and he had three siblings, who were also children of the slave master. He had two older sisters, Ann Turner and Mariah Turner, and one younger brother, whose name was Scott Turner.

Jesse Turner, with his second wife and their four children, traveled to Texas from Columbia, Missouri, bringing along his four unacknowledged, enslaved children. In 1862, Jesse Turner died, leaving a deathbed will in which he directed that his enslaved children were to be divided among his wife and their children. The will further

(Continues)

Continued

stipulated that, in order to sustain an income for the family, they were not to be sold but rather hired out to work.

Taylor Turner was willed to his older half sister and her husband, and he was hired out to the nearby Huffhines family as a farm hand. He continued to work there as he grew into manhood, working alongside those enslaved by the Huffhines family. Following emancipation in 1865, he remained on the Huffhines farm as a paid farm hand.

In 1874, he married Laura Hines, who had migrated to Texas from Kentucky with the Huffhines family, to whom she was enslaved. She, too, had remained as a worker on the Huffhines farm after gaining her freedom.

Taylor and Laura Turner continued to work for the Huffhines, and eventually they bought property next to the Huffhines farm. Their land holdings grew to about ninety acres, bounded by today's Willow Lane on the south, Preston Road on the west, Interstate 635 on the north, and Hillcrest Road on the east. They continued to live on their namesake Turner Way until their deaths.

Taylor and Laura Turner had nine children between 1874 to 1898: Georgia, Hemilla, Van, Robert, Millie, Gertrude, Cassie, Jessie, and Wylie.

Notable in the Turner lineage was Taylor Anderson Tarpley, the son of Taylor's sister Ann Turner Tarpley. Likely named for his uncle Taylor Turner, he married Mary Jane Coit, and they became one of the most acclaimed families in northern Dallas County.

Additionally, the well-known and revered attorney, J. L. Turner, was the nephew of Taylor Turner. He was the son of Taylor's sister Mariah, whose husband also had the Turner surname. *Courtesy of George Keaton Jr.*

On the farm of Taylor and Laura Turner, Laura poses in the carriage while her sons, brothers Robert and Wylie Turner, stand nearby. Wylie Turner was the grandfather of coeditor George Keaton Jr. *Courtesy of George Keaton Jr.*

White Rock Chapel Church was organized in Upper White Rock on November 15, 1884.[22] The Reverend C. C. Christian was the first pastor. The first trustees were Jack and George Coit, B. F. Turner, Felix Bingham, and Willie Harris.

The church was located on Celestial Road, between Preston Road and Montfort Road. Nearby White Rock Creek flowed past the only cemetery for Blacks in the area, White Rock Colored Union Graveyard. It has been said that Whites were buried in the cemetery during slavery.[23]

---

22. Recent research has confirmed that White Rock Chapel had been organized earlier, in the homes of formerly enslaved people who had settled in the area, and that November 15, 1884, marked the date on which the small congregation purchased land on which to build their first church, which was near a cemetery they had already established.—Eds.

23. Research shows that the first parcel of property for the cemetery was purchased by George Coit from a White family named Scott and that only four burials date to pre-emancipation days.—Eds.

The church was renamed White Rock Christian Chapel CME, and in 1960 [most of the congregation] relocated to Montfort Road near Spring Valley Road, where it now stands. The original site was purchased from plantation-owner Obier for the price of ten dollars. Additional church land was once owned [and later donated] by the White farmer S. S. Noell. The present pastor is Reverend Paul Freeman.[24]

St. Paul African Methodist Episcopal Church was organized in 1884. A small structure with thatched roof was built at the site that is now Hillcrest and LBJ Freeway. The one-half acre of land it occupied was donated by Mack Thomas, who, along with Taylor Turner, Mose Jackson, Washington Daniels, George Wells Sr., and Jeff Bush, was an organizer.

In 1887, Washington Daniels donated one and one-half acres of land on Buffalo Creek, across the road from the original site, for a larger building, where it remained until 1919, when a new church was built on Forest Lane at Hillcrest and was renamed St. Paul AME Church at White Rock.

During the mid-1930s, the church was moved to Coit Road. It stands beside a modern structure which was completed under the pastorage of Rev. N. A. Burton, who was assigned church minister in 1972. The present pastor is Reverend Walter McDonald.

According to available records, Mt. Pisgah Baptist Church is considered the oldest Black church in Dallas County. In 1864 a few slaves and a White Richardson minister, Rev. Butler, "met under a large elm tree, one half mile west of Preston and Spring Valley Roads. There the church was organized."[25]

Its first deacons were John Huffman, Dan Howard, Sam Fowler, William Phifer, Tobe Howard, and Jack Sanders. A land deed points

---

24. A small number of congregation members remained at the Celestial Place location, where they continued to worship with the name White Rock Chapel until 2018, when the property was put into receivership during a dispute among the members. For up-to-date information about the White Rock Chapel, see www.whiterockchapelofaddison.org.—Eds.

25. Note: Minutes of all organizational meetings since the founding have been kept by the church.—Eds.

Founded in 1884, St. Paul AME was started in Lower White Rock at what is now Hillcrest Road and Interstate 635. It was relocated four times, and the 1919 building shown now stands on Clark Road in Cedar Hill, where it serves as a wedding chapel. *Courtesy of George Keaton Jr.*

out that land was donated for the church by a former slave, William Wilkerson. The church building was located at Preston Road at Spring Valley Road. On April 30, 1981, the church relocated on Webb Chapel Road due to the need to expand. Rev. Cecil Smith presently [1987] pastors Mr. Pisgah Baptist Church, and Rev. N. Dorsey is Pastor of Latter Rain Holiness Church, occupants of the old church structure.

Around 1870 the first school for Black children in Upper White Rock was built on Keller Springs Road at Noell Road [later renamed Montford Road]. It comprised first through third grades. Founder of the private school was John Wesley Ray of Tennessee and Virginia. He was the first teacher in the school. He later became principal of York School in Elm Thicket. The school was later established on Celestial Road by the Addison School District and named the Addison Colored Elementary School. It was a two-room building and was extended through seven grades. George Wells Jr. was a teacher there during the 1930s. Edna Steptoe and Ruby Hickman also taught there.

Prior to increasing the grades, parents sent their children to Dallas or Corsicana schools. They paid room and board for the privilege of giving their children educational advantages.

Crispus Attucks Elementary School was established during the 1950s. It replaced the Addison School near Montfort and Spring Valley Roads. Mary Heads Carter, granddaughter of the formerly enslaved Mose Jackson, served as principal.

In Lower White Rock, a community school was organized in the Masonic Lodge Hall after Emancipation. It was located on Cottonwood Branch and White Rock Creek in what is now Hamilton Park. Years later it was relocated on Hillcrest Road at Forest Lane, where gradually all high school grades were added.

Armstrong School was named for local physician S. W. Armstrong. During the 1930s, Phillip James Hicks was principal, and some of the teachers were Reverend Fred Williams, Willie Turner, Melrose Moore, Pearl Isaacs, Ella Hicks, Myrtle Mae Sadler, A. C. Partee, Waymon Wells, Berniece Phillips Stewart, and M. R. Turner.

During the mid-1930s, the school was moved to Coit Road near the AME Church. It was then in the Vickery School district and was renamed Vickery Colored High School. During the 1940s, it was named Anderson Bonner School, in honor of a local pioneer family, and remained so until the opening of Hamilton Park School in 1954, in the Richardson School District.

Upper and Lower White Rock became a vibrant and thriving community, with many of the Black landowners becoming very prosperous. During the mid-century, with the expansion of Dallas city limits, the growth in land value, and the fall in productivity of the land, owners began to sell. Many families became wealthy as a result of the sales.

With the ending of the slave institution and the passage of many decades of Black ownership of the land, Black pride developed to the highest level. The ex-slaves purchased land, built homes, raised their children, erected their educational and religious facilities, educated their children, and profited from their labor. They walked proudly and taught the new generations to strive to become whatever they wished to be. Some continued as farmers, while others sought careers in education, medicine, law, engineering, and other sciences. The ex-slaves and their descendants made great strides during this period and laid a firm foundation for those who will follow in their ancestral footsteps.

West Dallas Community
Historians: Chloe Baker and W. B. Anderson

The West Dallas of the pre–World War II years was not the same as the West Dallas of today. West Dallas, a rather large rural Dallas community, was bounded on the north by the Trinity River, on the northeast by Beckley Avenue, on the south by the Dallas–Fort Worth Turnpike [I-30], and on the west by Dallas's city limits. Singleton Boulevard runs through the center of the community.

Although at that time the community was not annexed to the city, patient inhabitants kept hope alive by assuring themselves that the community would one day grow, that flood control would come, and that all conveniences would be enjoyed. That day did arrive.

Little is available regarding the reason for the establishment of this community. Perhaps it was the dream of one James E. Flanders, who in 1844 established a small community at [the current] Sylvan [Avenue] and [I-30].

Very soon after the Civil War, maybe around 1867, people came to the West Dallas area in wagons; some walked, while others had to pull their wagons because they had no mules. Many were slaves and ex-slaves who came to Dallas County from the "Black Belt" of Texas (southeast and northeast Texas). The underlying reason for the settlement of their community was mainly economical, because of the location of the Trinity River, many gravel sites, and the fertile soil.

Socially and politically, the land provided a neighborhood for Black families. The dirt roads led to cattle trails and railroads. Pioneers who came to West Dallas purchased land for the purpose of establishing a home and supporting it by the agricultural use of the rich soil. The pioneers proved the area had potential for a growing community, and other families came while the pioneer families grew. Some twenty or thirty years later, West Dallas became a suburb of Dallas [within Dallas] County.

Many of those who came found work on the Texas and Pacific (T&P) and the Missouri, Kansas, and Texas (MK&T) railroads laying crossties and putting them together with spikes. Individuals who did this work were known as "Gandy Dancers." Gandy Dancers were numerous as railroads extended their lines. Many followed railroading for years. As the [rail]lines moved, so did some of the families, many of whom lived in the section houses provided for their families.

The land in the extreme western part of the community was white rock suitable for making cement. Soon large cement manufacturing plants were established. The plants provided jobs for those in West Dallas and other surrounding areas.

Men came from far and near seeking employment. Soon the area was heavily populated and became known as "Cement City." Trinity Portland Cement Company was established, also at Eagle Ford, which provided jobs for men living in that and other surrounding areas. The cement company in Eagle Ford is still in operation; however, the name has changed several times.

There were several oil companies in West Dallas that provided jobs for men in the area and in Eagle Ford. Farming was the other means of making a living during this time for many of the families.

The community was sequestered and sparsely settled by close-knit, friendly, church-going families whose pride was in home ownership, however modest. White, Black, and Hispanic ethnic groups made up the population. Most were acquainted with each other. Middle-income Anglos dominated the business establishments along West Commerce and Singleton. Some Blacks were self-employed or supported their families by working in the city.

The Black churches and schools provided the culture for the inhabitants, who had very strong ties to one another. Two churches served the Black community around the turn of the twentieth century: Mt. Gilead Baptist and Jackson Temple (now Carter Temple CME). During the early years, one school was provided for each ethnic group. Additional schools were provided later.

The first school was held in the Mt. Gilead Baptist Church. One of the pioneer members of the church, Mrs. Sadie Shields, saw the need for a school in the community and decided to engage residents in raising money to purchase the land. Mrs. Shields took it upon herself to go through the community door-to-door soliciting money from residents to purchase land for the school.

The residents contributed liberally. Mrs. Shields then went to the county, requesting a school for Black children in the community. Her request was granted, and the first school was erected on the plot where the old Frederick Douglass Elementary was located. She was founder and organizer of the school. It is hoped that someday a school will be named in honor of this great educator.

Later, the schools serving the Black and the White communities were both named Cedar Valley—one for Anglo children and one for Black children. As early as records reveal, the established Colored Cedar Valley School was first taught by a Ms. Davis in 1894. When Dallas annexed West Dallas, the name of the school was changed to Fred Douglass for the great Black abolitionist and orator.

Other early teachers were Mrs. Sadie Shields Henderson, Ms. Lillian E. Hicks, Ms. John Ella Patton, and Ms. Eloise Jones. Other schools, which were constructed in later years, were: Gabe P. Allen Elementary School; C. F. Carr Elementary; George Washington Carver; Jose Navarro; Benito Juárez; Sequoyah Junior High; Thomas Edison; and L. G. Pinkston.

A listing of West Dallas African American residents, businesses, shops, stores, and churches follows:

Religious Institutions

- Jackson Temple CME, a Colored Methodist Episcopal Church
- Mt. Gilead Baptist Church, one of the oldest Baptist churches
- Rising Star Missionary Baptist Church
- Mt. Zion Primitive Baptist Church, whose ritual was washing the feet
- Holiness Church

Cultural Institutions

- Free and Accepted Masons
- Odd Fellows
- Eastern Star
- American Woodmen
- Court of Calanthas

Businesses

- Texas Portland Cement Co., West Commerce Street
- The Lead Plant, Singleton Boulevard
- Cement City General Store, West Commerce Street
- Texaco Oil Company, Singleton Boulevard (Gates)

- Gates Oil Assn., Singleton Boulevard
- Wyatts Boiler Works, West Commerce Street
- Austin Bridge Co., Singleton Boulevard
- Goodwill Stores 1 and 2, Singleton Boulevard
- Mr. Tom King proved to be a valuable asset to the community. He owned a fleet of large trailer-trucks which he contracted out, hauled lumber from the freight yards, and made deliveries throughout the city. This operation provided jobs for numerous young men for a period of years.

Stores

- Phillips Grocery and Market, Singleton Boulevard
- Shoe Shop (Mexican), Singleton Boulevard
- Will Marsh Service Station, Singleton Boulevard
- Second-hand Furniture Store
- Ray's Gun Sales and Repair Shop, Singleton Boulevard
- Feed Store (plants, vegetables, and flower seeds)

Residents, Beginning from the Western Part of the Community

- John Tate (Emma) and children: Geneva, Lucille, Willie
- Mr. and Mrs. Stevenson (Stella)
  Areata Yarborough, Thomas
- Mr. and Mrs. Watson
- Mr. and Mrs. Henderson
  Lois Henderson, Calyp Henderson
- Mrs. J. P. Bell (widow)
  Willie Bell, Anthony Bell
- Mr. and Mrs. Will Johnson (Blanche)
  Cynthia Mae Johnson
  Augustus Johnson
  Charlesetta Johnson (adopted)
- Grandmother Graham
  Lizzie Graham

- Mr. and Mrs. Robert Whittington (Mary) Cecil
- Mr. and Mrs. Manual Baker (Pearl)
  Mr. and Mrs. Luke Young (Pearl)
- Mr. and Mrs. Silas Scott (Anna)
- Mr. and Mrs. Eli Long (Mattie Lee)
- Mr. and Mrs. Roy Williams (Everline)
  Lula Mae (niece)
- Mr. and Mrs. John White (Priscilla)
  Willie B. Garrett Blankenship, Curtis
  Lucy Garrett Smith
  James Smith Jr.
  Lelia Mae Blankenship, who became Mrs. Melvin Davis
  Edna Blankenship
  Curtis Blankenship Jr.
- Mr. and Mrs. Ben Franklin Scott—Annie Rosetta Hill
  Chloe Videlle Scott, Lee, Baker
  Earnest Benjamin Scott
  Juanita Schott, Hunt, Germany
- Mr. and Mrs. Joe B. Hawthorne (Mattie)
  Charles W. Asberry II
- Mr. and Mrs. J. Potts
  Jessie Baker
- Mr. and Mrs. Rance Cole Sr. (Wessie)
  Mary Francis Cole
  Wessie Mae Cole
  Rance Cole Jr.
  Sam Cole
  Raymond Cole
  Willie Cole
  Cleveland Cole
- Family next door to the Coles
  R. M. Anderson
- Mr. and Mrs. Raymond Cole (Erma)
  Rai Lorene Cole

Singleton Boulevard

- Mr. and Mrs. Tommy Williams (Allyne)
  Lois Williams
  Mattie Asberry
- Mr. and Mrs. Dave Kyles
  Davetta Kyles
  Clifton Kyles
- Mr. and Mrs. Jessie Jenkins (Josie)
  Dorothy May Williams
- Mr. and Mrs. Will Marsh (Ada King)
  Edgar Allen Marsh
  Will Marsh Jr.
  L. K. Marsh
- Mr. and Mrs. Jack Cleveland Lee (Cloe Videlle)
  Jack Cleveland Lee Jr.
  Ava Marie Lee
- Mr. and Mrs. Walter L. King
  Le Ester King
- Mrs. Mamie Wright
- Mr. and Mrs. George Crockett
  Berneice Crockett
  Helen Ruth Jenkins, Berneice's daughter
- Mr. and Mrs. Robert Hadnot (Lula)
  Dorothy Hadnot
- Mr. and Mrs. McKinney (Lula)
- Robinson family
  Mr. L. Robinson
  Ms. Jeanette Robinson
  Imogene Fuqua Robinson
- Mr. and Mrs. Will Arnold
- Mrs. Moody (a widow)
- Mrs. Elnora Belcher Hilliard
  Drelay Hilliard
  Rudolph Hilliard

Ralph Hilliard
Annie Lowe Hilliard, Love
Jackie Love
Alvin Love
Owen Love
- Mr. and Mrs. Clarence B. Lee (Mary Hunt Lee)
Mr. and Mrs. Clarence Lee Sr.
Doris Jean Lee-Humphrey
Clarence Lee Jr.
- Mr. and Mrs. Elbert Flemming—Mary Jane, Grandma, and Grandpa Flemming
Mattie Flemming King—Oscar King
Richard Flemming
Addie Flemming
- Mr. and Mrs. Will Thomas
Charlie Thomas—Areatta Thomas
Mr. and Mrs. Maurice Thomas—Lurline
Inez Thomas
Mary Louise Thomas, Ware
- Mr. and Mrs. Davis (Sarah)
Mr. Ira Davis
Mr. Jenaire Davis
Mr. Jerome Davis
Mr. Wayman Davis
Ms. Davis Sewell

Part II
Schools

Schools for African American Children in Dallas: 1875–1940

By Dr. Mamie L. McKnight

Public school education officially began in Dallas on June 16, 1884, when the Dallas School District was organized. However, records indicate that both volunteer and quasi-public schools for African American children existed as early as the late 1860s.

Immediately following the Civil War, the Freedman's Bureau established a school twice for the children of ex-slaves. The first one lasted about two months and the second one a little over a year. At least three African American churches in Dallas reported that schools "to teach Colored children how to read, write, and compute" began in the early 1870s.

According to New Hope Baptist Church history compiled and written by Dr. Melvin Banks (1973), when Rev. Griggs built a new house of worship [for New Hope Baptist Church] in 1875, the old building became New Hope Grammar School: "The school grew and by 1877 there was a need to add higher grades. Rev. Griggs reported the need. Dr. [Robert Cooke] Buckner [a White Baptist minister who came to Dallas in 1875] called on Whites to help support missionaries among Negroes and to help establish high schools for them. The [Baptist General] Association took up money to help found a Colored Baptist High School in Dallas. The school opened under Professor S. H. Smothers. Thus, under the leadership of New Hope Church, the first high school for Blacks in Dallas was begun."

[The following] is noted in the 1980 [edition of the] St. Paul United Methodist Church Pictorial Directory: "In 1875 under the pastorate of Rev. Harry Swann a day school was organized for Negro children in Dallas. This school served the Negro children until the city schools opened in early 1884. Rev. Swann preached on Sunday and taught in the school during the week. Other teachers were assigned to the school by the Freedman's Aid Society. Two outstanding products of this school, whom many knew, were Mr. George Shirley, a business-man, and Mr. T. D. Marshall, a Dallas school principal."

When John Wesley Ray came to Texas in the winter of 1878–79 after teaching in East Tennessee and Virginia, there were no public schools in Dallas and the vicinity. He organized private schools at Plano, Jefferson, White Rock, and Dallas. The Dallas school was taught at Evening Chapel CME Church (Boll Street CME Church).

The first quasi-public schools for Black children in Dallas were built in 1882. The first building on South Lamar was known as the Cedars School. The building was the old City Hospital, which had been discarded. J. W. Ray was elected principal.

A DISD school source book reports that, in August 1882, there were "three Colored schools whose teachers were A. H. Jones, north-ern Dallas; S. H. Smothers, eastern Dallas; and H. W. Howell, the Cedars." An 1883–84 record indicated that "the city owned six public school houses—four devoted to White and two to colored children." When the Dallas School District was organized in 1884, only two schools for "colored children" were included in the system. It appears that the third school cited above in northern Dallas [possibly White Rock] was outside the city limits.

According to Rose Mary Rumbley in *A Century of Class* (1984), on the first day of school—September 15, 1884—there were sixteen White teachers and six Black teachers for the five hundred and twenty-two White students and the eighty-one Black students in the newly organized Dallas School District.

In 1884, the two schools for African American children were Colored School No. 1 and Colored School No. 2. Colored School No. 1 was located on the corner of Canton and Cockrell Streets, near the present School Administration Building. H. Howell was principal. In 1902, Colored School No. 1 was changed to Wright Cuney School, and Charles Rice was made principal. In 1908, the school address was listed as Canton and Santa Fe Streets. B. F. Darrell was listed as principal. J. W. Wilson was principal in 1912. In 1913, the building was "sold for $10,000, because Negroes had almost deserted the area."

The first high school grade for African American children was in the 1888–89 Dallas School District Report. Seven eighth-grade children were taught at Colored School No. 1.

Colored School No. 2 was located at Flora and Burford Streets. Dr. R. Stokes was principal in 1884. Other principals were B. E. Spratlin, 1888–1890; N. W. Harllee, 1890–1902; H. S. Thompson, 1902–1908; and Charles Rice, 1908. In 1902, the name of this school was changed to Booker T. Washington School.

In 1888, White School No. 2 was moved to Welborn and Alamo Streets. The building opened as Colored School No. 3 in the fall of 1888. N. W. Harllee was principal from 1888 to 1890, and J. P. Starks from 1890 to 1899. In 1900, Colored School No. 3 no longer appeared in the records.

Colored School No. 4 was also established in 1888, on Fuqua Street in Ninth Ward, east of Central Railroad. H. S. Thompson became the first principal and was followed by F. L. Hall. This school disappeared from the records about 1896. Another Colored School No. 4 was built on South Preston Street. J. P. Starks was principal. In 1902, the name of the school was changed to Fred Douglass School. The school was rebuilt later, on South Preston at Gano Street, and was given the name J. P. Starks School. It remained in use until the 1970s and was later used for DISD storage.

In 1889, Colored School No. 5 opened in the Odd Fellows Hall on Juliette Street, with E. T. Albert as principal. Wayne Manzella served as Principal from 1890 to 1892. Colored School No 6 was also opened in 1889, on Sutton Street. J. T. C. Newsome served as principal for the first year, and W. W. Jones was principal from 1890 to 1892. In 1890, Colored School No. 7 opened on Juliette and Fairmount Streets, with H. S. Thompson as principal.

In 1938, J. Mason Brewer, a former Dallasite and renowned writer, explained the next developments: "In 1891 the colored citizens of the Ninth Ward, led by Reverend R. Griggs, pastor of New Hope Baptist Church, appointed Lawyer F. K. Chase to write a petition to the City Council and to the School Board asking that a brick school be built in the Ninth Ward as the city was building brick schools throughout the city for White people."

This petition was presented to the Council and School Board by Rev. Griggs and Mr. Chase, and the request was granted. Prior to the opening of the new brick school on Hall Street in 1892–93, there were three small schools in that neighborhood: Smother's School on Hall Street in the New Hope Baptist Church building; Colored School No. 4, on Fuqua Street; and Colored School No. 5, on Juliette Street. All three schools were combined in the "brick school," and W. W. Manzella, from the Smothers School, was appointed principal.

The only school at this time with upper grades was Colored School No. 1. After the brick school was built, the citizens petitioned again—this time to have the advanced pupils placed in the brick school and to call it the "High School," until a separate facility could be built. Since W. W. Manzella was a college graduate, the citizens also asked that he be appointed high school principal.

On June 14, 1892, a resolution by the Dallas Board of Education established the first high school for the colored children of Dallas. The resolution read as follows: "Wayne Manzella is to have charge of the higher grades, and, if his work is satisfactory when the new building is completed in the Ninth Ward, he is to have charge of the same on probation."

The enrollment at the beginning of the 1892–93 school year in the new Dallas Colored High School was thirty-three. There were twenty-five eighth graders, seven ninth graders, and one tenth grader.

Wayne Manzella was principal of the school for two years. He then resigned to accept the presidency of Langston University, which was known as the Oklahoma State College of Negroes.

Several additions were made to the combination high school and elementary school. The original building had eight recitation rooms, a basement with four rooms for a heater, a fuel room, and two storerooms. The basement was later changed into recitation rooms. In 1910–11, the annex facing Cochran Street was built, consisting of twelve rooms. This building was named the Dallas Colored High School. In 1926–27, eight rooms and a cafeteria were added to the Cochran building. Also, a lavatory and heating apartment for both buildings were added.

In 1904, Oak Cliff was annexed to Dallas. The Ninth Ward Colored School at Eighth and Miller (Anthony) Streets became a part of the Dallas School District. A new building was opened in 1928 and named the "N. W. Harllee School." H. B. Pemberton was principal of the new school until 1953.

In 1908, the Carroll Avenue Colored School was listed as a Dallas school. There was no record of the school after 1908. In 1909, the Pacific Avenue Colored School was established on Pacific and Fletcher Streets.

In 1920, the Lagow Colored School and the Queen City Colored School became part of the Dallas School System by annexation. The Lagow Colored School was later replaced by other area schools. The Queen City Colored School was closed when the new Phyllis Wheatley School was completed in 1928.

In 1922, the new Booker T. Washington High School opened at 2501 Flora Street. All Black high school students in Dallas and in neighboring county schools attended Booker T.—at one time on half-day schedules to accommodate the heavy enrollment. When the new school opened, the old Dallas Colored High School building was used to house B. F. Darrell Elementary School children.

In 1952, Booker T. Washington High School was enlarged and became Booker T. Washington Technical High School. In the mid-1970s, the facility was enlarged again to house the Arts Magnet at Booker T. Washington High School.

On November 12, 1989, Booker T. Washington was officially dedicated as a Dallas Historical Landmark. It became the first standing DISD school facility to be so designated. A few days earlier, the DISD Board of Trustees renamed the school the Booker T. Washington High School for the Performing and Visual Arts.

In 1927, the West Dallas Independent School District became a part of the Dallas School System. The Cedar Valley Colored School was renamed the Fred Douglass School.

In 1929, the York School in the Elm Thicket area was established. The K. B. Polk School, which was completed in 1964, eventually replaced the York School.

Julia C. Frazier School was constructed on Spring Avenue in 1929. Mr. T. W. Pratt was the first principal.

Although dates have not been established for the opening of the school, the Lincoln Manor Colored School appeared in the 1924 Audit Report of the Dallas schools. This school later became the H. S. Thompson School. The new building was constructed in 1951.

The Wesley School was established in the North Dallas community known as the Booker T. Addition. It was included in the 1924–25 DISD records. Indications are that it became a part of the school system by annexation.

The last two schools for African American children that were built in the era prior to World War II were Lincoln High School and J. W. Ray School. Both schools opened in 1939, Lincoln in January and J. W. Ray in September.

Two Catholic schools for African American children in Dallas were established during the period from the early 1900s through the 1940s. St. Peter School was located in the North Dallas area on Cochran Street. St. Anthony School was built in South Dallas on Romine and Myrtle Streets.

In 1908, Father John Ferdinand, a Josephite priest, erected St. Peter Academy and placed it under the direction of Sister Servants of the Holy Ghost and Mary Immaculate of San Antonio. Called "Sisters' Institute," the school opened September 4, 1910, as a boarding and day school. Two classrooms were occupied by forty pupils, ten of whom were boarders. St. Peter Academy, which served both elementary and secondary students, closed at the end of the 1986–87 school year.

St. Anthony Colored Catholic Church and School was built in the late 1930s, in the South Dallas area. After White residents in the area openly opposed building the school and church, it was eventually opened at the proposed site. The school closed late in the fall of 1989.

A *Dallas Times Herald* article dated January 20, 1938, reported that the erection of a new building by St. Anthony Colored Catholic Church in South Dallas was protested by White residents in the area. They felt that the building would "depreciate value of their property." The leader of the protest stated, "We feel that the Bishop understands our problem and will do everything within his power to help us. We want the people of Dallas to know that we do not object to the church because it is a catholic church, but merely because it is a Negro church erected in a White area."

It has been reported that two small schools existed in the Oak Cliff area prior to the opening of N. W. Harllee School. The Dunbar School was reportedly on Eighth Street near the Moore Street Park. Mrs. Wallace was the teacher at another school referred to as the Trinity Heights School. It is conceivable that the schools existed in the Bonnie View and Trinity Heights School Districts, respectively, prior to the annexation by Dallas. Also, the 1900 Dallas Directory reported an Oak Cliff Colored School at eleventh and Betterton Circle Streets. John F. Farris was the teacher.

Mr. Floyd Wilkerson, a native Dallasite and retired DISD teacher and principal, provided his memories and insights:

Before 1920, Dallas city schools continued to expand and increase in enrollment. Paved streets and public utilities ended at the city limits. Black communities both in and outside the city limits had unpaved streets and no public utilities in most areas. The progressive families in these communities wanted churches and schools. Churches were easier to begin—in most instances, in the homes. They later embraced the idea of getting the county's permission to use church buildings for instruction provided there was not more than one teacher. The teacher would instruct forty or fifty pupils from grades one through seven. The county paid the teacher, provided coal for a potbellied stove, and little else. Parents bought books and all school supplies for their own children. As did Black students from many of the county schools, children from the Wesley School in the Booker T. Washington Addition, traveled five miles each way to attend the Dallas Colored High School.

During the late 1800s, many persons living in Dallas sent their children to Corsicana to attend high school. [Black families in Corsicana boarded students from Dallas for a fee.] Indications are that the Corsicana school for Black children was better equipped than the one in Dallas. The school was housed in a brick building, and there were more teachers at the high school level.

Colored School No. 1 [in Dallas] turned out the first Black high school graduates. The three graduates were John E. Reed, valedictorian, Elizabeth Hall, and Martha Smith. The graduation exercises were held in the Negro building at the state fairgrounds at two o'clock in the afternoon, June 3, 1892. Dr. J. W. Anderson delivered the commencement address.

[Later] John Reed graduated from medical school and practiced in Denver, Colorado. Mrs. Elizabeth Hall Lindley taught at Booker T. Washington. Ammon Wells, class of 1895, was the first lawyer who was a Dallas school graduate, and Charles Morgan, class of 1897, was the first graduate to become an accountant. The total enrollment of African American students in Dallas in the 1924–25 school year was 4,040.

Part III

First Families

James H. and Mamie B. Abernathy Family

Family historians: Virginia Abernathy Douglas and Mamie Abernathy McKnight

James H. (December 25, 1901–March 4, 1986) and Mamie Bell Mitchell Abernathy (July 9, 1903–) moved to Dallas immediately following their wedding on April 26, 1924, in Bivins, Texas.

James was the grandson of Elick Abernathy (circa 1840–1905), who migrated to Avinger, Texas, from Alabama as a freedman some-time during or immediately following the Civil War. It is reported that he came to the area with the Hearne family. His granddaughter, Pettie Lee Abernathy Johnson, remembers as least two trips her grandfather made back to Alabama to visit his brother, a college professor in or near Birmingham, Alabama.

Elick laid claim to more than three hundred acres of farmland in Avinger and bartered to pay for it by "delivering varying amounts of middling cotton to the County Clerk each year." According to land deeds, all indebtedness for the land was cleared in 1899. Most of the farmland was purchased by James H., a grandson, when the heirs sold it. It remains family property today.

Elick later married Susie, and to that union eight children survived: Emma, Ora, Sophia, Clydia, John, James Elick, Jenny, and another sister who died as a child.

85

James Elick, Sophia, and Clydia remained on their allotted portions of the farm throughout their lives. Sophia's grandniece, Gladys, is the only family member still living on the farm. Her mother was killed during a tornado (circa 1918) as she ran toward a railroad track with her infant child, Gladys.

James Elick (1879–December 20, 1964) assumed major responsibility for a large portion of the farm after his father's death. He married Pearlie C. Cheatham (1883–December 19, 1916), who was one of the seventeen children of Henry and Amy Cheatham. They had four children: James Hovie, Mira Lee (died in 1917 at thirteen years of age), Roy (June 12, 1905–February 1936), and Ceola Abernathy Royal (July 30, 1907–December 1947). All three surviving children eventually moved to Dallas.

James Hovie was sent to Prairie View Normal College in 1915, as a fourteen-year-old. He returned from Prairie View and taught several years at the New Zion School in the Aberdeen Community, Bivins, Texas. While teaching in Bivins, he met his wife-to-be, Mamie B. Mitchell.

Mamie B. was the daughter of Samuella Virginia Ann Baugus Mitchell (January 25, 1861–December 25, 1945) and Robert Mitchell. Cass County records indicate that Samuella was one of four mulatto children of the house servant Lydia Baugus and farm owner Major Robert Baugus. She had one sister, Agnes Baugus (September 6, 1858–circa 1865), and two brothers, Robert Washburn Baugus (January 3, 1863–circa 1950) and George Baugus, who died very young.

Major Baugus also had children by his [previous] wife, who died before Lydia's children were born. Lydia later married a Wiley and had a second family of five or six children. Lydia died when Samuella was seventeen years of age. Samuella reared the Wiley half-sisters and -brothers on her father's farm. When her father died, he willed the house and a share of the farm to her.

Samuella's mother [Lydia] was the daughter of an African slave and a Cherokee Indian. She [Samuella] remembered her grandfather,

John Lewis, and often told stories about him. Born a slave somewhere in North Carolina, he ran away as a young boy and was taken in by the Cherokee Nation. He grew up in the Indian village and subsequently married an Indian maiden. It is not known when John [Lewis] and his wife came to Texas, but it is believed they came with the Baugus family in the 1840s. He later fought in the Civil War.

Another story Samuella remembered about her grandfather had to do with his behavior when he became ired with the work overseers. He was known to "sit on a fence and whittle wood." Both the farm owner and work overseer were afraid to bother him and force him to go back to work.

Samuella remained on the farm until 1925, when she joined her daughter in Dallas. She married Robert Tyson and Robert Mitchell and had four children to survive. They were Pearl Mitchell (–circa 1909), Ambus Seamon (August 22, 1892–June 18, 1972), Elaska Tyson (June 9, 1898–1974), and Mamie Bell (July 9, 1903–). Her daughter Pearl died while in her early twenties and left two young children: Mary Rambo (April 9, 1906–January 18, 1982) and Arthur Johnson (1909–). They were three years old and several months old, respectively. They were both reared by their grandmother, Samuella.

When James and Mamie moved to Dallas as a young married couple, they settled in Oak Cliff. Except for a ten-year stay in the San Francisco Bay area, from 1954 to 1964, they maintained their home in Oak Cliff. James worked at the Dixie Wax Paper Company in Dallas and San Francisco. His wife, Mamie, was a seamstress and domestic worker, as well as a housewife. Their seven children are: Attorney James Roy Abernathy, San Francisco; Dr. Robert O. Abernathy, Orangeburg, South Carolina; Dr. Mamie L. McKnight, Dallas; Mrs. Virginia Pearlie Douglas, El Cerrito, California; Norman Ray Abernathy, Dallas; Gary Richard Abernathy, Houston; and Arthur Douglas Abernathy, Houston.

The sixteen grandchildren are: Kevin, Christopher, and Tracy (James); Ginger Laurie (Mamie); Edward W. III and Valerie Perene

(Virginia); Rodney, Jerome, Jamie, and Janine (Norman); Karen, Michelle, Gary Quinn, and Jerrod (Gary R.); and Areika Daun and Ashlei Daun (Arthur). Nichole Lynette (Edward III) is the only great-grandchild.

John and Anna Anderson

Family historian: W. B. Anderson

John Anderson, the eldest of eight children born to John and Mary Robinson Anderson, came to Dallas as a section foreman for the Texas & Pacific Railroad Company early in the twentieth century. He had begun work on the railroad at the age of fifteen. Although older men considered him to be too young for the task, his stature and commanding personality soon won him the honor and respect of all those who worked under him. Honesty, fearlessness, and hard work were his guiding philosophy throughout his life.

Born in Elmo, Texas, Kaufman County, John and his brother, Henry Anderson, were the paternal grandsons of Lizzie Hardin, the respected matriarch of the Hardin family of Elmo, Texas. He was married to Anna Thomas, the youngest child of Frances and Thomas Tulton Thomas of Elmo, Texas, in 1906. Five children were born to the couple: Edward, Orie, Hallie, Billie Burke, and Evelyn.

As the T&P Railroad continued to press westward, influencing the growth of Dallas from a prairie settlement to a great metropolis, John was assigned to work west of the Trinity between Dallas, Eagle Ford, and beyond. Blacks and Mexican Americans worked under his supervision, giving John an opportunity to communicate in Spanish.

John settled on railroad property in West Dallas, off West Commerce Street. This was to be a temporary move for him before going on to El Paso, Texas, with the railroad.

As Mr. and Mrs. Anderson began rearing a family, World War I was raging in Europe. Some of Mr. Anderson's half-brothers (by his mother's second marriage, following the death of her first husband) served Uncle Sam in that war. In the aftermath of WWI, the economic picture changed. Mr. Anderson was replaced by Mexican labor by the railroad company. He was later employed by the Briggs Weaver Company and, afterwards, by the Southern Plow Company of Dallas, where he remained until the age of retirement. His brother, Henry, was employed by the Portland Cement Company of Eagle Ford.

Mrs. Anderson, having been a schoolteacher at the age of fifteen in her hometown, had aspirations for her children: a good basic education and sound spiritual guidance. She enrolled her children in the community school named, at that time, Cedar Valley Colored Elementary School. The school for Anglo children bore the same name, but the term "colored" distinguished the two county schools. Cedar Valley Elementary School later was renamed Fred Douglass Elementary School when the community was annexed to the city. Jackson Temple CME Church (later renamed Carter Temple CME) was the source of inspiration and spiritual guidance for the Anderson family.

As the world of work and marriage beckoned the three older children, Edward, Orie, and Hallie Anderson, higher education was pursued by the two younger children, Willie Burke and Evelyn.

Evelyn, a former student of Texas College, Tyler, Texas, is married to Mr. T. B. Smith Jr., a native of Streetman, Texas, a graduate of Jarvis Christian College, Hawkins, Texas, and Tuskegee Institute, Tuskegee, Alabama. Her first son, Reynauld, was born in Tuskegee. They are the parents of three sons: Reynauld, a teacher and basketball coach in Washington, DC; Kenneth, who is employed by Kaiser Permanente; and Keith, an instructor of flight attendants for Pan American Airlines.

Upon graduation from Texas College, Willie Burke was the first student from her community to become an instructor at her alma mater, Texas College in Tyler, Texas. Miss Anderson later returned to her home city to teach English and speech at her high school alma mater, Booker T. Washington. Deeply devoted to her work and to her students, Miss Anderson found pleasure in coaching dramatics as an incentive to developing positive attitudes and self-confidence in her students. She organized the first class in French for the Black students of Dallas. Before retirement, she spent several years as a classroom teacher in the following high schools: James Madison, Lincoln, Skyline Career Development Center (Cluster Coordinator), and Adamson High School.

During her active career, she continued to pursue advanced studies in French at Atlanta University, Atlanta, Georgia; Teachers College, Columbia University in New York; and at Alliance Française in Paris, France. She was invited by the United States Department of Education to serve as an exchange teacher in the Far East. Instead, she chose to teach English as a Foreign Language in Jose Diego High School of Puerto Rico, and in the extensions of Catholic and Inter-American Universities during her stay in Aguadilla, Puerto Rico. She extended her studies to include Spanish at the Universidad de Cultura in Saltillo, Mexico.

Descendants of John and Anna Anderson

Edward Anderson married Pearl Anthony, and their children were Edwin Samuel, Gerard, and Warren Lee Anderson. Orie Anderson married Eunice McCauley, and their only child was Evelyn Anderson Rutledge. Orie married a second time to Elnora Houston, and their only child was Orie Annette Anderson Trigg. Evelyn Anderson married T. B. Smith Jr., and their children were Reynauld, Kenneth, and Keith.

The five children of the John and Anna Anderson family engendered twenty-two great-grandchildren, and by 1989, the children of five of those great-grandchildren had engendered offspring of their own.

Jasper Sr. and Edna Nixon Baccus

Family historian: Annie Baccus Bell

The greatest strength of the Baccus family lies in a strong support system that is based on the principles of Christianity. Jasper and Edna Baccus of Dallas, Texas, established those principles in their home. The family was taught to exhort, aid, and counsel one another; admonish each other to overcome their faults; aid their neighbors, friends, and those in need; and most of all, always put God first. Also, the family recognizes the importance of preserving its unique history.

Jasper Baccus married Edna Nixon. Their union produced nine children: Doris Baccus McMath, Jasper Baccus Jr., Ruth Baccus Murray, Annie Baccus Bell, Fannie Baccus, Brooksie Baccus Rogers, Carl Baccus, and Bobbie Baccus Lanham. Their ninth child, a son who was never named, died at birth. Jasper Baccus's wife, Edna, and their eight children survive.

Emma Estelle (Stella) Baccus married Melvin Houston. To their union two children were born: Melvin Houston Jr. and Adlee Houston Trezevant. Emma Baccus Houston died April 7, 1968. Her husband and son are both deceased. Adlee survives and lives in Fort Worth, Texas.

Jasper Baccus Sr. was born December 1, 1885, and he died August 26, 1966. He married Edna Nixon (born 1902), the daughter of William Edward and Giley Nixon. Edna, a native of Midway, Texas, moved to Dallas in her early teens and married Jasper March 31, 1926. Edna's parents wanted their eldest child to attend Dallas schools, where they thought she would receive a better education. Thus, she was sent to live with her aunt and uncle, Robbie and Henry Pearson, who owned the Two Brothers Cafe on Pacific Avenue. Jasper Baccus was a frequent customer and met Edna Nixon there while she worked after school as a waitress.

Jasper, anxious to move his wife to a new, growing community in South Dallas, purchased a large tract of land with a house on it from Dick Barkley, the owner of Dallas City Market. The market is now known as the Farmer's Market. The property which he purchased extends from Waldron Avenue to Octavia Street. Since Jasper, known as "Jap" to a lot of his friends, and "Jap Baccus" to those who respectfully asked for a loan, telephone, etc., was a thrifty person. He was able to pay cash for the property and the house.

Mr. Baccus and his family were among the first Black people to reside in South Dallas. At the time, the area was mostly populated by a few Whites and a wealthy group of Jewish residents. Everybody was his friend. With his natural talent for comedy, he had a knack for turning any potentially volatile situation into a profusion of laughter. He was known for his honesty, his forthrightness, his common sense, his wonderful sense of humor.

He ran his house like a monarch, not a tyrant, just a loving father, who said all the right things and made all the right moves—whatever it took to "get those kids through school." He used to remind his family that he never finished the fourth grade, and since he was doing alright, he challenged them to stay in school and to reach for their respective dreams.

Besides being a happy family man, Jasper was used to hard work. His father, Patrick, pulled him out of school to help out in his various enterprises in downtown Dallas. But Jasper had a mind of his own and decided early to go into business for himself.

Jasper knew that Dallas was growing by leaps and bounds. That meant people were going to need transportation to move things around. Therefore, he decided to start his own transfer and trucking business. He chose a location at Pacific Avenue and Central Avenue behind Hart's Furniture Store, which still exists on Elm Street. Jasper's business prospered because he had clients from every walk of life. Among them were Dallas's elite, rich and poor, famous and infamous. If they could pay (or make good on a promise to pay), he hauled their belongings anywhere and everywhere. Between hauls from Union Station and various parts of the city and outlying countryside, he would almost daily go down to the Farmer's Market and get food to share with families in his neighborhood.

Jasper's wife, Edna, also had a business background. She graduated from Booker T. Washington High School and soon after worked as a secretary for Dr. M. H. Leach and Attorney J. L. Turner, prominent Black businessmen in the city of Dallas. Later, she worked as an insurance agent for Henderson and Wren Funeral Home. (To this day, she doesn't miss a funeral, and the family always teases her about her apparent morbid proclivity toward attending these sad events.) Her dream, however, was to go on to college to become an English teacher. But the dashing Mr. Baccus swept her off her feet. Wedding bells were ringing in her ears—school could wait. And it did—eight kids and numerable grandchildren later.

After caring for eight children (she has often told the story of how five of them had whooping cough simultaneously, keeping her up day and night until they got well) and getting them through college, Edna Baccus then decided it was time that she pursued her original goal and somehow get into the field of education. So, even though some thought it was rather late in life to be "chasing rainbows," she became a teacher's aide at Charles Rice Elementary School while Floyd Wilkerson still served as the principal. She was crowned "Miss PTA" at the school by Mr. Wilkerson and cherishes the memory.

Later, she transferred to James Madison High School under the able leadership of Leon King. He had attended Lincoln High School with Carl and Bobbie, her two youngest children. She calls him "Son" and he calls her "Mother Baccus" to this day.

Mrs. Baccus continues to be a dedicated member of the Church of Christ. Her love for teaching young children made itself evident in the church as well, since she has been a church schoolteacher for over sixty years. She also was instrumental in forming the "Annual Youth Conference," an outreach program for children, teens, and young adults which engages them in seminar-style week-long sessions every year in August in different US cities.

For Jasper and Edna Baccus to have influenced so many children in their own neighborhood, adjacent communities, and throughout the nation, it makes sense that their primary realm of concern was for their eight children. Their two sons and six daughters have gone on to excel in their respective fields of endeavor, making notable strides amid early familial difficulties. The Baccus children followed the family's tradition in business and education.

Doris Baccus McMath is a graduate of Wheatley Elementary, Lincoln High School, and Tuskegee University (BS degree in Elementary Education). She earned a Master of Arts degree from Southern Methodist University and received an honorary doctorate from the American Bible Institute. McMath has served in the Dallas Independent School District for twenty-four years. Presently, she is an Instructional Resource Teacher.

Jasper Baccus Jr. has been in the cleaning business for over thirty years, serving all areas of Dallas. Presently, he operates Baccus Cleaners on Martin Luther King Boulevard.

Annie Baccus Bell graduated from Wheatley Elementary and Lincoln High Schools. She received her BS Degree from Tuskegee University and a master's degree from Prairie View University, with further study at North Texas State University and the University of Colorado. Bell has been a professional educator for thirty years—serving in the Dallas Independent School District for twenty years.

Fannie Baccus graduated from Wheatley Elementary, Lincoln High School, Tuskegee University, and Hampton University. She majored in business. For several years, she served as secretary for Blue Cross Blue Shield Company located in Dallas. She later transferred to the Blue Cross Blue Shield Company in Los Angeles, California, where she served as an office director. Later, she worked in electronics and became an outstanding worker at Texas Instruments.

Brooksie Baccus Rogers received her education from Wheatley Elementary and Lincoln High School. She is a graduate of Baylor School of Nursing. She worked at Baylor University Medical Center for over twenty years before retiring. She is active in the Parent Teacher Association. She is best known for decorating cakes for all occasions.

Dr. Carl C. Baccus is a graduate of Wheatley Elementary, Lincoln High, Pepperdine University, and California Graduate School of Theology, Glendale, California. He has traveled extensively in the United States, Canada, Aruba, Bermuda, Jerusalem, and the Caribbean and Hawaiian Islands. The Southside Church of Christ in Los Angeles, California, where Dr. Carl C. Baccus is the evangelist, is committed to meeting the needs of the community. Carl Baccus created the "Concerned Citizens Community Involvement Project" to enable them to respond to community needs. An annual "Baccus Scholarship Award" has been established for the worthy youth, and over $30,000 has been awarded. He presents these awards on his birthday each year.

Since the early days in Watts, Carl Baccus and the Southside Church of Christ congregation have maintained a close working relationship with the community, feeding the poor, aiding senior citizens, and addressing many social needs. He has received several plaques, trophies, and other awards from church, school, and the community. The Board of Supervisors of the County of Los Angeles gave him a special award in the dedication of Jesse Owens Park in Los Angeles, California. Carl Baccus is the author of the book *Let Freedom Ring Through Christ*. He will continue to stir Californians and people in the West Indies by way of radio and television with his unique preaching style.

Bobbie Baccus Lanham is a Wheatley Elementary, Lincoln High School, and Southern University, Baton Rouge, Louisiana, graduate. She worked for the City of Los Angeles as director-in-charge of several of the city's recreational centers and parks. Presently she serves as Educational Director of the New Focus Day Care and Christian School, 1655 West Manchester, Los Angeles, California.

The Baccus family lived and fought through the struggles of South Dallas. They witnessed the advances made by many Black families in the areas of business, education, government, the arts, religion, and the sciences. The Baccus family helped keep Black Dallas alive by passing on stories of the past to the younger generation and actively working in the community. They helped make South Dallas a place of pride, progress, and promise.

Anderson and Eliza Bonner Family

Family historians: Eunice Bonner Turner
and Odessa Bonner Hill

The amazing accomplishments of Anderson Bonner (circa 1835–circa 1920) as a farmer and owner of extensive land holdings north of Dallas along White Rock Creek and Cottonwood Branch have not been fully credited.[26] A former slave, Anderson Bonner signed his name with an X on deeds for hundreds of acres of land. He purchased the property with funds earned from his farm products and houses he leased to sharecroppers. The fact that all of his business transactions were handled with legal consultation and documentation tends to verify his brilliant business sense and knowledge of measures needed to secure his massive holdings. Records indicate that the warranty deed for one of his earliest land purchases (over sixty acres) was filed in Dallas County, August 10, 1874.

According to members of the family, it is not known how Anderson Bonner, his brother, Louis, and sister, Caroline, came from Alabama to the farm area north of White Rock Creek. There are indications that they may have lived in Arkansas for a while. Also, it was

---

26. The 1870 census shows Anderson Bonner's birthdate as 1846; however, his headstone in White Rock Cemetery Garden of Memories records his birth and death dates as 1843–1920.—Eds.

Formerly enslaved Anderson Bonner became one of the largest landowners in Lower White Rock, including where today's Medical City Dallas stands. *Courtesy of Remembering Black Dallas, Inc.*

reported that at some point Anderson was given to a White family as a Christmas gift.[27]

Anderson Bonner married Eliza, and nine known children were born to that union: Newton, William, Ed, John, Andy, Mary, Martha, Charlie, and Nash. Eliza was originally from Arkansas. The children helped work the farm. They grew cotton, corn, and fruit, along with other types of crops.

Eliza died as the result of a lamp explosion and fire in their home. Those who saw the explosion said she placed her hands over her head when the lamp blew up in her face and caught fire. Later on, Anderson Bonner married Lucinda, from Waxahachie, Texas.

The first school for Black children in the area was the Vickery and Hillcrest School. It was later moved to Coit Road and was renamed the Anderson Bonner School. The school was closed by the Richardson Independent School District when Hamilton Park School opened in 1955.

Prior to World War II, many Black groups held picnics on a section of the farm on Forest Lane, including the property where Medical City is now located (Forest Lane and Central Expressway). Central Expressway was cut through the farm. The City of Dallas officially named the park west of Medical City on Forest Lane the Anderson Bonner Park. Bicycle trails built by the city are along the White Rock Creek area that was a part of the farm.

There are four surviving grandchildren of Anderson Bonner: Charlie and Hallie Bonner's three children, Eunice Bonner Turner, Henry A. Bonner, and Marie Bonner, and Odessa Bonner Hill, the child of John and Pearl Turner Bonner. Odessa is the only survivor of the nine children of John and Pearl Bonner.

The sister of Anderson Bonner, Caroline, married Ed Fields. Pearl Turner Bonner, wife of John Bonner, was from the Turner

---

27. Sometime between 1850 and 1865, Anderson Bonner and his brother, Lewis, were brought to Texas from Limestone County, Alabama, by their slave holder, Mahulda Bonner, widow of Willis Bonner. In 1869, Anderson and Lewis registered to vote in Precinct 5 in Dallas County.

family. One of the Fields descendants married a Giddings. This established linkages among several of the pioneer African American families who migrated to the farmlands along White Rock Creek in settlements known as Upper White Rock and Lower White Rock. These families, along with others, had extensive land holdings along a line between Dallas and Richardson from Garland to Carrollton.

Frederick Douglass Bookman

Family historians: Madelyne Williams, niece,
and Dr. Walter Bookman, nephew

Frederick Douglass Bookman Sr. and Viola Turner Bookman were the father and mother of the Bookman clan. Rev. Frederick Douglass Bookman [Jr.] was born in Grimes County near Navasota, Texas, in the Flyellen Branch Community. He was the fifth of nineteen children born to Fred and Viola Bookman. Only five of the children lived to adulthood: Frederick, Charlie, Addie, Lee (Craig), and Florida (Morris).

In 1908, Frederick Bookman Jr. graduated from Burnett High School in Terrell. In 1909, the family moved to Dallas as sharecroppers and settled in Mill City. Prior to coming to Dallas, they lived in Ennis, Terrell, and Elmo, Texas. The first family home in Dallas was near Hatcher Street. It is alleged that when the house burned down, it caused his father to suffer a fatal heart attack.

Rev. Bookman owned a grocery store on Foreman and Baldwin Streets. He lived in the rear of the building, while his mother and youngest brother, Joe, lived upstairs. As a young man, Rev. Bookman played baseball with the Terrell Black Devils and the Dallas Jacks.

His sisters, Florida and Lee (Mrs. L. L. Craig), left home to work for the [Dallas] pioneer Munger family, where they lived in servants' quarters. A brother, Charlie, moved to Chicago and worked as a Pullman porter on the Southern Pacific Railway Line. He died November 20, 1969. Members of the family state that he fled to Chicago from Dallas by freight train when their family home was set fire by area Whites. He was a member of the sleeping car porters' union.[28]

Another brother, Tom, worked as chauffeur and janitor for the Sanger family in their downtown store and lived in the servants' section of the family's home on Akard Street. His niece, Madelyne Williams, recalls how handsome and impressive he was in his chauffeur's uniform, "leggons, boots, and cap."

Rev. Bookman was converted in the Baptist faith in Elmo, Texas, under the pastorate of Rev. G. F. Hood. After arriving in Dallas, he joined Mt. Rose Baptist Church and served as Sunday School superintendent and president of the Baptist youth group and sang in the choir. He was licensed to preach in 1916 while at Mt. Rose and was ordained in 1918 under the pastorate of Rev. W. M. Johnson.

In 1913, he married Louise Moton of Lenore, Louisiana. They built a home next door to the grocery store. He and Louise raised and educated her daughter, Mary Dell Connally. Louise and Mary furnished music for the church. Mary Dell was one of the first teachers at Julia C. Frazier Elementary School. She died while young, and her mother followed her in death in 1941.

In 1918, Rev. Bookman became pastor of Antioch Baptist Church in Dallas. In 1922, he served as pastor of Trinity Baptist Church in Dallas. Rev. F. D. Bookman was founder and first moderator of Greater Rising Star Association. He remained in this position until his death.

---

28. The Brotherhood of Sleeping Car Porters—BCSP, which was active from 1925 to 1978.—Eds.

In 1930, he was called to pastor the Bethlehem Baptist Church. He sold the store in order to purchase more land to expand the church at Baldwin, Metropolitan, and Foreman Streets. He and his brother, both master masons and carpenters, laid the foundation for the building. Rev. J. R. Stewart, Rev. F. U. Howard, and Rev. C. L. Rainey also contributed their talents in building Bethlehem Church. They also helped remodel the church after additional land was acquired from the Richardson family.

During that time, the only utility convenience in the area homes was the telephone. Rev. Bookman led the neighbors and church members in working to acquire electricity, water, and gas for the community. They were successful. Mrs. Madelyne Williams, Rev. Bookman's niece, remembers the joy and celebration in each household as the old outhouses were burned.

Rev. Bookman established the first funeral home south of Elm Street, the Lone Star Funeral Home. Originally, it was located on Oakland Avenue in Queen City. It was across from the old cemetery, on the site where New Bethel Baptist Church now stands. Later it was moved to Spring Avenue on the old Thomas Tolbert Homestead. The funeral home and church still stand on the property which Rev. Bookman purchased for each institution.

Rev. Bookman was first vice president of the Dallas Chapter of the NAACP when Rev. B. R. Riley was president. As a 33rd-degree Scottish Rite Mason, he served as Worshipful Master of his chapter. He was also president of the BYPU Congress [Baptist Young Peoples Union Congress], a member of the St. John Landmark Association, the Black Chamber of Commerce, and the YMCA. He was an officer of the Morticians Association and one of the first directors of the *Star Post* newspaper.

He died in 1951 after pastoring more than twenty years at Bethlehem Baptist Church. After his death, his brother, Joe, managed the funeral home, and Joe's wife, Vivian, served as secretary-treasurer. Joe died in 1988, and his wife is presently manager of the funeral home.

Rev. Bookman, as a pioneer and minister, set many high stand-ards that are remembered today. He was a family man, a minister, a businessman, and a community leader. But most of all, he was a humanitarian. In the words of A. W. Jackson of Houston, author of *A Sure Foundation*, Rev. Bookman was "a man of courage, tact, initiative. In other words, he was a go-getter, a high stepper and a far-reacher."

Tobe Bosh and May Elder Wilkerson Bosh

Family historian: Mrs. Lucille C. Bosh McGaughey

Mr. Tobe Bosh was born in La Grange, Georgia, October 5, 1874, and died in Dallas, Texas, December 7, 1949. May Elder Wilkerson Bosh was born in Lineville, Alabama, May 28, 1889, and died in Dallas, Texas, November 30, 1969. The parents of both individuals were born during slavery. May Elder Bosh's father, Mr. John Wilkerson, was eighteen when slavery ended. His father was the White owner of his slaves in Alabama.

Mr. John Wilkerson lived to be ninety-nine years old before he died in Hutchins, Texas. His grandchildren knew him and remem-bered his stories about slavery. John Wilkerson was not allowed to work in the fields—he was the slaves' water boy and a servant in his father's house.

The parents of Tobe Bosh are unknown. He and May Elder Bosh married in 1909 in Lineville, Alabama. Tobe Bosh had four children by two previous marriages, and May Elder Bosh had three children by her late husband, Mr. King Phillips.

Mr. Tobe Bosh's children were Mrs. Gertrude Bosh Brewer, Mrs. Rosa Lee Bosh Jackson (Los Angeles, California), Mr. Macceo Bosh, and Mr. Mingo Bosh. Mrs. May Elder Bosh's children were Eugene Phillips, Olan Phillips, and Owen Phillips. All three are deceased.

Nine more children were born to the union of Tobe and May Elder Bosh. They were Mrs. Euollis Bosh McGregor, Mr. Jack Bosh, Mrs. Pauline Bosh Sallie (Trenton, New Jersey), Mrs. Beulah Mae Bosh Jackson, Miss Irene Bosh, Mr. Thomas Bosh, and Mrs. Mildred Bosh Hamilton (San Antonio, Texas).

Mr. and Mrs. Tobe Bosh moved from Lineville, Alabama, to Dallas County, Texas, in the Lisbon area in 1923. They settled on the Simpson Farm, where Mrs. May Elder Bosh's two brothers, Henry Wilkerson and Willis Beasley, lived with their families. The Simpson Farm was later sold to Bishop College, long after these families moved to Dallas. Bishop College moved from Marshall, Texas, to this location in the early 1960s.

The Bosh family later moved to Mitchell Langdom's farm near Hutchins, Texas. They lived there until they moved to Dallas in the early 1940s.

Mr. Tobe Bosh was known as an excellent farmer and a dedicated community worker. He believed in providing the best possible educational opportunities for his children. He visited the schools often and, if he was not pleased with the teacher and/or the curriculum, he transferred his children. They attended N. W. Harllee Elementary School in Dallas, the Lisbon Colored School, and eventually the Rock Crest school in Lancaster, Texas, where he paid their tuition for several years and often furnished their transportation.

Mr. and Mrs. Tobe Bosh attended elementary schools in Georgia and Alabama but did not graduate. They decided that their children would finish high school and college. Religious beliefs and devotion to God were practiced in their home. Family prayers and Bible readings were held each night after the children's study period at home ended. Blessings and Bible quotations were said before breakfast each day.

Mr. Tobe Bosh did not keep his children out of school to cultivate his or anyone else's farm. They were financially poor, especially during the great depression of the late 1920s and '30s, but they managed to stay in school and survive.

Mrs. May Elder Bosh was a wonderful mother, an excellent cook, and a self-taught seamstress. She made her daughters' clothes and pieced quilts for her family. She was also a very thrifty shopper for food and clothes for her family. She traveled to Dallas each Saturday in a buggy to sell butter and eggs and sometimes chickens. This money enabled her to purchase groceries in Deep Ellum, where they were cheaper than in the store near the farm. Her strong religious beliefs and faith gave her the strength that she needed to endure the difficult ordeals of rearing a large family while often suffering with asthma.

Lucille and Louise Bosh attended the Lisbon Colored School in the seventh grade, after leaving N. W. Harllee Elementary School. They had also attended this school before it burned a few years earlier. They were the only two students in their graduation class in 1932.

The Booker T. Washington High School was the only high school in Dallas County for colored children. The building was so small that grades nine and ten attended school in the afternoon, and grades eleven and twelve held classes in the morning. There were no recesses and gymnasiums. The football team had to practice on the Hall Street Recreation Park.

Mr. Bosh could not afford to pay room and board and other expenses for two girls to attend Booker T. Washington. Therefore, Louise decided to let Lucille attend. Lucille roomed with Mr. and Mrs. J. Barbee the first year and with her widowed sister, Rosa Lee Jackson, and her children the following three years. She worked part-time to help pay her bills and save for her tuition and bus fare to Tuskegee Institute in Alabama.

The younger sisters and a brother attended elementary and junior high school in Lancaster, Texas, and later graduated from Lincoln High School or Booker T. Washington High.

Lucille C. Bosh was the first in her family and the first student from Lisbon to graduate from college. While in college, she worked on the NYA [National Youth Administration] programs during President F. D. Roosevelt's tenure in Washington. There were no loans or scholarships available. Lucille graduated from Tuskegee with honors. She received her bachelor of science degree in social science and received her ME degree from Prairie View College. She did further graduate work in guidance and counseling at the University of Colorado, North Texas State, and Harvard University.

Pauline Bosh Sallie and Beulah Mae Bosh Jackson graduated from Tuskegee Institute as commercial dietitians. Pauline worked as a dietitian and later a supervisor until she retired at the State Hospital in Trenton, New Jersey. Beulah Mae Bosh Jackson was employed as a dietitian in Hot Springs, Virginia. Later, she worked for the Los Angeles post office until she retired.

Mildred Bosh Hamilton received her BS degree from Prairie View College, where she met and married her husband, Mr. Hilton Hamilton. He graduated from Prairie View in electrical engineering. They presently live in San Antonio, Texas, where they worked until they retired. Mildred taught school and Hilton worked at a military base.

Lucille Bosh McGaughey taught two years in the Colored High School in Cartersville, Georgia, followed by fourteen years as health and physical education teacher at Lincoln High School, Dallas, Texas. She also directed the famous Purple Flash Pep Squad at Lincoln, where they won twelve first-place awards on Colored Folks Day at the State Fair of Texas in Dallas.

Later, Mrs. McGaughey served as the Dean of Students and Counselor for eleven years at James Madison High School. In 1967, she went to Bishop College, where she served as a counselor in the Thirteen College Curriculum Program (TCCP) and [as] a part-time consultant to counselors in other Black colleges. Mrs. McGaughey also served as a faculty and community leader in Bishop's annual fundraising drives, for which she received several awards. She is the recipient of several achievement awards in education, religion, and community activities. After retiring, Mrs. McGaughey continued to expand her involvements in real estate and other investments.

Miss Irene Bosh attended Prairie View College in the field of nursing until she left because of illness.

Mr. Jack Bosh was a roofer and carpenter, who was widely known for his proficiency. He sent all five of his children to college.

Mrs. Rosa Lee Jackson was an outstanding businesswoman before she became disabled. Her husband died when her children were very young, but she provided well for them and invested in real estate from her small salary as a maid and laundry woman. Several of her sisters came to Dallas and lived with her free of charge while attending high school.

Mr. Amos and Euollis Bosh McGregor were married longer than anyone in their family—fifty-eight years. Amos was an excellent provider and loving father. He was a devoted deacon of his church. Euollis is an excellent housewife, loving mother, and seamstress. Mr. McGregor died in 1987.

The other Bosh children received their education in the public schools of Dallas and Dallas County, married, and became wonderful fathers and mothers. They earned decent livings for their families and sent several of their children to college.

Mr. and Mrs. Tobe Bosh were the proud parents of seventeen children, thirty-three grandchildren, and thirty-nine great-grandchildren. Fourteen of their children and grandchildren graduated from college, while others are presently attending college.

Abraham and Udora Brewer Family

Family historians: Jesse Brewer
and Constance Davis

Abraham Brewer (July 4, 1855–1937) came to Dallas about 1876. As a child in Tyler, Texas, he and his mother were freed from slavery following the signing of the Emancipation Proclamation.

Unable to care for her son, Abraham's mother gave him to an Irishman by the name of Milligan. Milligan taught the obviously precocious child a number of crafts, including carpentry, winemaking, gardening, and the care of farm animals. Abraham also developed a keen sense of business, which enabled him as an adult to capitalize on the many crafts he learned.

Abraham came to Dallas as a worker with one of the two railroads servicing Dallas. He married Udora Ann Johnson (September 30, 1865–1951) in 1878. Udora came to Dallas from Lufkin, Texas. In Dallas, they established residence in the South Dallas area east of Fair Park. This area had not been annexed by the City of Dallas at that time. Abraham built a home for his family at 4812 Second Avenue. The house still stands in the original location. Abraham began to acquire additional land from area White residents.

The Brewers had nine children: Burlema (1878), Sidney, Carrie Brewer Fucher, Willie, Annie Mae, Estella Brewer Cofield McCoy, Doris Gwendolyn Brewer Fulcher (August 1, 1910), Ella, and Jesse (August 5, 1897). Burlema and Sidney died in childhood. Mr. Brewer named a street for his son, Sidney, by joining two sticks in the form of a cross, writing the name Sidney on it, and securing the sign in the ground. When this area became a part of Dallas, the street retained its name.

In addition to the land Mr. Brewer owned, he leased sixty-two additional acres for a truck farm. The plot was bound on the south by Pine Street, west by Oakland Avenue, east by Exline Street, and north by the Oakland Cemetery. On this land, he developed one of the most productive truck farms in the Dallas area. He also raised cattle and a number of other farm animals and fowls. He would carry fresh vegetables to the Old City Market to sell at least two or three times a week. He would leave home in his wagon very early in the morning and return late in the evening. At the peak of his truck farming career, he employed as many as thirty people to work the farm and care for the animals.

The husband of Estella Cofield, Silas Cofield, was one of the founders of the Excelsior Life Insurance Company. Members of the family recall how Estella and her husband, during the early days of the company, would ride horseback to nearby towns in order to pay claims for burials that were to take place the next day.

Jesse and Doris are the two surviving children of the Brewers. Jesse married Lenora Byrd (February 3, 1901—July 31, 1971) from Forney, Texas. Jesse and his father built Jesse's home next door to the family home on Second Avenue.

Leonora's brother, Rev. Bernard Byrd, built and pastored Munger Avenue Baptist Church for a number of years. Records indicate that he led a protest movement to prevent the government from displacing Black homeowners to build Roseland Homes in the North Dallas area. Obviously, his group lost the battle, but not without a gallant attempt to save one of the nicest Black-owned and Black-built neighborhoods in the city at that time. Using a Black contractor, he rebuilt the church.

Jesse Brewer vividly remembers growing up and eventually rearing a family in Dallas. He attended elementary school, from 1905–1912, in a one-room schoolhouse in the old Mt. Moriah Church. His first teacher was Mr. T. D. Marshall, former teacher and principal in the Dallas schools. Jesse graduated from the Old Colored High School in 1915 with thirty-three other classmates. One of his high school classmates was Alvernon King-Tripp, a local civic leader. He remembers riding the trolley car from his home to the end of the line and then walking the remainder of the way to school. As a seven-year-old, he watched his first funeral procession while perched on a fence as the pallbearers walked down Oakland Street carrying the casket and playing music "New Orleans" style.

His early work experiences included a job at the Adolphus Hotel and work with a civilian team that was sent to the East Coast to build an Army camp in Philadelphia. He also worked with his brother-in-law in the early days of Excelsior Life Insurance Company. His major interest, however, was in electronics. Using his own ingenuity, he built a radio. He furthered his education by taking a correspondence course in electronics. He studied very hard at night after work. The course was offered by RCA Electronics and Radio School. After completing the course, he was able to secure a job at Southwestern Life Insurance Company as an electrician. He became chief electrician in the old company building, which was on the corner of Akard and Main Streets. He worked there until he retired in the 1960s.

While working at Southwestern Life, he remembers going to the second-floor window and witnessing the lynching of a Black man on the "arch." After the man was removed from the hanging scaffold, he was dragged down Commerce Street behind a Model T Ford.[29] He also saw the Ku Klux Klan march several times in downtown Dallas.

Jesse A. Brewer provided well for his wife and three children. He purchased his second home in North Dallas at 2211 Allen Street. He and his wife also bought a home in Oak Cliff. His three children are Bernard Constance Fairfax Brewer-Davis (October 9, 1919) of Dallas; Jesse A. Brewer, Jr. (October 11, 1921), Los Angeles, California; and Silas Hamilton Brewer (January 3, 1929) of Brentwood, California.

---

29. On Sunday, July 18, 2021, the Dallas County Justice Initiative and the national organization the Equal Justice Initiative (EJI) held a ceremony in recognition of this heinous act, honoring the memory of the man who was killed, Allen Brooks. The ceremony, part of the EJI Community Remembrance Project, included collecting soil from the ground of the site, now Pegasus Plaza, at the southeast corner of Main and Akard Streets, as well as a scholarship award ceremony hosted at the Remembering Black Dallas, Inc. headquarters at 1408 N. Washington Avenue. Allen Brooks will also be recognized with a Texas State Historical Marker in Dallas's Martyrs Park.—Eds.

Constance attended Wiley College and has been an entrepreneur with her husband, William, in Dallas. Jesse is second in command, Deputy Chief of Police, with the Los Angeles Police Department. He was a consultant for *Hill Street Blues*, a highly rated television police story. He graduated from Tuskegee Institute as a Second Lieutenant and served in the Army until his retirement as a Colonel. He has three sons: Jesse III, Jonathan, and Kenneth.

Silas is in government service in Brentwood. He has one son, Anthony. The grandfather of Lydia, Silas's first wife, was Oscar DePriest, the first Black Congressman from Illinois.

Jesse Jr.'s wife, Odessa, is a retired nurse. Constance's husband, William, is a Dallas businessman. Silas's wife, Jimmie, teaches in Brentwood.

There are now three great-great-grandchildren in the pioneer Brewer family. Each generation has made outstanding contributions in the tradition of the first young man, Abraham, who migrated to Dallas. Though born in slavery, he became one of the most enterprising young men of his time.

James and Ellen Brown

Family historian: Alma Elaine Brown with Gladys Jernigan, Charles Brown, and Chestine Brown

In the early 1800s,[30] James and Ellen Brown were married in Granger, Texas. Four sons and one daughter were born to this union: James Jr., George, Mollie, Lee Edward, and John Milton. The members of the family (with the exception of James Jr.) moved to Dallas as early pioneers, after the children received an elementary education. A few years after George, Mollie, Lee Edward, and John Milton were grown, James and Ellen passed away.

---

30. It is likely that the events in this narrative began later, in the mid- to late 1800s.—Eds.

James Jr. remained in Granger, Texas, and married Carrie Smith. To this union six children were born—one son and five daughters: Allen, Lela, Ellen, Carrie, Miranda, and Marie. When the children were young, James and Carrie passed away. The younger ones, Miranda and Marie, were brought to Dallas and reared by their Aunt Mollie and Uncle George. The others remained in Granger and were reared by the parents of their mother, Carrie.

Miranda and Marie received their education in the Dallas public schools. Marie received her BA degree from Prairie View State University and taught in Hillsboro, Texas, for several years. The members of the entire family are now deceased.

George married twice. Clara was the first wife and Julia Ray was the second. George and both wives are now deceased. He was a member of the Knights of Pythias Lodge.

Mollie married Tom Wilkins, who was a member of the Knights of Pythias Lodge. To this union was born one daughter, Lela. Lela married Cleveland Turner, and to their union was born one son, Cleveland Jr. Lela received her education in the Dallas public schools and was valedictorian of her class. She received her BA degree from Prairie View State University. She taught writing at J. P. Starks Elementary School for a number of years. She was a charter member of the Royal Art Club of Dallas. Tom, Mollie, Cleveland, and Lela are now deceased.

Their son, Cleveland Jr., graduated from the Dallas public schools and also was the valedictorian of his class. He received a scholarship from the Kiwanis Club and attended the University of Michigan for several years. He also spent several years in the Army Air Force. He received computer education training. At the present time, he works in the computer system of Sacramento, California, where he resides with his family. He is married to the former Velma Dawson, who is a certified public accountant. They have a son and a daughter: Cleveland III is a senior in college and a member of Tau Kappa Epsilon fraternity, and Alicia, a junior in high school, is quite active in athletics.

John Milton married Mary Etta Williams, and to this union four children were born. There were three daughters and one son: Johnnie Mae, Mabel, Lorine, and Charles. John was an agent for the Excelsior Mutual Benefit Insurance for several years. He collected his door-to-door dues traveling by horse and buggy. He received a very outstanding promotion to the position of secretary-treasurer of the insurance company. This position he held until his death. He was also a member of the Knights of Pythias Lodge, and his wife, Mary Etta, was a member of the Courts of Calanthe Lodge. John and Mary Etta are now deceased.

Johnnie Mae received her education in the Dallas public schools and later attended Bishop College. She had one daughter, Gladys, by an early marriage. Later she married James Francis and remained with him until her death. She was a licensed beauty operator during her lifetime.

Gladys received her education in the Dallas public schools and graduated from Huston-Tillotson College with a BA degree. She did further study at East Texas State University and Southern Methodist University. She taught for several years in the Richardson public school system, from which she retired. She is presently married to Ladell Jernigan of Longview, Texas.

Mabel received her education in the Dallas public schools. She attended Wilberforce University and received her BA degree from Bishop College. She taught a few years in the Dallas public schools. She was a member of Delta Sigma Theta Sorority. She married Floyd Wilkerson, a retired principal of DISD and remained his wife until her death.

Lorine received her education in the Dallas public schools and received her BA Degree with a major in music from Bishop College. She did further study at Howard University. She studied under outstanding voice teachers and traveled extensively with major groups. She taught for several years in the Dallas public schools, at N. W. Harllee Elementary School and Phyllis Wheatley School. She was presented as a debutante by the Idlewild Club of

Dallas. She was married for several years to Julester Lee, who is now deceased.

Charles received his education in the Dallas public schools and received his BA degree from Bishop College. He is married to Chestine Bass of Dallas. They presently live in Los Angeles, California. To this union were born two sons, Charles Jr. (now deceased) and Cedric. Charles Sr. is an electric contractor, and Cedric works with his father in the electrical business.

Lee Edward married Ella Abram, and to this union were born two daughters, Bertha Lee and Alma Elaine. Lee Edward was in the hauling and transfer business during the horse-and-buggy days. He transported freight from A. G. Spaulding, Practical Drawing Company, Texas School Book Depository, etc., in a horse-drawn wagon to the Railway Express Office. Lee Edward was a member of Knights of Pythian Lodge and Ella was a member of the Knights and Daughters of Tabor. Lee and Ella are now deceased.

Bertha Lee attended the Dallas public schools. She received a BA degree from Wiley College, with further study at Prairie View State University and North Texas State University. She married an Army veteran, which ended in divorce. She taught for many years in Dallas, at Wheatley, Dunbar, and Roger Q. Mills. She retired after forty-five years of service. She was a member of Zeta Phi Beta Sorority. She is now deceased.

Alma Elaine received her education in Dallas public schools. She began studying piano with Mrs. Maurine Bailey and later [studied with] Mrs. Portia Washington Pittman, the daughter of Booker T. Washington. Mrs. Pittman also taught choral music at Booker T. Washington High School in Dallas.

Alma received her bachelor of music degree from Fisk University, with further study at Ball State University. She graduated from Roosevelt University with a master of music education degree. She performed in a four-piano concert held at the State Fair Music Hall. She taught choral music in various schools in Dallas: H. S. Thompson, Phyllis Wheatley, Erasmo Seguin Learning Center, and Lincoln High

School. Also, she taught music education at the Montessori Creative Learning Center (private school).

She is a member of the National Association of Jazz Educators and a member of the National Alliance of Black School Educators. She has given several piano recitals in Dallas and elsewhere. She won an award for appearing in a talent show held on a Hawaiian cruise ship in 1986. She is a member of Alpha Kappa Alpha Sorority and composed the Alpha Xi Omega Chapter Hymn, "Alpha Xi Omega Dear."

This is the conclusion of the Brown family history from the early 1800s to 1988. This is one of the pioneer families of Dallas. The information was compiled by Alma Elaine Brown, the oldest surviving member of the Brown family.

John and Reathy Brown

Family historian: Lillie Belle Brown Hall

Mrs. Lillie Belle Brown Hall is the daughter of John and Reathy Brown. John was born April 1, 1882, in Marshall, Texas. He was the son of Jack Brown and Ellen Calvin Brown, who were descendants of slave parents. His father was brought from Tennessee to Marshall. Jack Brown married Ellen Brown, and to this union six children were born: John, Ben, Peter, Eli, Hurbert, and James. All are deceased.

After Jack Brown's death, Ben migrated from Marshall to Dallas in search of work in 1904. He began work at the Dallas Car Barn, which was a good-paying job for an unskilled worker in the early period of Dallas. He purchased a home in what was then known as Booker T. Addition, an area of Dallas which at that time looked more like a swamp. However, now it has been transformed into one of Dallas's elite sections.

John Brown remained in Marshall and married Reathy O. Taswell of Jefferson, Texas. While in Marshall, one son was born: John Esters Brown. Later John and Reathy migrated to Dallas in search of work. Although John was a farm-reared boy, it was not difficult for him to locate a job, because he had worked as a plumber, carpenter, and mechanic, as well as an employee for a box factory, a foundry, and the Texas Pacific Railway. He mastered many skills without a formal education.

He and Reathy lived on Hill Avenue near the Dallas Fair Park. Here their second child, Lillie Belle Brown, was born. She was named for the daughter of her Uncle Ben, the first-known Black mayor of Bollie, Oklahoma. Lillie Belle began her school days at an early age. She attended the No. 4 School, located on the corner of Preston and Gano Streets. This entire section was called The Prairie. While she was in attendance, the school name was changed to J. P. Starks. It was named for a former principal, Professor J. P. Starks. Her first teacher at the No. 4 School was Mrs. Eva Weems. Other teachers were Mrs. Fannie Gipson, music supervisor of all Black schools, Mesdames Mason, Lela Wilkins, Pocahontas Rochon, Overton, Hardley, Thomas, Edna E. Ezell, M. L. Island, and Williams, and Mr. K. B. Polk.

Lillie Belle was indeed happy to finish the seventh grade with top honors. She remembers distinctly speaking at the graduation exercise held at the Pythian Temple on Elm Street. The Temple was remembered by the students because Mrs. Overton, their history teacher, emphasized that Mr. Sydney Pittman, the husband of the daughter of Booker T. Washington, was the architect of the building. Little did she know that soon she would have to compete with Booker T. Washington's grandson, Sydney Pittman Jr., in her history class at Booker T. Washington High School.

After finishing J. P. Starks, Lillie Belle had to spend one semester at B. F. Darrell while Booker T. Washington High School was being completed on Burford and Flora Streets. The 1922 class was moved to Booker T. Washington at mid-semester and graduated in 1925.

She was a member of the first four-year graduating class of Booker T. Washington High.

In the 1920s Lillie Belle's father and Uncle Ben came back into the picture. Her graduating year from high school in 1925 was during the Depression. Her father always remembered that from age three she had always wanted to be a schoolteacher. He started planning to find a way to send her to college.

Three years before her graduation, he purchased a mule and a horse and kept them in a barn in his back yard on William Street. He began building a wagon out of scraps picked up on the streets and in the junk yards. He wanted to have it ready to travel to his home farm in Marshall to make enough money to pay for her schooling. His job, as well as most others around, was playing out in those Depression days.

After Lillie Belle graduated from high school, her father completed his covered wagon, hitched the back yard–reared horse and mule to the wagon, and drove with his son from Dallas to Marshall to start making what he could to pay for Lillie Belle's schooling at Bishop College. After two years at Bishop, she was able to get a teaching job on a two-year certificate.

Born the only daughter of two children of the late John and Reathy Brown, Lillie Belle Brown became one of the distinguished educators of the time. She received her bachelor of science degree from Bishop College in Marshall, Texas, where she graduated cum laude. She began her teaching career while a student at Bishop College. She met Mr. J. D. Hall, who was to become her husband, life confidant, and friend. They were married when she began work toward the master of arts degree at Columbia University in New York City.

Mrs. Hall was the first resident of Upshur County school system to receive a master's degree. She received the master's and professional degree from Columbia. She also completed graduate work at North Texas State University and Prairie View University. She completed all academic requirements for the doctor of philosophy degree from

Columbia University and needs only a one-year residency to have the degree bestowed upon her.

Lillie Belle Hall taught in the public schools of East Texas and Dallas and at Bishop College on both undergraduate and graduate levels. She has the distinction of having missed only eight days from the classroom in the fifty years of her teaching career.

She began her teaching career at Rains Elementary School, Point, Texas. She was principal at Snow Hill School, Gilmer, Texas, and remained there thirty-one years. She taught at Bishop College seven years; Lancaster, Texas, six semesters; Lincoln High, three years; Hillcrest High, nine years; and L. G. Pinkston High, Dallas. She taught English and was head or co-chairman of the English department at three of these schools.

She organized or was founder/sponsor of several supportive organizations for student growth and development. She was director of the county Interscholastic League for Upshur County and later district director of the Interscholastic League for five counties. She was the only woman to serve as director of the District Interscholastic League. She was named Teacher of the Year at three of the high schools where she taught.

Lillie Belle has continually been an active participant in religious, civic, and professional organizations. She was baptized at Mount Rose Baptist Church, Dallas, Texas, located on The Prairie. She affiliated with Galilee Baptist during her sojourn years in Marshall. She has been a member of Good Street Baptist Church since returning to her home city, Dallas. Her active and professional affiliations include NAACP, YWCA, Chamber of Commerce, Zeta Phi Beta Sorority, County Principals' Wives of Dallas, and regional director of Bishop College.

Lillie Belle is the recipient of many outstanding awards, among which are Educator of the Year, Elite News; Excellence in Education, United for Action; Zeta of the Year, Kappa Zeta Chapter; Bishop College Hall of Fame; Extra Mile Award, Bishop College; Appreciation Award, Maria Morgan Branch YWCA; sustaining Membership

Drive, YWCA; Love, Devotion, and Understanding of Children, L. G. Pinkston; and Hall of Fame, Valley View High, Gilmer. She recently received the NAACP Juanita Jewel Craft Award. Club offices held include: president, Zeta Phi Beta Sorority, Kappa Zeta Chapter and vice president, Upsilon Zeta Chapter, Marshall.

J. D. Hall, husband and confidant of Mrs. Lillie B. Hall, was born in Marshall, Texas, Harrison County. He had two brothers, Robert and Percy, and one sister, Veral Hall. He has since early childhood been an aspirant for educational, religious, civic, and political leadership. His career has shown upward mobility through a variety of job responsibilities. The jobs include brick yard worker, hotel bell boy and captain, teacher, principal, and assistant superintendent.

After graduation from Bishop College, Marshall, Texas, Mr. Hall began his teaching career at Rocky Crest, Lancaster, Texas. After one year, he was elected principal, and later assistant superintendent, of Lancaster Independent School District. He retired in 1984, after thirty years of service.

He has been an active participant in civic and political activities. Politically, his aspirations were fulfilled when he ran for office and became the second Black trustee of the Dallas County Community College District. He has held this position for eleven years and is now serving as a vice chairman of the board. Mr. Hall was appointed director of the Guaranty Bank, Dallas, in 1970 and remained director until the bank dissolved in 1988.

His civic and fraternal services include Moorland Branch YMCA Board, Goals for Dallas, Urban League, YWCA, Bishop College Club, Dallas Manpower Board, Lancaster Recreation Board, Red Cross Board, Knights of Pythias and Masonic Lodges, Phi Beta Sigma Fraternity, Elk's Club, and others. He is a member of Good Street Baptist Church, Dallas, Texas.

Mr. Hall is the recipient of numerous awards, namely Service Awards as a teacher, principal, and counselor, Lancaster Independent School District; Extra Mile Award, Bishop College; Spirit of America Award, Guaranty Bank; Meritorious Service Award; L. Storey Stemmons Award, Urban League; Gulf Coast Regional Award and Man of the Year Award, Phi Beta Sigma Fraternity; Lancaster Chamber of Commerce; and many others.

T. C. and Hannah Clayton

Family historian: Sarah Clayton Finley,
interviewed by Willie C. Abney

T. C. Clayton was born in East Texas. He later moved with his parents, Smith Clayton and Caroline Fisher Clayton, to Kaufman County, where he met and married Miss Hannah Teal. To this union twelve children were born. In 1908, the family moved to Dallas and located at 1905 South Haskell Avenue, where they lived for more than forty years. The Claytons were members of St. Mark Baptist Church. T. C. Clayton served on the Board of Deacons and the Finance Committee.

T. C. and Hannah Clayton had twelve children: Verble Clayton Sheppard, Obelia Clayton Humble, Irene Clayton, Dorothy Clayton Lyde, T. C. Clayton Jr., Alton Clayton, Sarah Clayton Finley, Luther Clayton, James Earl Clayton, Helen Clayton Bryant, Eugene Clayton, and Harvey Clayton. The Clayton children attended the Dallas public schools. Verble Clayton Sheppard and Dorothy Clayton Lyde are graduates of Booker T. Washington High School.

T. C. Clayton was a landscaper and was responsible for many beautiful lawns throughout the city of Dallas. T. C. Clayton passed September 1948, in Dallas, Texas. Hannah Clayton passed several years later in Los Angeles, California, where several of the children had migrated earlier in their lives.

Elija and Charity Davis Family

Family historians: Herman D. Washington,
Doris Washington Bluitt, and V. Jewel
Washington Meshack

Mother Charity Davis was born in Parksville, Kentucky, to Joe and Elizabeth Fry in 1861. After moving to Dallas in 1880, her husband, Reverend Elija Davis, supported her love for God and man with an inspiration to create a Christian community for their children and others.

On a warm summer night in 1895, Reverend Joshua Goin, Reverend W. F. Love, and several others met in the home of Reverend Elija and Mother Charity Davis to plan for their dream—a new church. The Saint Paul African Methodist Episcopal Church had its beginning from this modest and humble group of Christians. The church is still located in the South Dallas community at 2420 Metropolitan. The name of Reverend Elija Davis can be found on the first cornerstone of the Saint Paul African Methodist Episcopal Church, as one of the first officers of the church.

The Charity Davis Missionary Society was named in honor of Mother Charity. She died on Monday, December 23, 1957.

Reverend and Mrs. Elija Davis had fifteen children, who were baptized and grew spiritually in the Saint Paul African Methodist Episcopal Church. Lovater Charlotte Davis was born to Reverend and Mrs. Elija J. Davis in Dallas, Texas, on May 16, 1894. She married Claude Washington and founded the Deluxe Beauty Shop on Romine Street. It was a successful business venture for Lovater and her daughter, Evelyn. The Dallas community patronized this beauty shop for expert hair care. Ten years after the death of her husband, Claude, Lovater married Young Aaron, who was also in business as a successful barber. They combined their resources and worked together harmoniously in the family, church, and business. He preceded her in death. Lovater Charlotte Davis Washington Aaron died on Friday evening, March 1, 1985, at the Shiloh Park Hospital in Garland, Texas.

Reverend Elija Davis is shown with his wife, Charity Fry Davis, and eight of their fifteen children in about 1900. *Black Dallas Remembered, Inc.*

Claude worked as a Pullman porter until his duties as a father of a growing family demanded his attention at home rather than the constant travel required for this vocation. He later worked as shipping clerk and deliveryman for Firestone Tire and Rubber Company and also the Lee Tire and Rubber Company.

Claude's family worshipped at the Friendship Baptist Church in the South Dallas community where several churches were organized. The closest church to this Baptist church was the Saint Paul African

Methodist Episcopal Church, which was the church of his wife's family. During her early years of motherhood, Claude's wife, Lovater, was unable to attend church on a regular basis. The Washington children attended worship services with their father at the Baptist church, the Methodist church, and other churches in the community.

Claude was a talented pianist whose melodic tunes could be heard at the local recreational center in the days of their youth. His family was nurtured in love and discipline. Eight survivors are James L., Evelyn L., Herman D., Claudia D., Vivyan Jewel, Abner D., Doris L., and Jessye L. The children of Claude and Lovater Washington continue the Davis legacy and the Washington discipline with a love for God and man in places of worship throughout the world. One son, Abner D. Washington, and his son, Ronald P. Washington, are ministers of the Worldwide Church of God. They serve as pastors of congregations in Los Angeles, California, and Ann Arbor, Michigan, respectively.

Three of the Davis descendants chose the ministry as their vocations. The ministers are: the late Reverend A. S. F. Jones of the African Methodist Episcopal Church; Abner D. Washington, Los Angeles, California Congregation of the Worldwide Church of God; and Ronald P. Washington, Ann Arbor, Michigan Congregation of the Worldwide Church of God.

William and Sarah Jones Davis

Contributed by Ezell Fuqua Carwile with interviews by W. B. Anderson

Sarah Jones Davis was born in July 1856 and died February 9, 1938. She organized the Jackson Temple CME Church, which is now Carter Temple CME Church in West Dallas. She served the church as Sunday

School superintendent for a number of years. Her daughter Wiletta served as pianist there for several years. Sarah Davis was known for her beautiful creations from crocheting.

William M. Davis, the husband of Sarah Davis, was born in 1846 in Missouri. He fought in the Civil War. The Davises had nine children, and only eight were living in 1900. The children were Willetta Davis, Ira D. Snaky Davis, Jimmie E. Clarntine Davis, Wayman Davis, Sarah Ella Davis, Katie Enderanes Davis, Lule Gorganer Davis, and Janaro Davis. William had one sister, Carrie Davis Hill.

The Davis home was a large, well-built house with a huge porch and garden on the side. It was located on the corner of Sylvan Avenue and Singleton Boulevard in West Dallas. The Davises had a wood yard and sold wood throughout the area.

Dr. William Knox Flowers Sr. Family

Family historian: Merle Flowers

William Knox Flowers Sr. was born in Raleigh, Mississippi, in 1886. The death of Dr. W. K. Flowers's sister prompted his interest in the medical profession. Therefore, he chose to attend Meharry Medical College following his graduation from Alcorn A&M College in Mississippi. He graduated from Meharry in 1913, and he did postgraduate work in Chicago.

Later he left Mississippi and travelled to Terrell, Texas. There he met Dr. L. G. Pinkston. Dr. Pinkston recommended that Dr. Flowers move to Sulphur Springs to commence his medical practice.

During his tenure in the medical profession at Sulphur Springs, an influenza epidemic became widespread in 1918. Physicians, Black and White, felt helpless because of their inability to develop a remedy for the illness. However, Dr. Flowers proceeded to develop a remedy for the epidemic for Black patients. Others in the medical profession remained completely unsuccessful in their attempts to aid in the creation of a remedy. Subsequently, White physicians referred their patients to Dr. Flowers.

Dr. Flowers married Bonnie Pearl Perry, and to that union four children were born: William K. Jr., Perry J., Madelyn M., and Edwina L.

In 1924, Dr. Flowers moved his family to Dallas, Texas, and purchased a home on Hall Street. Dr. Flowers Sr. was also eager to establish his practice in Dallas and constructed a two-story office building in 1925, at 2317 Hall Street. Prior to this development though, Dr. Flowers worked with Dr. Walter McMillan.

The two-story office building provided office space for other businesses. Some of the businesses were Atlanta Life Insurance Company and Universal Life Insurance Company. Dr. A. E. Hughes, Dr. Cleaver, and Attorneys Dwayne and Roger Mason leased space in the building. Dr. Flowers Sr. practiced at this location until he died in 1957.

Dr. W. K. Flowers was a dedicated member of Boll Street CME Church, an original charter member of the Negro Chamber of Commerce, and a major contributor to the YMCA.

J. S. Giddings Family

Family historian: Ora Giddings Clayton

Born in 1865, Joseph Sherman Giddings (Joe) was a native of Georgia and the son of Felix and Ira Giddings. As a young boy he moved to Dallas with his parents, sisters, and brothers. His parents were slaves before moving to Dallas.

Joe studied hard and at the age of nineteen was given his first assignment to teach in one of the rural schools north of Dallas.

Joseph Sherman Giddings. *Black Dallas Remembered, Inc.*

Estella Fields Giddings. *Black Dallas Remembered, Inc.*

Determined to further his education, he enrolled in Paul Quinn College, mastered his subjects with honor, and became one of the most deserving and respected teachers of that time.

Joe taught in the one-room schools where all grades and subjects—primer through high school—were taught. The school term was four to six months a year. He was known to teach students who are now considered slow learners. His style of teaching was most unique. He taught for more than fifty years, from the small community of Bear Creek to many communities in Dallas, including Little Egypt and Fields Settlement. Friends and neighbors referred to him as Professor Giddings, the lawyer. They felt that only a lawyer could help with the many problems he helped resolve.

In 1885, he bought more than two hundred acres of land from Captain Emmerson, whose grave marker stands tall in the cemetery on Hall Street, Dallas, Texas. Sharecroppers lived on the premises and were very successful with agricultural products.

In 1886, he married Mallie Hill, whose parents were part owners of Little Egypt, where he taught for many years. To this union seven children were born. Mrs. Hill and five of the children preceded him in death.

Many years later he married Estella Fields, a former student. They were blessed with five children: Ola M., Kenneth, Ora, Vella, and Dartrell. All married and made their homes in Dallas, except one who lives in Oklahoma City.

Joseph died in March 1951, and he was buried in the family cemetery, which is known as the Fields' Cemetery. This cemetery is in North Dallas on Skillman Avenue. The first person to be buried there was in 1910. His granddaughter, Gigi Clayton, the daughter of Ora Giddings Clayton and Ezra Clayton, and the great-great-granddaughter of Anderson Fields, is also buried there. She was the sister of Gary R. Clayton and the fiancée of Tony Dorsett (star running back for the Dallas Cowboys).

————————

Charles Randle Graggs Family

Family historian: Ouida Graggs Chambers

Mr. Charles R. Graggs—author, lecturer, archivist, shoe repairman, lover of art, books, and civil rights—was a man born with visions ahead of his time.

Mr. Graggs was a product of slave parents in Marlin Falls County, Texas. He migrated to Dallas in the early 1890s and spent seventy-five years there. He never received the honors his deeds would ordinarily have merited. Nevertheless, the *Dallas Morning News* paid a special tribute to his family upon his death for his contributions to the *News*.

Mr. Graggs matriculated at Howard University in Washington, DC. Before the turn of the [twentieth] century, he attended the Boston Conservatory of Art at Boston University, Boston, Massachusetts. After attending college, he collected more than 1,200 books and works of art. He used his pen as a weapon in fighting the battles for freedom of his fellow African Americans.

Graggs was the father of five children. His wife and three of his children preceded him in death. He told his children that he was born with a three-fold taste for art, books, [and] questioning and attacking segregation as applied solely to Negroes. This premise is character-ized in his myriad works, a few of which are listed here: *Education—An Essay*, 1921; *The Fallacy of Racial Segregation*, 1924; *An Open Reply to the Foes of Civil Rights*, 1949; "N.A.A.W.P. (National Association for the Advancement of White People)," 1955; "Negro Women," 1955; Two Open Letters to Governor Allan Shivers, 1955; Answer—Rebuttal to Georgia's Attorney General, 1956; *Is It Hate or Is It Fear?*, 1957; *Nuggets—Events—Education*, 1959; *Education—Its Priceless Assets*, 1959.

Mr. Graggs was always self-employed. He owned and operated his own shoe repair and used clothing shop, located on Hall Street across the street from the B. F. Darrell School. He was a charter member of the NAACP and the first Black to witness the act of violence when a porter was literally thrown from the [Dallas County] Court House after having been summoned for jury duty.

Graggs stated, "After the advent of Christ, no great painting or poem has given men even the slightest hint to uphold or kill anyone merely on account of his immediate racial kin."

Mr. Graggs has two loving, proud daughters, Mrs. Vabel Graggs Reid of Santa Monica, California, and Mrs. Ouida Graggs Chambers of Dallas, Texas.

A Special Tribute: Mrs. Ouida Graggs Chambers, daughter of Charles Randle Graggs, was a well-known church leader in New Hope Baptist Church. She worked enthusiastically with the Black Dallas Remembered Steering Committee to write her family history. On March 8, 1987, she suffered a heart attack from which she did not recover.

Jeff and Hannah Hill

Family historian: Lela Hill Wicks with Arleanor Hamilton Peters and Della Hill Dunham

Among the early settlers of Little Egypt were Jeff and Hannah Hill. According to family records, they purchased property in Little Egypt in 1883. Deeds reveal the purchasing date as October 15, 1883.

Little Egypt, an all-Black community, was one of the freedmen's towns for former slaves and their offspring. It was located near [today's] Northwest Highway and Abrams Road in [what is now] the White Rock Lake area near White Rock Creek.

Jim Schutze, in his book *Accommodations*, writes: "the neighborhood was on land deeded in 1865 to former slaves, Jeff and

Hannah Hill, the residents, who named their church Little Egypt Chapel Baptist Church because the neighborhood and the church were associated with deliverance from bondage."

Little Egypt ceased to exist in May 1962, when it was bought out by a real estate syndicate for a shopping center. Among the more than two hundred residents at that time were William and Commodore Hill, sons of Jeff and Hannah Hill.

William Hill, the patriarch of the remaining Hill family, was eighty-seven when Little Egypt was bought out. He was known to family members as "Uncle Dood." Commodore, who was seventy-six at the time of the move, was born in Little Egypt. The property was in the family for seventy-nine years. Jeff and Hannah Hill were the parents of ten children. The other offspring were John, Henry, Peter, Pierce, Joe, Olivia, Bristol, and Mollie. All were deceased by 1962. Some of the siblings of Peter Hill are still living in Dallas County. They are Otha Hill Henry, Millie Hill Dunbar, and Pete Hill.

Earlier, Hannah was married to Lafayette Nash. This union produced two children, Emily and Cassandra. Family history has Jeff as a youngster coming to Texas from Missouri with his former slave master, whose surname was Hill.

Jeff used his acreage for farming—a combination of farmland and bountiful orchards. Jeff and Hannah Hill were also longtime owners and operators of a grocery store located on their property at Northwest Highway.

According to Egypt Chapel Baptist Church history, the church was organized April 10, 1880, by Rev. A. R. Griggs, an early pastor of New Hope Baptist Church and a well-known community organizer.

The Hill family played a prominent role in the history of Egypt Chapel Baptist Church. The church building was constructed on the property of Jeff and Hannah Hill. The cornerstone was laid on July 11, 1920, under the leadership of Rev. R. L. Robertson. The names on the cornerstone were H. A. Hill, J. A. Starks, O. Drake,

Mr. Matthew, and Mr. Hill. For years the church was under the leadership of John Hill.

During the 1940s, under the leadership of the Rev. J. B. Body, the church purchased property from Commodore and Sarah Hill on Ferndale Road in the White Rock area. A red brick structure was built at this location. Sarah was very active in the church and served as a trustee. She also served as clerk and secretary of the church. In 1962 the church moved to its present location, 1122 Hutchins Road in East Oak Cliff.

The Hills were very active in the Little Egypt Community. Henry Hill served as a trustee of Egypt Lodge of Odd Fellows, No. 6072. Many of the deceased members of the Hill family and their loved ones are buried in the McCree Cemetery on Audelia Road.

At this writing, it is not known when Jeff and Hannah Hill died. However, it is known that he preceded her in death and that she attended the Texas Centennial State Fair in 1936. At that time, she was 100 years old.

At the exodus of Little Egypt Community in 1962, the Jeff and Hannah Hill family had expanded to include twelve grandchildren, twenty-five great-grandchildren, and thirty-five great-great-grandchildren.

Little Egypt pioneers, Jeff and Hannah Hill, would have been proud of their descendants who went on to earn degrees in higher education. Included among them were the following:

- Lela Hill Wicks, MEd from the University of North Texas (daughter of Elijah Hill and the late Earlie B. Hamilton Hill)
- Ann Cheryl Turner Neal, bachelor of social work, Texas Woman's University; and Godfrey Turner, Bachelor of Science from Texas Tech (daughter and son of Willie Sue Hill Turner Jefferson and the late Sidney Turner)
- Conchetta Yvonne Hill, BS from Texas Tech (daughter of William Earl Hill and Silverne Hill)

- Candace Elaine Wicks, BS from Huston-Tillotson (daughter of Lela Hill Wicks and Samuel Wicks)
- Tyrone Collins, MD, and L. C. Collins Jr., MD, Meharry Medical School (sons of Dr. and Mrs. L. C. Collins Sr.). Their mother, the former Billye Jean Peters, is the daughter of Rozetta Hill Peters.

John E. Jr. and Ruby G. Hill

Family historian: Marion Hill James

John Edward Hill Jr. was the only son of Mr. and Mrs. John E. Hill. He was born May 24, 1898, in Austin, Texas. He was educated in the public schools of Austin. He moved to Dallas about 1920. He was a government employee and retired as a maintenance supervisor at the Federal Building, 1114 Commerce Street.

Ruby Roberts Gipson Hill was born to Mr. and Mrs. Dan Gipson in Weatherford, Texas. She moved to Dallas at an early age. She was educated in the public schools of Dallas and graduated from Dallas Colored High School in 1917. She retired from the workforce as a sick claims clerk at Excelsior Life Insurance Company.

John Edward Jr. and Ruby Roberta Gipson were married on May 22, 1924, by Rev. C. C. Harper, pastor of St. John Baptist Church, where they were members. To this union one child was born, Marion Frances Hill. The Hills bought a home in Wheatley Addition, at 3732 Dunbar Street, in about 1926.

Marion married Herman Lee DeVaughn Sr., and to this union two children were born, Tanya Reneé DeVaughn and Herman Lee DeVaughn Jr. Marion later married John Alfred James. To this union one child was born, Rosalyn Rubette James.

Herman DeVaughn Jr. married Kim Yvette Willis of Houston, Texas. To this union one child was born, Nichelle Quinteé DeVaughn.

Descendants of John E. Jr. and Ruby G. Hill include daughter, Marion Hill James; grandson, Herman Lee DeVaughn Jr.; granddaughters, Tanya Renee DeVaughn and Rosalyn Rubette James; and great-granddaughter, Nichelle Quinteé DeVaughn.

Tom Hill Sr. and Nicy Foster Hill; Ben F. Scott and Annie Hill Scott Families

Family historian: Chloe V. Baker

The recorded history of the Foster families had its beginning with Nicy Foster, a slave, who is credited with having been the mother of twenty children. The children were fathered for the most part by her slave master and other slave men. She was the first known generation of the Foster family.

Her children comprised the second generation. Her slave daughter, Priscilla, was the mother of eight children. There is no record to indicate that there was a husband in the picture. The assumption is that, like her mother, she too was the victim of a slave master and other slave men.

The trend changed when Priscilla's fifth child, Nicy Foster, married her husband, Tom Hill Sr. (date and place unknown). They became parents of seven children—the third generation.

Annie Rosetta Hill, the third of the Hill children and the fourth generation, married Ben Franklin Scott, January 17, 1903, in Millican, Brazos County, Texas. Ben, the son of Alex Sr. and Mary McGregor Scott, was twenty-three years old, and Annie was eighteen.

Annie Rosetta Hill Scott was born on December 9, 1885, and lived until June 5, 1971. *Black Dallas Remembered, Inc.*

In 1905, the Scotts became parents of a baby girl, who died in infancy. After the death of their first baby, they moved to Dallas in 1906 and established a residence among other Dallas pioneers at 2512 Juliette Street. This location is now the north side of Booker T. Washington Arts Magnet School campus.

Prior to 1906, the Scotts and Hill families lived on a 285-acre farm purchased in 1875 from the H&TC Railroad by Alex Scott and three other Black men. They organized the Black community called Petersburg. It was named in honor of their leader, Peter Morgan. Petersburg became a thriving community of twenty families. It still exists today.

Ben and Annie were blessed again with three more children. Chloe, the first child to live, was born July 10, 1909; Earnest was born December 7, 1910; and Juanita was born August 12, 1912. A total of five children were born to this union, marking the fifth generation.

The Scotts joined St. Paul Methodist Episcopal Church in 1907, under the pastorage of the Reverend N. J. Johnson. The children were brought up in Sunday School, church, and the Epworth League, where they were nurtured in learning Christian and moral principles. Along with family training, the church helped mold their lives into worthwhile Christian citizens.

Chloe's early education began at age four. From 1913 to 1915, she and her brother, Earnest, attended Mrs. Georgia Hall's Kindergarten School, located in the 2700 block of Juliette Street. Her elementary education began in 1916 at Booker T. Washington School (Old No. 2) as a second grader. Ms. Callie Hicks taught the second grade and was her first public school teacher. She enjoyed her childhood days on Juliette and made many friends.

Ben Scott established a successful moving business in 1910, which he operated from his residence. His first mode of transportation was a one-horse-drawn Express Wagon used to do light moving and hauling. The business grew rapidly, forcing him to relocate to a large building with office and storage space. It became necessary for him to purchase a large moving van (two-horse-drawn), which would accommodate moving an entire household of furnishings, and to hire a secretary. He relocated at the corner of Hawkins, Montezuma, and the Central Railroad tracks.

He managed the moving business for fifteen years, pulling up by his own bootstraps. It was the first Black business of its kind— B. F. Scott Moving, Transfer, and Storage Company. The business growth became more than he and his two helpers could handle. Therefore, he took on a partner, Mr. J. R. Perkins, a friend and grandfather to Thomas and Lonnie Tolbert.

They enjoyed a thriving business. After the advent of the automobile, the motor truck captured most of the local transportation, causing the horse-drawn vehicle to become obsolete. Ben was then faced with the necessity of purchasing a motor truck. He chose not to go that route and accepted a job in the public sector. Mr. Perkins, his partner, owned a truck and fell heir to the business.

The family moved to West Dallas in the spring of 1922. This time, residence was established at 2205 Snyder Street in a newly built home designed by Mr. Scott for his family. It was the first such home built in that community. The family enjoyed living in the community but maintained church membership at St. Paul. Chloe entered high school in the fall of 1922, in the newly built Booker T. Washington High School. Chloe married Jack C. Lee Sr., the father of Jack C. Lee Jr. and Ave Marie Lee. He died August 23, 1926. She married Leslie V. Baker on March 5, 1943, and they established residence at 2905 Lagow, in their newly built home. In February 1964, they moved to the present location.

Leslie spent forty-two years on the railroad as a Pullman porter. He retired from service on November 1, 1967. Chloe and Leslie were married for forty-two years and enjoyed a beautiful marriage until his demise on May 20, 1985. He was a devout husband and father.

Chloe established Baker's School of Sewing, Designing, and Millinery in October 1943 and followed this line of work for 20 years. She was employed by the Dallas Independent School District in 1960, as a classroom teacher. Before retiring on May 30,

1977, she was an advisory guidance counselor and the first Black career counselor.

Earnest Scott and his wife, Irene Johnson, were the parents of one son, Earnest B. Scott Jr. He has five children and four grandchildren. Juanita Scott Hunt married William Hunt, both deceased. They were the parents of two sons, Marvin McKinley and George Paul. Marvin did not have children. George Paul and his wife were the parents of seven children and grandparents of seven grandchildren, making a total of sixteen members of the eighth generation. Chloe's immediate family—mother, father, brother, and sister—are all deceased. She is the sole survivor.

The ancestral lineage includes two Fosters, one Hill, one Scott, one Lee, one Hunt, one Smith, and one Traylor—the eight generations. The first Foster family reunion was held in Dallas on July 22, 1956. The last thirty annual reunions have been held in Millican, Petersburg, and Bryan, Texas.

Earline Goins Hoover

Family historian: Gussie Hoover Montgomery

Earline Goins Hoover, daughter of Rev. and Mrs. Augustus W. Goins, was a native of Natchitoches, Louisiana. Her uncles, Reverends Edward and Milton Goins, were prominent pastors in the Louisiana area. Rev. Edward Goins pastored the Asbury Methodist Church in Natchitoches, Louisiana.

Earline Goins Hoover had six brothers and one sister: Oscar, Malalieu, Darris, Richard, Earl, Edward, and Julia. Her twin brother, Earl Goins, was active with a boys' club organized by him. He became an excellent speaker and leader in the community. Earl was the founder of the Goins Foundation. A newspaper article stated that he was one of the most influential persons with delinquent boys. They all called him "Uncle Earl." At the time of his death, he was the pastor of Carver Methodist Church in Dallas.

Earline Goins Hoover attended Wiley College in Marshall, Texas. She taught school for a short time. The piano and violin were her first loves. Mr. K. B. Polk was her violin teacher. Love for music was passed on to her children. A piano was always in the home. The family would frequently have a songfest around the piano— especially during the holidays. Each of her children was given responsibilities in the household. She was an excellent seamstress, which was certainly helpful with growing children.

Earline Goins Hoover settled in North Dallas during the [early] 1900s. She was married to Edward Henry Hoover Sr., who was a truck driver for Vermont Marble Company, located on Wall Street. The community was called "The Bog." Edward Hoover was the son of Jack and Luvenia Hoover. Both were natives of Louisiana. Mary Hoover, grandmother of Edward Hoover, lived to be one hundred and thirteen years old.

Earline and Edward Hoover joined the Plymouth Congregational Church, which was located on Hawkins Street in Dallas. They became the parents of ten children: Edward Hoover Jr., Lorrayne, DeLois, Carmena, Henry, Earline, Juanita, Julia, Earl, and Gussie. The family moved to South Dallas in November 1933. The children attended Phyllis Wheatley, B. F. Darrell, Booker T. Washington, and Lincoln High Schools.

Earline Goins Hoover became active in civic and religious activities in the Wheatley community. The gracious lady had membership in a flower club, Delta Mothers, a canning club, and the Ministers' Wives and Daughters Organization. She was designated as Mother of the Year in 1949.

Edward H. Hoover Jr., now deceased, married LaBelle Channel. They were the parents of two sons: Larry and Kenneth, both of whom moved to Los Angeles, California. Edward Hoover Jr. died in January 1973 and is buried in Ross Hills Memorial Park in Los Angeles. LaBelle Hoover died [circa 1987] in Los Angeles. Lorrayne M. Hoover, a pianist, died June 22, 1983, and is buried in Lincoln Memorial Cemetery, Dallas.

DeLois M. Hoover Love, retired teacher, married Roy H. Love, son of Professor and Mrs. E. W. D. Love. They have two children, Rodney and Roland Love. Carmena Hoover Adams, a legal secretary, married Reuben Adams. They have three children: LaVelle, Reuben Jr., and Toni. Henry Augustus Hoover, a postal review clerk, married Earline Harvest, and they have two children: Adrienne Brewster and Anthony Hoover.

Earline Hoover Powell, who works for Northrop Corporation in Los Angeles, married Marvin Powell. Marilyn is a product of this marriage. Juanita Hoover Benjamin, a machinist, married Bobby Benjamin. They have three daughters: Ronelda, Valetia, and Dianne. Julia Hoover Viney, a computer operator, married Charles Viney, and they have two daughters: Denise Davis and Dinah Elmore. Earl Goins Hoover, manager of the NCO Club, is not married. Gussie H. Montgomery, retired teacher, married Keisler William Montgomery, and they have one daughter, Gloria Jean. Gloria was cited in Who's Who Among Students for outstanding work in music education in 1982. Gloria married Douglas Lee, and three children were born to this union: Pamela, Keith, and Sonya. Keith A. Lee married Kellian White. They are the parents of one child, Ketra Sharon Lee. Ketra is the great-great-great-grandchild of Augustus Goins, great-great-grandchild of Earline Goins Hoover, great-granddaughter of Gussie Montgomery, and granddaughter of Gloria Montgomery Lee Roque. Ketra Sharon represents a sixth generation of this lineage.

Earline Goins Hoover's life was like beautiful flowers. She brought sunshine to everyone she touched. Flower arranging was her hobby, and she had a green thumb. Her devotion to her family was superb. She was a member of St. Paul United Methodist Church at the time of her death on November 12, 1951. The Earline Hoover Circle of the United Methodist Women's Unit was named in her honor at the church.

Samuel W. and Emmie Mae Hudson Sr.

Family historians: Mr. and Mrs. Samuel Hudson Jr.,
with a member of each family providing
his/her family narrative

The first generation in this narrative began with Samuel W. Hudson Sr., the son of ex-slaves, who began a tradition which has continued and borne fruit for four more generations—a tradition of toil and sacrifice so that children in the family are given the opportunity to receive a college education. To date, all descendants have earned college degrees.

Samuel W. Hudson Sr. was born February 22, 1877, of ex-slaves Josiah Hudson and Jane Hudson in Jackson, Mississippi. Before coming to Texas in 1898, he attended Tougaloo College, which had been founded in 1869 in Jackson, Mississippi. After coming to Dallas, he met Emmie Mae Allen, whose family moved to Dallas from Jefferson, Texas. They were married in 1910.

Mr. and Mrs. Hudson had seven children: Samuel Jr., Allie Mae, Dorothy, Elsie, Jacob, Joe, and Emmie Jean. The senior Hudson had one son by his first marriage, Johnny Hudson. The family home was located in the Booker T. Washington Addition at 5211 Central Avenue.

Both Mr. and Mrs. Hudson Sr. inspired their children, relatives, and friends to attend college. The seven children graduated from Bishop College. One of Mrs. Hudson's cousins, Adolph E. Jordan, whose mother passed when he was five years of age, was assisted by the family in attending Tillotson College and Meharry Medical University. He received a degree in pharmacy from Meharry. Most of these degrees were obtained through financial sacrifices of the Hudson's during the depression years.

Mrs. Hudson was a housewife but found ways to earn funds for special events. Mr. Hudson made several successful business investments but spent the major part of his career as an employee of Mobil Oil Company in the Magnolia Building, downtown Dallas. He was the assistant to the manager and supervised all of the custodial help until his retirement in 1941. He was part owner of Jordan Drug Company in Dallas and operated the business for twenty years.

In 1916, Samuel W. Hudson Sr. was one of the organizers and founders of Trinity Methodist Church, located in the Booker T. Washington Addition of Dallas. He remained a member of this congregation for thirty years before becoming a Seventh Day Adventist.

He was a member of the Roseland Homes Chorus, he was very active in the campaign for funds that created and founded the Moorland Branch YMCA, and he helped develop the Dallas Negro Chamber of Commerce and many other civic and community organizations.

Samuel Hudson was born on February 22, 1877, and he married Emmie Mae Allen in 1910. They had seven children. Emmie Mae died in 1934, but Samuel lived until December 15, 1972. *Black Dallas Remembered, Inc.*

Mrs. Hudson died in 1934, and Mr. Hudson, who lived to be ninety-five years of age, died on December 15, 1972.

The second generation began with Samuel Hudson Jr., who was the oldest of the seven children of Mr. and Mrs. Hudson. He attended Wesley Elementary School in the Booker T. Washington Addition as well as B. F. Darrell Elementary School, and he graduated from Booker T. Washington High School. He graduated from Bishop College with majors in science and education.

His first job after graduation from college was boy's work secretary at the Moorland Branch YMCA. He then taught mathematics at Booker T. Washington High. The major portion of his career was spent in public housing, which he began in 1942 as the manager of Roseland Homes Housing Project. He worked his way up the ladder in this area, and when he retired on August 30, 1986, he was equal opportunity compliance specialist, Department of Housing and Urban Development, Region VI.

While a student at Bishop College, Mr. Hudson met Ella Lois Johnson of Houston, Texas. They married on July 31, 1937, at Antioch Baptist Church in Houston. Their marriage lasted forty-three years until Mrs. Hudson's death in July 1978.

Mrs. Hudson Jr. was a product of the Houston public schools, where she was elected queen of B. T. Washington High School. She graduated salutatorian of her class in 1930. After graduation, she enrolled in Bishop College and was elected college queen in 1932. Her college work was completed at Oberlin College, Oberlin, Ohio, where she received the bachelor of arts degree and the bachelor of public school music degree in 1935.

While a student at Oberlin College, she composed the orchestral arrangement for "Juba Dance," by Nathaniel Dett. This number was used by the Oberlin College Student Symphony Orchestra and played by the student orchestra at her commencement. The Dallas Symphony also played the arrangement on April 30, 1969, and on two other occasions. Her employment included teaching at Houston College for Negroes, which later became Texas Southern

University; Talladega College; and in the Dallas Independent School District.

In addition to being a wife and mother, Mrs. Hudson was an accomplished musician and participated in many community activities through which she could share her exceptional talents. She was a member of the Dallas Educational Association and other groups interested in education and music. Among her most cherished honors was the Woman of the Year Award presented to her by the Florence B. Brooks Art and Literary Club of Fort Worth in 1969. Equally important to her was a resolution passed by the [Texas] House of Representatives, 64th Legislature, congratulating her for her many achievements in music education and community affairs when she retired from the Dallas Independent School District.

Mr. and Mrs. Hudson Jr. were the parents of five children: Mary Lois Hudson Sweatt, Samuel W. Hudson III, Estrellita Hudson Redus, Camellia Hudson Franklin, and Clifford Hudson. The three daughters graduated from Mills College in Oakland, California. Samuel III attended the University of Puget Sound in Tacoma, Washington, for two years and completed his work at Texas Southern University with a degree in law. Clifford graduated from Morehouse College in Atlanta, Georgia, with a BA degree in business administration.

Mary Lois Hudson Sweatt, owner of the Mary Lois School of Dance, Dallas, is married to Dr. James L. Sweatt III, a local thoracic surgeon. Dr. Sweatt, a graduate of Middlebury College (BS) and Washington University (MD), also grew up in Dallas. The Sweatts have four children: James IV, William, Alisa, and Mary Elizabeth.

James IV graduated from Westchester College in Fulton, Missouri, and is now employed by McDonald-Douglas in St. Louis. William graduated from Amherst University and is presently employed by Merrill Lynch Company in New York. Alisa is a 1988 graduate of Carleton College in Minnesota. Mary Elizabeth has completed her sophomore year at Colorado State.

Samuel W. Hudson III has been a member of the Texas House of Representatives for seventeen years. He is married to Henri Hudson, and they have eight children: Samuel IV, a student at Southern University in Baton Rouge, Louisiana; Cynric, a student at Southern University; Lela Lois, and Samzie, high school students in Dallas; Stacy, Traci, and Frenchell, elementary students, and William, a preschooler.

Estrellita Hudson Redus, a sales representative with Xerox Corporation in Oakland, California, is married to Caleb Raleigh Redus IV. Caleb is an employment representative with Chevron Resources Company, Chevron USA., San Francisco, California. The Reduses have two children: Caleb Raleigh Redus V and Nyjeri Ellita Redus.

Camellia Hudson Franklin is a public relations and special events consultant. She recently served as western development director for the Western Regional Office of the NAACP Legal Defense and Educational Fund, Inc. She desegregated the sport of ice-skating for Blacks in Dallas and the State of Texas in 1960, when her parents successfully won the right for her to enroll in ice-skating classes at Dallas's Fair Park Ice Arena. Immediately upon graduating from Mills College in 1973, she launched a professional ice-skating career that spanned a period of seven years as a member of the corps de ballet in Ice Capades and as "Ice Angel" on the Donny and Marie [Osmond] Show. Camellia is married to Attorney Maurice Edward Franklin Sr. They reside in Los Angeles, California, with their two children, Maurice II and Ella-Pauline.

Clifford J. Hudson is presently an insurance investigator with the State Board of Insurance, Austin, Texas. He worked for Golden Gate Mutual Life Insurance Company in Los Angeles, California for three years before taking his present position in 1987. He is married to Doris W. Hudson, a graduate of Spelman College, who is presently a sales associate with Foley's in Austin. The Hudsons have two children: Clifford J. Hudson Jr. and Jason W. Hudson.

On February 15, 1987, Mr. Samuel Hudson Jr. married Mrs. Geneva Anderson, widow of the late Dr. N. H. Anderson of Marshall, Texas. She has two children, Major Nolan H. Anderson Jr. and Major Ronald Charles Anderson, and five grandchildren.

Mrs. Allie Mae Hudson Jones is the second child of the late Mr. and Mrs. Samuel W. Hudson Sr. She remembers many "happy and cherished memories of growing up in a family of seven children with loving parents. The value of education was instilled in each of us at an early age, and we knew we were expected to acquire a college degree."

In addition to graduating from Bishop College, Mrs. Jones did graduate study at the University of Southern California, the University of California at Los Angeles, and Pepperdine University. She began her teaching career in the Dallas city schools and worked in the Grand Prairie District before moving to Los Angeles. She taught twenty-nine years in the Los Angeles Unified School District.

In 1937 she married the late Rev. James Lafayette Jones, a graduate of Wiley College and Drew Theological Seminary. They began their married life in Dallas, where their two daughters, Berthann and Jean, were born.

Their daughters are also in the field of education. Berthann Jones Heath, a graduate of Pepperdine University and the University of California at Los Angeles, is currently an administrator in the San Diego City Schools. Jean Lafay Jones Tidwell is a graduate of Pepperdine and is currently an early childhood educator in Silver Springs, Maryland.

The pride and joy of Mrs. Jones are her three grandchildren. John Heath is a recent graduate of Morehouse College and the Georgia Institute of Technology. He has started his career as an electrical engineer. Djenaba and Moriba Tidwell attend school in Silver Springs.

Mrs. Jones states: "The legacy left by my parents and continued by my husband and me, is still being perpetuated through my children and grandchildren. We believe not only in the value of education, but also in contributing our efforts towards helping others."

Dorothy Lois Hudson Jones was an educator, scholar, counselor, community leader, wife, and mother—all of these endeavors depicted the third child of Samuel W. and Emmie Mae Hudson. During her lifetime (1915–1980), Dorothy's involvement in her community and state, particularly in the areas of education and concern for the under-privileged, was monumental.

Dorothy graduated from Booker T. Washington High School in Dallas and received her baccalaureate degree from Bishop College in French and English. She specialized in guidance and counseling at the graduate level and earned additional hours in this area from the University of Arkansas at Pine Bluff; University of Arkansas at Fayetteville; North Texas State University at Denton; Henderson State University; and Syracuse University, Syracuse, New York.

Marriage to her college sweetheart brought Dorothy to Texarkana, Arkansas, in 1937. She began her teaching career in the Texarkana, Arkansas School System in 1942, as a first grade teacher. In 1946, she was selected as one of three persons in the state to initiate guidance and counseling programs in Black schools, where she served as counselor for twenty-seven years. She was recognized throughout the state as a leader in the field of counseling and guidance, and the program she developed became a model for other school districts across the state. She served for many years on the State Advisory Council on Secondary Education and on a state committee for the selection of tests.

Dorothy helped to open many doors for the Black community of Texarkana. She was a member of the first Interracial Committee— serving as its secretary. The committee was established to promote peaceful integration of public facilities in Texarkana. Through persistent contact with the National Girl Scout Office, she was instrumental in bringing girl scouting to Black girls in Texarkana. She sponsored the first Junior Red Cross organization for Black students. Many students would not have attended college had it not been for the persistence of Dorothy H. Jones.

Her professional and community affiliations included: the National Education Association; Arkansas Education Association; [Arkansas] Classroom Teachers Association; Arkansas State Counselors Association, of which she was secretary and member; National Sorority

Phi Delta Kappa; Debonair Civic Club; Baptist Ministers' Wives Club; and the Semper Fidelis Club; and she was a board member of the Texarkana Sheltered Workshop. She received a life membership in the PTA.

She and her husband, Rev. Nathan E. Jones Sr., sponsored numerous school-related activities. He was a coach and science teacher for forty-five years. Except for two years (1955–57) when he coached at his alma mater, Bishop College, he worked at the same high school as Dorothy. In the area of coaching, he is a legend. He has the distinction of having served longer than any other coach in the history of Arkansas athletics. Rev. Jones is now the minister of Munn's Chapel Church in Prescott, Arkansas. Nathan and Dorothy have four children.

The first, Nathan E. Jones Jr., is a graduate of Washington High School, Texarkana, Arkansas, where he was a varsity basketball player, football star, and honor graduate. He attended TSU before graduating from California State University, Los Angeles. He worked in Los Angeles as a coach before moving to West Germany to serve as football coach at Mannheim American High School. Currently, he is serving as girls' athletic director at Liberty-Eylau High School, Texarkana, Texas. He was voted as Coach of the Year in 1983. Nathan is active in the Lake Drive Baptist Church and many civic organizations. He is a former president of Kappa Alpha Psi and the Pan Hellenic council. He is presently president of the WHS Alumni Association and vice president of the National Alumni Association.

Nathan is married to Ethel P. Jones and father of Nathan E. Jones III and Caroline Nathasa. His wife, Ethel, is principal of Dunbar Elementary in Texarkana, Texas. Nathan III attended Morehouse College. He graduated from Prairie View College. Nathan III is currently residing in Dallas, Texas, where he is a claims adjuster for State Farm Insurance Company. Caroline, a recent honors graduate of Liberty-Eylau High School, is attending Howard University.

Emmie Jo Jones Gamble, the second child of Dorothy and Nathan, is a mathematics teacher at Arkansas High School in Texarkana,

Arkansas. She is married to retired Sgt. Eddie Lee Gamble Sr., who is currently working with the United States Postal Service. They have three children, Pelvin, Eddie Jr., and Vincent. Pelvin is currently a student at the University of Arkansas at Little Rock, pursuing a career in the writing field. Eddie Lee Jr. is a captain in the United States Army, having graduated from West Point Military Academy in 1984. Vincent is in his third year of a pre-pharmacy program at Texas Southern University, Houston, Texas.

Emmie received her bachelor's degree from the University of Arkansas at Pine Bluff and her master's degree from East Texas State University, Texarkana. She is quite active in civic and community activities. As the first Black appointed to the board of trustees at Southern Arkansas University, Magnolia, Arkansas, she served six years and became the first Black and first woman elected chairman of the board. She was selected as one of "100 Women of Achievement in Arkansas" by the Arkansas Women's Press and received a Distinguished Citizen Award from the City of Texarkana and the State of Arkansas. She and her husband Eddie have been active in such organizations as Boy Scouts, Girl Scouts board, Southwest Mental Health Board, parent-teacher organizations, and numerous community activities.

Delphynne is the third child of Dorothy and Nathan Jones Sr. She now resides in Los Angeles, California, and is married to Alcus "Al" Davis. They have two children, Rodney and Regina. Alcus worked in the wholesale beer business for eighteen years and is presently operations/community relations manager for KACE-FM radio station. Rodney is a student at Grambling State University, and Regina is a senior at St. Bernard High School in Playa Del Rey, California.

Delphynne received her Bachelor of Arts degree from the University of Arkansas, Pine Bluff, and her master's from Pepperdine University. She has worked for the LA Unified School District for twenty-two years and is presently a reading specialist/coordinator. She and her husband, Al, are actively involved in various organizations in the Los Angeles area.

Yates Roderick Jones, the fourth child of Dorothy and Nathan Jones, is a cost accountant with the International Paper Company, Domino, Texas, where he has worked for twelve years. He is a graduate of the University of Arkansas at Pine Bluff, with a bachelor of science degree in business administration and has certification in accounting.

Ricky has two sons, Derrick, a tenth grader at Arkansas High School, Texarkana, and Roderick, who is two and one-half years old. Ricky's activities include membership in the Kappa Alpha Psi Fraternity, officer of the International Paper Company Credit Union, and service as a loan executive for the United Way Program.

Elise Hudson Jackson, the fourth child of Mr. and Mrs. Samuel Hudson Sr., attended public school in Dallas and graduated from Bishop College in Marshall, Texas. She married Rev. Clifford Jackson Sr., and to that union were born two sons and one daughter, Clifford Jr., Andrew, and Carol. Both Rev. and Mrs. Jackson are retired teachers. Mrs. Jackson taught in the Grand Prairie schools for twenty-five years. Rev. Jackson worked in the Dallas schools for thirty-two years. The Jacksons reside in Grand Prairie.

Clifford Jr., a graduate of Bishop College, works for Sears. Attorney Andrew Jackson is the director of the Paralegal Program at the Community College in Hurst, Texas. Their daughter, Carol, is also a teacher.

Jacob Eugene Hudson, the fifth child of the late Samuel William Hudson Sr. and Emmie Rogers Hudson, was born in Dallas, Texas, and educated in the Dallas public school system. He graduated from B. F. Darrell Elementary School in June 1934, Booker T. Washington High School in June 1938, and in 1942, he received a bachelor of arts degree from Bishop College, Marshall, Texas. He majored in history and minored in sociology.

He was drafted into the United States Army in August 1942, and he served overseas in France, Italy, and North Africa during World War II. He received an honorable discharge in December 1945.

In March 1946, he moved to Los Angeles, California, where his service continued with the United States Government. He began graduate studies at the University of Southern California to pursue a master of arts degree.

In February 1948, he married Doris Guster, a native Dallasite and the daughter of the late Reverend Samuel George Guster and Hanna Sockwell Guster Eldridge. Doris attended B. F. Darrell Elementary School and graduated from Booker T. Washington High School in 1939. She is a 1945 graduate of Talladega College, Talladega, Alabama, with a bachelor of arts degree in elementary education. She taught two years at Talladega College's Demonstration School for training teachers.

Doris has a Golden Life Membership in Delta Sigma Theta Sorority, Inc. She is a member of the YWCA, NAACP, Laguna Arts Festival, National Council of Negro Women, and numerous other charitable organizations. She did graduate work at the University of Southern California, Pepperdine University, Cal-State LA, and the University of California at Los Angeles. She retired from the Compton Unified School district in June 1983.

Jacob and Doris have one daughter, Sylvia, and one grand-daughter, McCall Fallon Johnson. Sylvia did her formal education at: the Montessori School, Santa Monica; Le Lycee Francais De Los Angeles, Bellagio Road; and Faith Lutheran, Saint Mary's Academy High School; and she studied for one year at Cal-State University, Northridge. She married John Eric Johnson.

Jacob retired from the United States Department of Justice, Immigration, and Naturalization in May 1983, where he had served thirty-two years. He is a member of the Congregational Church of Christian Fellowship U.C.C., NAACP, Crenshaw Chamber of Commerce, Crenshaw Neighbors, NARFE, and the Urban League. He formerly held the office of treasurer for a church club, Fellow League, and was a member of the board of directors for Crenshaw Neighbors. He received numerous honors, certificates, and plaques from the government, city, county, and state.

Joe A. Hudson Sr. is the sixth child of Samuel Sr. and Emmie Mae Hudson [born circa 1921]. He received a BA from Bishop College and an MA from California State University at Los Angeles. His work experience includes: physical education director, Moorland Branch YMCA, Dallas, Texas, 1943–47; PE teacher, Fred Douglass Elementary, Dallas, Texas, 1947–52; teacher, Los Angeles city schools, 1952–63; pupil services and attendance counselor, Los Angeles city schools, 1963–74; and adviser, Work Experience Education, Los Angeles city schools, 1974 to present.

He married Dorothy Elliott Hudson in April 1947. She has a BS from Clark College and did graduate work at the University of Southern California. Her work experience includes home visitor, Dallas Housing Authority, 1950–52; admissions worker, Los Angeles County Hospital, 1952–1957; and teacher, Los Angeles city schools, 1957–85.

Joe and Dorothy Hudson have two sons, Joe Jr. and Michael. Joe A. Hudson Jr. was born in Dallas, Texas, in March 1948. He earned a BA from Bishop College and did graduate work at East Texas State University. He is project director of the Gain Program, Los Angeles City College. His wife is Elaine Robinson Hudson. She received a BA from Texas Woman's University and an MA from East Texas State University. She is a teacher in the Compton, California, school district. They have one son, Steven Elliott Hudson, who was born in August 1980.

Michael E. Hudson Sr. was born in Los Angeles, California, in January 1955. He received a BA from Pacific University, Forest Grove, Oregon, and an MBA from Loyola University. He is a personnel analyst in the Los Angeles Unified School District. His wife is June Grundy Hudson. She received a BA from California State University, Long Beach. She is an employment representative, Archdiocese of Los Angles. They have one son, Michael E. Hudson Jr., who was born in June 1982, and one daughter, April Hudson, born in July 1985.

In reflecting on his experiences in Dallas, Joe Hudson Sr. states:

I grew up in a small community called Booker T. Washington Addition. My mother and father were very strict, but loving and dedicated parents. They both were very supportive of their children and wanted the best for them. They made many sacrifices to see that we were educated and lived a well-rounded life. My father worked six days per week which left my mother at home to guide and direct us in our daily lives. My mother was very active in community affairs and the church. She was very active in the drive to build Moorland YMCA, a place that her boys could greatly benefit from. As soon as I was old enough, she carried me to the Y and enrolled me in their program. The YMCA helped me to grow spiritually, mentally, and physically. It was there that I learned to swim, became a member of the gymnastic team under Fred Young, and I was taught many values that have been helpful to me throughout life by David Howell. With this training, I was able to become physical director at Moorland YMCA upon graduation from college. This created in me a desire to work with young people. My whole career has been spent working with youngsters. While there, I organized a tumbling team known as "The Flying Torpedoes." They were featured in one of the National Negro Newsreel programs which at that time were shown in the Black movie houses across the country. I also became the first Black in Dallas to be sent by the American Red Cross to a National Aquatic School. I spent two weeks at West Virginia State University getting training in Water Safety, Lifesaving, Row Boating, Canoeing, and First Aid Instructors training.

The five years that I spent at Fred Douglass as Physical Education teacher stands out as a highlight in my life. At that time, West Dallas was supposed to be a tough assignment for a teacher. They previously had not had a male PE teacher and had not fared well in intramural sports. While I served, we won three city track meets for elementary schools and were softball champions once. Many of the boys then began to participate in athletics at Booker T. Washington High School.

While in high school, I went into the ice business with my brother-in-law, James Jones. We had an ice route that covered all of North Dallas and Booker T. Addition. I stayed in this business until I finished college. The money helped to pay my way through college. I also waited tables at the Old Plantation Club and the Columbian Club which helped greatly in paying for college.

Dallas was an excellent place for a person to grow up. Since my parents were very education oriented, I knew at age seven that I was going to college. This was the year that my oldest brother, Samuel Jr., went to college. One of the last things that I heard my mother say on the morning she passed was "Sam, be sure that all of the children go to college." Looking back, I appreciate my father very much for the many sacrifices that he had to make for these dreams to come true.

Growing up in Dallas enhanced my life in many ways. I think of my oldest sister, Allie Mae, who looked after me as a mother after my mother passed. I think of my oldest brother, Samuel Jr., who taught me to hunt and helped to shape and guide me into the man I am today. I think of the many dedicated teachers in Dallas that touched my life. They were interested in seeing that you received a good education and were prepared to enter college. Any of the successes that I have had can be traced back to the influences that Dallas had on my life. It makes me very happy and proud to say that Dallas played an integral part in the shaping of my life.

Emmie Jean Hudson Whaley, the youngest of the seven children of Emmie Mae Hudson and Samuel W. Hudson Sr., was born in Dallas, Texas, [on July 29, 1924] and educated in the public schools there. She graduated from Booker T. Washington High School in 1940. She received a BA degree from Bishop College in Marshall, Texas.

Soon after graduation from college, Emmie Jean joined the staff of Bishop College, where she worked as secretary to the public relations director. Her next secretarial experience was at the Moorland Branch YMCA in Dallas, Texas.

Teaching experience began for Emmie Jean in Dallas, Texas, at York Elementary School. Since that time, she has remained in the field of education, having taught in Phoenix, Arizona, and Los Angeles, California, where she retired in 1984. During her teaching career in Los Angeles, Emmie Jean served as training teacher for USC, UCLA, and USA Teacher Job Corps. She later coordinated specially funded programs: Title I, Early Childhood Education, School Improvement, and Bilingual Education.

Emmie Jean completed graduate study at Pepperdine University, where she earned an MA degree in Public Administration. Previous graduate work was taken at Arizona State University, Tempe, Arizona, in the field of education.

Emmie Jean is the mother of three children by her first husband [Oliver Wendell Phillips Jr., whom she married in 1944. In 1964, she married Leon E. Whaley, and they combined his five children with her three for "a great loving unit for 36 years of marriage"].[31] Leon E. Whaley is a graduate of Bishop College, Marshall, Texas. He earned an MA degree in business administration from Pepperdine University, where he joined the staff as part-time instructor in the Department of Business Administration and served for three years. Leon has been active with many community organizations and activities. He recently [1987] retired from Recreation & Parks, where he was recreation supervisor.

Emma's children are Cecellia Jean Phillips Simmons, Oliver W. Phillips III, and Jacqueline Lynnette Phillips Jackson. Cecellia received a BA degree from San Jose State University and an MA from San Francisco University. She is an assistant principal in the Los Angeles Unified School District. Oliver Wendell earned a BA degree from Cal Poly University, San Luis Obispo, California, and he did further study at Hunter College, New York City; Literature College, London, England; and University of Geneva, Switzerland. His studies were in theatre production and French. He is employed as production assistant by OPV Production Company.

Jacqueline earned a BA degree from Mills College and an MS from Boston University. Her graduate study was in television production, filmmaking, and broadcast structure. She served as production assistant and field producer for KABC-TV's "Eyewitness Los Angeles" weekly magazine show. She is now a law student at USC. Her husband, Attorney T. Warren Jackson, graduated from Cornell University and earned a juris doctorate from Harvard Law School. He is employed by Hughes Aircraft Company as senior

---

31. Obituary of Emmie Jean Whaley, Forest Lawn Memorial-Parks & Mortuaries, Los Angeles, California, 2015.—Eds.

counsel, legal/human resources. They are parents of a daughter, Lindsey Cecellia Jackson.

Emmie Jean Whaley's concern for children has been paramount in her career, and she has worked diligently to provide meaningful experiences and to maintain high educational standards for all children who have been so fortunate to have her touch their lives. She has been involved in many community and volunteer projects, including: chairman of the Education Committee and director of Girls Camp for United Christian Church; advisory committee member, Friendship Day Camp, Camp Fire Girls, and Woodcraft Rangers; volunteer assistant, Ethnic Family Camp; and chairman of education committee, Women & Girls Workshop, Los Angeles City Human Relations Bureau.

Emmie Jean is a member of Crenshaw United Methodist, where she has served on the Finance Committee and the Christian Education Committee. She is a member of the following professional and civic organizations: Delta Sigma Theta, National Sorority of Phi Delta Kappa; Top Ladies of Distinction; NAACP; California Retired Teachers Association; and Friendly Educators. Emmie Jean is listed in the 1981–82 edition of *Who's Who among Black Women in California*. She has received awards for her services to the school and community, including a resolution from Los Angeles City Council and certificate from California State Department of Education.

Dr. Arrie E. Hughes Sr. Family

Family historian: Arrie Hughes Jr.

Dr. Arrie Edmund Hughes Sr. graduated from Meharry Medical, Dental, and Pharmaceutical School in Nashville, Tennessee, in 1922. He practiced first in South Texas (Taylor, Giddings, Elgin, Bastrop, and Brenham) with the late Dr. Dickey. Moving to Dallas in 1925 with his new bride, Elna V. McDade Hughes of Elgin, Texas, he opened his office in the McMillan Sanitarium.

Upon completion of the Flowers Building in August 1925, he began a long and fruitful friendship and association with Dr. W. K. Flowers. He was in the Flowers Building for almost twenty years, before moving two doors over into his own building.

Dr. Hughes was preceded in his move to Dallas by his father, Lawrence Hughes, who came to Dallas from Palestine, Texas, in 1876. In 1882, Lawrence Hughes went back to Palestine to look after the family farm, which at that time contained 2,100 acres of land. Except for sixteen acres, all the other land was confiscated by nightriders.

The first year Dr. and Mrs. Hughes came to Dallas, they lived in a house on Fairmount Street. Seven months later, they moved in with his aunt, Katie Warren Wiggins, at 2830 Thomas Avenue (corner of Thomas and Allen Street).

Mrs. Hughes, a graduate of Prairie View A&M College, taught two years at B. F. Darrell School on Hall Street. She taught English and mathematics.

Dr. Hughes was a conscientious, dedicated dentist, who not only pulled teeth but early on worked voluntarily with his patients and school-age youngsters on preventive care and oral hygiene. He was the first minority dentist to visit schools in the Dallas School District in that capacity. He donated a full day each month for years.

He was a former president of the Gulf State Dental Society in Texas and for many years served as treasurer of the M. C. Cooper Dental Society in Dallas. He was an active member of the NAACP; director of the Dallas Black Chamber of Commerce; a member of the Meharry Alumni Association; and a trustee of Bethel AME Church. Dr. and Mrs. Hughes were active at St. Peters Academy, the YMCA, and many civic organizations.

Dr. and Mrs. Hughes were the parents of three children: Arrie E. Jr., Arthur L., and Norma J. Their grandchildren are: Cheryl Yavonne Hughes Haynes, Lea Lois Hughes Davis, Michael Hughes Gillam,

Teri Gillam, Traci Constance Gillam, Keli Elna Gillam, Linda Tyrone Greer, and Dietra C. Hughes. Great-grandchildren are: Jonathan Davis (Lea Lois), Tash V. Gillam (Michael), Justin Hughes Haynes (Cheryl), and Brandi Nicole Torte (Teri).

Andrew and Tempie Jackson

Family historian: Clifford J. Jackson

Andrew Jackson was born to slave parents on the plantation of Jed C. Adams Sr. in Henderson County, near Athens, Texas. Jed C. Adams was father of the late Judge Jed C. Adams Jr., of Dallas. Andrew was eight years old at the time of Emancipation. He was born Andrew Jackson Ody to Almstead and Sarah Jane Ody, chattel of Jed C. Adams.

When Andrew reached adulthood, he moved to Dallas, in the 1870s or '80s, to begin a new life. Like many former slaves, he chose to leave his slave name behind. By dropping the surname Ody, he became Andrew Jackson.

As a small boy, seven or eight years old, Andrew had been taught the rudiments of the Three Rs by Jed Adams Jr., who was a year or two younger. This knowledge kindled in Andrew a passionate desire for learning. Early in adult life, he bought a small farm outside Athens, in the community of Fincastle. Later, he sold the farm and came to Dallas, where he owned and operated a saloon on Jackson Street in downtown Dallas.

Soon after coming to Dallas, Andrew met and married Tempie Cloud, to whom nine children were born. The only surviving children are Mrs. Fannie Wheeler and Clifford J. Jackson.

In 1904, Andrew and Tempie Jackson purchased a nine-acre tract of land in East Dallas, in the community of Mill City. It was here that he began "truck farming" vegetables for the city market. He farmed this tract from 1904 until 1923, when he entered the retail grocery business.

After the passing of Tempie, his wife of thirty-six years and the mother of his children, he decided truck farming was too tough for him. He then built a combination home and grocery store, which he operated with his son until he passed in 1930.

Clifford Jackson operated the business until June 1931, when he received his BA degree in education. In the fall of 1931, he signed a contract with the Dallas Independent School District to teach social studies, a position he retained for forty-six years. He retired in 1977.

William Jackson Family

Family historian: Jimmie Jackson Moore

Great-great-grandmother Emily White is the earliest known ancestor of the Jackson-related families. She was born in South Carolina in 1821. Despite physical abuses and other indignities, she was a survivor.

Early in the summer of 1849, on a plantation in Alabama, a baby girl was born to Emily, the house slave. The child was named O'Shillie, surname of Emily's Irish slave master, the child's father. Emily's mother was herself a product of miscegenation. Soon after Emancipation, O'Shillie and her mother made their way to Millican, Texas, where O'Shillie married Joey Tom Ross. About 1867 they moved to Calvert, Texas, and became the parents of seven children: William, Annie, Jessie, Etta, Laura, Earl, and Fannie Ross.

In 1868, they purchased a small farm and house. On this piece of land, they raised corn, peas, potatoes, and other garden vegetables.

After Joey's death, Mama O'Shillie worked as a cook in private duty. She reared seven grandchildren: Annie and Blanche Caldwell, Alla Bell Ford, Hellen Hellman, Daisy and Charles Cowens, and William Jackson. The grandchildren tended the gardens and small crops. Emily White died about 1906. Later, O'Shillie added to her small holdings by acquiring the lot next to her property. Neither the legacy of slavery nor the uncertainties of freedom defeated her. She came to Dallas in 1924. At the time of death, she still owned the land. Her descendants continued to hold it. She died July 12, 1933, in Dallas and was buried in Beauty Rest Cemetery in Calvert.

Cloretta Lyons, maternal great-grandmother, was the first family member to settle in Dallas. She was born in Calvert, Texas, in 1866, and married Burl Johnson in 1885. They came to Dallas in 1886 and joined St. Paul Episcopal Church about 1890. She was a seamstress, and Burl was a carpenter. Their children were Ella, James, and Bishop. Burl Johnson died in 1916, and Cloretta died on March 2, 1931, in Dallas.

James Jackson and Fannie Ross Jackson were parents of William Jackson, who was born in 1895 in Calvert. (James died in 1950 in Wetumka, Oklahoma.) In 1901, Fannie moved to Dallas and married Granville Lacy in 1903. The three Lacy children were Nicholas, Evelyn, and Annie Lacy. Fannie Jackson Lacy died in 1919. During the late 1920s, the Lacy family acquired pieces of property in Old Wheatley Place.

William Jackson came to Dallas in 1910. He was employed at the Golden Pheasant Restaurant. During the summer vacations, he went to Omaha, Nebraska, and worked as a dining car waiter. He married Willie B. Fisher on March 4, 1917.

Willie B. Fisher was born in Calvert, March 4, 1900, the daughter of Samuel and Ella Lyons Fisher. After their father's death, she and her sister, Ruby Fisher, often lived with their aunt, Catherine Fisher Turner, and her children. Catherine's children were Mary Ella, Hattie, and Boyce, father of Judge Alvin Turner. Ella Fisher was born in 1885 and died in Dallas in 1969.

William Jackson and his wife, Willie, became the parents of three children: Jimmie Mae, Robert Samuel, and Edythe Marie. He was a very industrious and frugal man. Willie was a homemaker, and her life revolved around her family and the activities of her church. Both parents placed a high sense of value in college education for their children.

The first Jackson family home was built in 1923 in old North Dallas. This property was later sold to the City of Dallas. William died in 1956 and was buried in Lincoln Memorial Cemetery in Dallas.

Jimmie Mae Jackson married Sylvester Darnell Moore, son of Thomas and Myrtle Williams Moore, in 1943. Their daughter, O'Shelia Anne Moore, married Samuel L. Brown, son of Allen and Hazel Douglas Brown, in 1970. Samuel founded BMA Systems, Incorporated in 1976.

Robert Samuel Jackson married Elizabeth Hampton, daughter of David and Ellen Pipkins Hampton, in 1946. Their son, David Samuel Jackson, married Dian Hopkins, daughter of Marshall and Leueda Hopkins, in 1982.

Edythe Marie Jackson married Willie Collins, son of Robert and Emma Collins, in 1952. They had three children: Tonya Marie, Cedric Dion, and Williamena. Tonya Marie Collins married Charles Wingham in 1977. She later married Walter Rayford, and in 1986, she married Dewey Simmons. Cedric Dion Collins married Carrie Brown, daughter of Jim and Oratha Cuttley Brown, in 1977. Williamena Jackson-Collins was named in memory of her maternal grandfather.

Beginning with Cloretta Johnson, six generations have been members of St. Paul United Methodist Church. Her great-granddaughter, Edythe Collins, served as church organist for two decades.

The great-grandchildren of William and Willie Fisher Jackson are Samuell Darnell Brown, born 1974, Dallas; Damon LaDon Wingham and Letitia LaShawn Wingham, born 1974, Dallas; Watina Renee Rayford, born 1979, Dallas; Cedric Dion Collins Jr., born 1978, Los Angeles, California; J'Quanta Marie Collins, born 1982, Dallas;

Donnell Charles Collins, born 1982, Los Angeles, California; and William J'Quare Collins, born 1984, Dallas.

From great-great-grandmother Emily until now, seven generations later, the Ross-Jackson clan members distinguished themselves as persons engaged in farm life, health services, business, music, common labor, law, education, and other useful careers. Individual talents, hard work, and perseverance counted more than earthly possessions. Their lives reflected a story of difficulties, achievements, blessings, and an unparalleled pride in their heritage.

D. Edwin and Ila Walker Johnson

Family historians and Contributors: Gloria Rhea White, Lois Palfrey, and Rosa Elston

Rev. D. Edwin Johnson was born in Point, Texas, [circa 1899] to Rev. and Mrs. David E. Johnson. His brothers and sisters were: Berdie Johnson Anderson, Rosa Johnson Oliver, Rayphael Johnson, Roy Johnson, Genevieve Johnson Goodlow, Dona Johnson, Lela Johnson Elston, and John Johnson.

In 1922, he married Ila M. Walker, a native of Hallsville, Texas, and the daughter of Thomas and Cornelia Walker. She moved to Dallas at the age of seven and lived with an aunt. She graduated with honors from Dallas public schools and from Bishop College, Marshall. She completed graduate work at Texas Southern University, Houston, and earned a diploma in Christian Education at the Interracial Theological Institute, which has since been named the D. Edwin Johnson Bible Institute.

Rev. Johnson attended Houston College and was conferred the Doctor of Divinity at the North Texas College of Theology. In 1924, he began in the ministry and served as pastor in Melissa and Pilot

Point, Texas; Ardmore, Oklahoma; and Mexia, Terrell, and Texarkana, Texas. From 1951 until retiring in 1969, he was dean of the Interracial Baptist Institute in Dallas, Texas.

For twenty years, Reverend Johnson was president of the Baptist Ministers Conference / B. M. and E. [Baptist Missionary and Education] Convention; treasurer of the Home Mission Board, National Baptist Convention of America, Inc. for thirty years; and moderator of the Friendship District Association.

Rev. and Mrs. Johnson are the parents of four children: Mrs. Lois E. Palfrey, Mrs. Gloria Rhea White, Lacy Kirk Johnson, and David E. Johnson.

Before her retirement, Mrs. Johnson taught in Collin County for five years, in Texarkana for eleven years, and upon moving to Dallas she served as assistant manager of the Good Street Baptist Church Day Care Center for six years.

She also served as a substitute teacher in the Dallas Independent School District and was an active trustee of Bishop College. She received the honorary Doctor of Humane Letters from Bishop College during commencement exercises in May 1983.

Well known for her volunteer services, Mrs. Johnson worked for the Red Cross and taught classes in first aid and home health-care. As counselor and confidant of many people from all walks of life, Mrs. Johnson was able to get young people to return to school during and after World War II. She was a strong advocate of education. Her children and grandchildren exemplify her dedication.

As the wife of a minister, Mrs. Johnson assumed her responsibilities in religious and civic affairs with diligence. She served as recording secretary of the B. M. and E. State Convention for twenty-two years. She served as president of the women's auxiliary of the Friendship District Association for five years. She was elected president of the B. M. and E. Convention in 1969 and held the position until 1983. She was also a member of the board of directors of the National Baptist Convention, USA, Inc.

When the National Baptist Convention, USA, Inc. met in Dallas in 1976, she served as chairlady of the planning and arrangements committee for the women's auxiliary. Her ability to manage the movements and activities of a large number of people won her national esteem.

Widely known as a dynamic, informed public speaker, Mrs. Johnson served as the first Black teacher in a Home Mission Board seminar for the Southern Baptist Convention which met in Glorietta, New Mexico. She traveled throughout the United States and in eleven foreign countries. She attended the World Baptist Alliance in Stockholm, Sweden, and was a delegate to the National Alliance of Baptist Women in Ontario, Canada.

As a faithful member of Good Street Baptist Church since 1924, Mrs. Johnson served as director of the young people's department for many years. She worked with several auxiliaries and held a variety of offices with the missionary society.

She received a number of citations, plaques, and awards for her work and services. Among these were the Distinguished Service Award from the L. K Williams Ministers Institute at Bishop College, the Extra Step Award from Bishop College, the Women's Day Award at Good Street Baptist Church, and an award from the Interdenominational Ministers' Wives Auxiliary.

Within Good Street Baptist Church, she received the Mother of the Year award and was elected Woman of the Year. Along with many others, she received an award from the Social Service and Community Center in Dallas.

In support of Bishop College, Mrs. Johnson raised money to provide a tennis court for the college. She contributed her personal money to the college and furnished a room there in memory of her late husband.

Mrs. Johnson was a charter member of the National Council of Negro Women and held memberships in the YWCA, the Society for Crippled Children, Church Women United, the NAACP, Zeta Phi Beta Sorority, Inc., and Ernestine Chapter 285, Order of the Eastern Star.

Both Rev. Johnson and Mrs. Johnson are now deceased. They had six grandchildren: Mrs. Evelyn McKee, David Johnson, Lacy Claude Johnson, Vanessa Tisdale, Dawrence Leon White, and Dawrence Kirk Johnson.

Charles Etta Emory Jones Family

*Family historians: Helen Marie Hurd
and Ellen Ruth Larkin*

Fortunate indeed is today's woman executive who possesses grace and charm with her business-like qualifications. She is a rare find. Mrs. Charles Etta Jones, secretary-treasurer of the Excelsior Life Insurance Company, was richly endowed with these attributes. These innate qualities largely assisted her in attaining a unique position with a Negro-owned insurance company in Texas.

Mrs. Jones was born in Sherman, Texas, on December 9, 1892, and moved to Dallas with her family at the age of eight. In 1919, she was married to Simon M. Jones, a local businessman. This union was terminated prematurely upon his death in 1925.

Mrs. Jones completed high school in Dallas, after which she attended Langston University in Langston, Oklahoma, and Eureka Business School in Dallas. She was a member of Salem Institutional Baptist Church, a staunch supporter and contributor to every civic move[ment], and a member of Iota Phi Lambda Sorority and the Royal Arts Social Club.

Mrs. Jones gave an organ to Madison High School. The principal at the time was Dr. Thomas Tolbert. The auditorium at the school was named in honor of her mother, Katie Bruce Sims. Mrs. Jones's other family members included a sister, Mrs. Marie King, and two brothers, John Henderson and Cecial Emory.

In 1916, when the Excelsior Mutual Benefit Association began its operation, it was in need of a secretary-clerk. Mr. Strickland, founder and president, remembering how well Miss Charles Etta Emory had served him in this capacity when he was in the employment of American Mutual Benefit Association, contacted her. On May 22, 1916, she came to work for Excelsior Mutual Benefit Association. This began her insurance career. She was very proud of her position and was happy to break this good news to her beloved mother. What a beginning! What a first step!

Henry Keller Sr. Family

Family historian: Florence Keller Butts

Henry Keller was born into slavery in 1817, on a plantation in Greenville, Tennessee. Unlike most slaves, he worked as a gardener and did housework for his master. After the slaves were freed, he married Mary Jane Reed, who had grown up on the same plantation. It is stated by family members that he delayed marriage until slavery was abolished because he did not wish to have children born into slavery.

The couple migrated to Texas shortly after they were married and settled on a farm in Collin County. They lived in a house with a dirt floor. They lived and worked there for several years, saving their money to purchase their own farm. When they reached their first milestone, they purchased a farm in Dallas County, where they settled in the area that is now called Far North Dallas.[32]

During his first few years as a Texan, his interest in land ownership continued to grow, and he acquired several other parcels of farmland

---

32. The Kellers bought their farm in Dallas County because Collin Counter, where they had migrated earlier, prohibited African Americans from owning property at the time.—Eds.

Henry Keller, for whom Keller Springs Road was named, is shown in about 1880. *Black Dallas Remembered, Inc.*

in the general area known as Upper White Rock. He became one of the larger Black landowners and farmers in Dallas County. His holdings totaled six hundred and forty acres of land. He lived on his original Dallas County farm for the rest of his life.

The farm was located on a farm road, which later was named Keller Springs Road in his honor. There was an everlasting running spring on his farm that supplied water for him and many of his fellow farmers who needed water at no cost.

Even though he had no formal education, he and his wife worked and managed their holdings and enjoyed many of the better things in life. When they died, they passed much of their accumulated wealth on to their ten children. They were parents of six boys and four girls. The boys were Jim, Charles, John, Henry Jr., Thomas, and George. The girls were Laura Keller, Ninnie Keller Sowell, Florence Keller Barton, and Alice Keller Patterson.

Mr. Keller was a religious man. He and [his wife Mary Jane Reed Keller were among] the founders of White Rock Christian Chapel CME Church. The church was founded in 1886, and [it] was located on [White Rock Creek until 1918, when it was moved across the creek to] Celestial Road [where it remained] for many years.[33]

In [about] 1954, [the congregation divided, and] the church moved to its new location in the same general area on Montfort Drive and Spring Valley Road.

His wife preceded him in death. She died in 1898, at the age of fifty-three. He died in 1911, at the age of ninety-four. Seven of his grandchildren are now living. They are the children of his youngest child, George, who was born when his father was seventy-two years old.

Six of them now live in the same general area. They are Mrs. Freddie Allen, Mrs. Rubye Hervey, Mrs. Florence Butts, Mrs. Patricia Hervey,

---

33. Their son, John Wesley Keller, was listed among the fifty-five stockholders of the Colored Union Cemetery of White Rock, which had been established even before the White Rock Chapel built its first church beside White Rock Creek. The Colored Union Cemetery of White Rock later was renamed White Rock Cemetery Garden of Memories.—Eds.

Theodore Keller, and Oliver Keller, all of Dallas. One grandchild, Mrs. Audrey Thomas, resides in Detroit, Michigan.

Ben King Family

Family historian: Alvernon King Tripp

Benjamin King and Mary Elizabeth Walker were joined in matrimony December 24, 1897, in Fallis, Oklahoma, where Mary and her family had lived since 1879. They came from Charlestown, South Carolina, on a wagon train made up of two wagons, two horses, three mules, father Alex Walker, wife Courtney, and seven children, ages ranging from two years to twenty-two years. They were able to claim four hundred and forty acres of land in the territory of Oklahoma. Mary was the seventh of nine children, two having died as infants.

Ben King was born in Kentucky at the close of the Civil War. The family had been separated during the war when his mother was sold to another plantation. He was given to a family of Shoziers, who moved to Texas and settled in Clarksville. At age fourteen, he completed the fifth grade in school, which was considered high school for Blacks at that time.

Ben, in September 1882, was offered an opportunity to ride to Dallas with a farmer to sell his cotton. Seeing Dallas with its tall buildings (three stories), Ben decided to remain in Dallas. He immediately found work with the E. M. Kahn family as a "stable boy," taking care of the horses and yard. Larry Kahn noted his eagerness to learn new things and started spending evenings working with him, acquainting him with books and studies of which he had never heard. He became acquainted with the cook, Hattie, who told him of her younger sister, Mary. At this time, Mary was in school at Langston Institute [in Langston, Oklahoma—now Langston University], a Catholic school established for advanced education for young people during winter months when the crops had been "laid by."

Christmas season, 1896, Ben visited Mary carrying a gold watch from Linz Jewelers. The engagement was now official. Ben's visit on December 24, 1897, culminated the marriage. They returned to Dallas to begin a new life together.

Their first home was in Joppy, Texas (South Dallas), on ten acres of land. To this was soon added a horse and wagon, a milk cow, four pigs, and a dozen chickens. Three acres were cleared for planting. From this land, he managed to grow four bales of cotton and vegetables to share with others.

On January 3, 1898, the first child was born. The name had been decided—a boy, LaVerne; a girl, Alvernon. A girl it was, who is now eighty-nine years old. Twenty-one months later, the second child, John Robert, named for Mary's two brothers, was born.

Trinity River floods had become hazardous for living conditions, so the Kings decided to move to drier ground. They purchased their second home at Spence and Cooper Streets in 1900. The Dallas city line had not been extended this far south. In 1902, the third child, Conwallis (Connie), was born.

Ben's idea to be the head of his own business remained with him. Here at Spence and Cooper Streets, the idea of a wood yard came to fruition. The business grew rapidly, and two more horses and wagons were added. Deliveries were made in all sections of the city. Cord wood was selling for eight dollars per cord (cut into fourteen-inch lengths). Three persons were employed plus the help of Alvernon and John Robert, who could stack three to four racks after school.

The children were taught early to earn their own money in the business. They were among the early depositors with the "Penny Savings Bank of Dallas."

The fourth child, again a boy, was born in December 1911. All during these years, a milk cow had been added, bringing the stock to seven head. People from many blocks in Queen City walked daily to get milk fresh from the Kings' [dairy]. The parents allowed each child to have not more than three families to deliver milk to, at ten cents per quart, to earn school expense money.

World War I changed conditions, making it difficult to get sufficient wood shipped in from East Texas. Ben had gone each summer cutting wood and shipping it by freight train into Dallas. Milk was increasing in demand. The Kings decided to increase their cattle, and within four years, through reproduction and purchasing, the dairy had become a Jersey dairy with eighty milk cows and two bulls for breeding purposes. Ben had leased and purchased several acres of land, much of it in the area where Proctor and Gamble Company now stands.

Dallas was rapidly expanding its city limits southward and establishing laws against animals within city limits. After many court battles, the business was forced from Cooper and Spence Streets. Land was leased in North Dallas very near the White Rock Lake. By that time, the herd numbered more than a hundred head, [and the business had] seven employees.

Dallas continued its annexing to the north, and within four years, that area was within city limits. That same law applied. Ben was now in poor health. Alvernon and John Robert had graduated from college and had entered other fields of endeavor. The decision was reached to sell the cattle, thus ending the many years of striving for the "King Jersey Dairy" in Dallas, Texas.

Ben King died on February 22, 1930, at his early childhood home in Clarksville, Texas. Mary died in October 1951 in Dallas, Texas; John Robert in September 1962; Bennie Jr. in March 1963; and Conwallis in April 1972.

During these intervening years, Alvernon was a teacher in the Dallas Independent School District. She married Charles Evans, a native Dallasite, and moved west to Salt Lake City in 1926.

John Robert achieved fame as an inventor with many credits for his work. Also, he was an early postal clerk with the US government.

Conwallis and John Robert, while students at Darrell High School in 1914, built the smallest car to run on Dallas streets. J. W. Towns, manual training instructor, had guided them. The motor used for the engine came from a discarded Harley-Davidson motorcycle.

Conwallis was the first Black in Dallas to fly and own his own plane. He was an employee of the Pullman Company from 1926 to 1969, when he retired due to ill health.

Bennie Jr. became a master electrician and was employed by the US government from 1941 until his death.

Ben King was baptized in 1894 at the New Hope Baptist Church. Rev. E. W. D. Isaac was the pastor. Mrs. King and the four children were baptized at New Hope and actively served under Rev. A. S. Jackson Sr. The daughter, Alvernon, continues to work actively in the church.

Still surviving from this union is the one daughter, Alvernon King Tripp, an active community volunteer; one granddaughter, Jewel King Snaer, a retired DISD teacher; one grandson, Abdul S. Hassan, cab owner-operator, Houston, Texas; six great-grandchildren; and one great-great-grandson.

To my parents I dedicate these immortal words of Booker T. Washington: "Success is to be measured not so much by the position that one has reached in life, as by the obstacles he has overcome while trying to succeed."

Marion and Servilla Dawson Lee

Family historian: Doris Jean Lee Humphrey

Marion Lee, his wife Servilla D. Lee, and their two sons, Clarence and Jack, moved to Dallas in 1914, from Caldwell, Texas. They settled in West Dallas on what was known then as Terry Row. Clarence and his brother enrolled in Cedar Valley Colored School, which later became Fred Douglass Elementary School. Marion Lee became employed at the Portland Trinity Cement Company. He was employed with this company at the time of his death in 1918. [Servilla D. Lee] did day work for some of the rich families in the Kessler Park area.

Later, Clarence was employed by Portland and then by the C. F. Massey Co. This company made concrete pipes and other concrete supplies. He supported his mother and brother with his earnings.

Clarence Booker T. Lee became gainfully employed at age fifteen or sixteen. By age seventeen, he had bought a home and paid for it. He had a seventh-grade education. This was due to the fact that when his father passed, he became the breadwinner of the family. His aspiration was to become a medical doctor. His aspiration was never fulfilled, but he always encouraged young people to seek a college degree.

He and Mary Jane Hunt married on June 24, 1924. Their eldest child, Doris Jean Lee, was born a year later. Their son, Clarence Jr., was born two years later, on January 1, 1927. They always instilled in their children the importance of a college education. Mary Jane's aspiration was to become a schoolteacher. Her aspiration was also cut short due to the death of her father, William "Shep" Hunt.

Clarence and Mary Jane lived in the house with his mother; his stepfather, Henry Patterson; and his younger brother, Jack Lee. After the birth of Doris Jean, Clarence's mother and her husband decided to build a larger house on the same property and let Clarence and Mary Jane have the smaller house.

Everything was fine until the Depression of the late '20s and early '30s. Clarence's mother divorced his stepfather and [they] went their separate ways. Mr. Patterson remained in Dallas with his sister, Viola Clark, and her husband, Ed Clark. Everyone called them Aunt Vi and Uncle Ed. They lived in Queen City (South Dallas) on Cooper Street. Clarence's mother moved to Wichita Falls, Texas, and went into service as a maid for some rich people. During this time, things were getting worse financially. Businesses were being closed due to the Depression.

Clarence lost his job at the C. F. Massey Co. in 1931. Clarence and Mary Jane lost their home and bank account and had to move to a rental house. They moved into a three-room shotgun house on Terry Row.

Clarence made the decision to make his own job. It was during this time that the Federal Government came up with the [National Recovery Administration] NRA and the [Works Progress Administration] WPA, which gave unemployed men with families two or three days' work each month and stamps for food and clothes. The government also established soup kitchens to feed the poor.

Clarence was a very proud man and never asked for aid from the government or any other social agency. He had a green panel truck in which he transported people to and from the soup kitchen, to places of employment, and to food ration stations. He would charge each person five or ten cents each, or whatever they could afford.

In 1932, he decided to raise hogs for a living. He bought one sow hog that was expecting a litter of pigs. He went to the market, which is now the Farmer's Market, and worked out a contract with all the merchants to clean up every morning, with the stipulation that he could keep all of the fruits and vegetables that were thrown away. The merchants agreed. They also paid him a salary. His goal was to use all of these fruits and vegetables to feed his hogs. He would salvage all of the edible fruits and vegetables and give them to the neighbors and friends. Some of the people encouraged him to start selling these fruits and vegetables. This grew into a lucrative business.

He established a route with his truck, peddling fruits and vegetables in West Dallas, Eagle Ford, and Thomas Hill neighborhoods. One of his big specialties was bananas. He was known in the Spanish neighborhood as the Plátano Man (Banana Man). He learned to speak Spanish fluently by traveling in the Spanish neighborhood. This resulted in some lifetime friendships. Doris Jean and Clarence Jr. still have some friends from their father's business relationships.

As his vegetable route grew, his hog-selling business also grew. He contracted with bakeries and restaurants all over Dallas to clean up their places of business for their leftover bread, cakes, pies, cookies, and [other] foods. At this time, the depression was really bad. Some of the neighbors would scour the alleys of Oak Cliff and the City dumping ground daily for whatever food they could salvage.

Clarence Sr. and Mary Jane had very soft hearts and would help wherever they could. Clarence would offer food to neighbors, friends, and relatives. By this time (1934–35), he and Mary Jane had acquired two milk cows, chickens, turkeys, and ducks. Mary Jane had her own business, selling milk, butter, eggs, and chickens. This lasted until 1938, and they decided to open a grocery store named Lee's Grocery. Clarence's slogan was "C. B. Lee's Grocery, Sole Owner of My Name." They ran this business from 1938 to approximately 1955.

In 1939 they opened a dance hall for teenagers, which ended up with adults also hanging out. They did not allow alcoholic drinks but specialized in homemade chili, hot links, barbecue, hamburgers, and hams. They sold lunches and hamburgers to the teachers and students at the Fred Douglass School. Mary Jane also made homemade desserts.

During this time, Clarence became a mail handler at the Union Terminal Post Office (1940). He did this so Clarence Jr. could get a college education.

Mary Jane Hunt Lee was born in Tyler on December 5, 1905, to the parentage of William and Harriet Fleming Hunt. William was a native of Tyler, and Harriet was a native of Dallas. Harriet's parents were Elbert and Mary Jane Stell Fleming.

The Hunts moved back to Dallas in 1906, when Mary Jane was three months old. Mary Jane was the third child born to William ("Shep") and Harriet. Katherine and William II were born [in Dallas] prior to their parents moving to Tyler.

William Hunt's parents were Lucious and Katherine (Kate) Jackson Hunt. Mary Jane's maternal grandparents, Elbert and Mary Jane Fleming, came to Dallas in the 1800s and settled in what is now known as Little Mexico, then known as Frog Town. They owned a home there and had seven children: five daughters and two sons. The oldest son, Ollie, died in childhood, but the six surviving children grew into senior citizens. They moved to West Dallas in 1900 or earlier, and all of the children attended Cedar Valley Colored School, which later became Fred Douglass Elementary School.

Elbert Fleming became a farmer and overseer of rent houses for the Terry Brothers Real Estate Co. He held that position until the early 1940s, when his eyesight failed. Lucious and Katie Hunt were the parents of two sons, William and Delma, and two daughters, Essie and Nonie. All four of these children were born in Tyler. The parents moved to Dallas in the 1800s. Nonie died in her twenties after childbirth, leaving a baby son, Clarence Jackson, who was reared by her mother, Katie.

Delma and William both worked for Trinity Portland Cement Company. Delma left the company around 1915 or earlier and went to work for Sears Roebuck Company on Lamar Street. He was an asthmatic all his life and was forced to retire in the late 1920s. As a result, he started the first Black bus service in Dallas. He would go from door to door to pick up passengers and take them downtown to the square. This area is now where the [Dallas] County Court House, Records Building, and the Red Courthouse are located. There the people would be able to catch streetcars to their designated areas. He ran this jitney service until 1935, the year he died.

During his [final] illness, he turned the business over to his eldest nephew, William Hunt Jr. At this time, the City of Dallas had added city bus service to the West Dallas area. After Delma passed, William closed the business. That bus was then known as the Western Heights bus. It is now the Beverly Hills.

Doris Jean Lee graduated from Booker T. Washington in May 1942 and entered Texas College in Tyler, Texas, in September 1942. She graduated in July 1946, with a bachelor of science in home economics. She was employed at Fred Douglass Elementary School from 1946 until 1947 as a teacher. She was the first student to graduate from Fred Douglass and return as a teacher.

In 1953 Clarence Jr. was employed by the Farmersville Independent School District as principal of Welford School. He remained there for fourteen years. When the schools were integrated, he was appointed head of the mathematics department, a position he held until his retirement in 1985 after thirty-two years in the teaching profession.

In 1953, Clarence Sr. was employed by [Dallas] County as a porter (known as maintenance) in the old courthouse on the third floor. He held this position until January 1, 1963. He was then sworn in as the first Black deputy clerk in the [Dallas] County Clerk's office, a position he held until his retirement in February 1975.

Doris Jean has been employed as a case worker for the past twenty-one years for Dallas County Mental Health/Mental Retardation. She has one son, Keith LaWayne Humphrey, a 1986 graduate of East Texas State University with a degree in business administration. He is also a member of the Phi Beta Sigma Fraternity and is presently a policeman in Fort Worth.

Clarence Jr. and his wife, Johnnie Mae Bell Lee, are the parents of five daughters: Acquinetta Lee Payne, Atlanta, Georgia (two daughters); Linda Jean Lee Lush, Dallas (two sons); Cheryl Ann Lee Burr, Missouri City, Texas (one son, one daughter); Carletta Onease Lee, Dallas; and Adrienne Michelle Lee, Farmersville, Texas.

Claude Sr. and Julia Carter McCain Family

Family historian: Mae Frances McCain Traylor

One of the prominent pioneers of Dallas County, Claude McCain Sr., was born in Avinger, Texas, December 6, 1884. He was one of seven children (four boys and three girls) born to Maynard and Susie Peppers McCain.

In 1922, he came to Dallas, Texas. After marrying Julia Carter, he settled at 5306 Keating Avenue in North Dallas, between the Central and Katy railroads. The community was known as Booker T. [Washington] Addition. Keating is now North Central Expressway and is the location of Roger Electrical Company, on the corner of North Central Expressway and McCommas.

In 1934, Claude McCain Sr. moved his family to 1904 Crockett Street in North Dallas, two blocks north of Ross Avenue and two blocks west of Booker T. Washington High School. They remained at this address until Borden Milk Company purchased the property in 1952.

Claude and Julia McCain then moved to 3211 Carpenter, where they remained until their deaths in 1978 and 1985, respectively. They are buried in Lincoln Memorial Cemetery.

Claude McCain, Sr. was employed by the Magnolia Petroleum Company, later Mobil Oil Company, home of the flying red horse in downtown Dallas. He retired after thirty-seven years of service. He supplemented his income by serving as an agent for Continental Casualty Insurance Company.

Claude McCain Sr. and his wife, Julia, became parents of three children: Lera Louise, Mae Frances, and Claude Jr.

Lera McCain Garret lives in Inglewood, California, with her son, Shelly. She attended B. F. Darrell and Booker T. Washington.

Mae Frances attended B. F. Darrell and Booker T. Washington. She married Samuel L. Traylor in 1950, and to this union two daughters were born: Lera Francine and Claudette Maria.

Claude Jr. also attended both Darrell and Washington Schools. He married Ramona Franklin of Houston in 1954. They are the proud parents of one son, Michael, and one daughter, Demetria. Velma McCain Moore and the late John Desmond Walker were children from previous marriages for both.

John Wesley McKinney

*Family historian: Jere L. McKinney
Blanton, granddaughter*

Mr. John Wesley McKinney migrated to Dallas in the early 1920s as a worker for the Texas and Pacific Railway. Mr. McKinney worked all over the state of Texas, living in houses provided by the railroad system. You can still see some of these houses today on the side of railroads. They are usually painted red or yellow.

Mr. McKinney, his wife, and five children lived in railroad communities that were at that time integrated with various migrant workers. Mr. McKinney learned to read and write and also converse in Spanish. With these skills, he became section foreman for the T&P Railroad and had an office in the round house located at Gaston and Fitzhugh. He kept records, made payroll, and also hired and fired workers.

Mr. McKinney lived for a while on Hamilton Street (known as the Magnolia Addition), renting a house from the Shivers, who at that time owned many houses on that street. This house was in walking distance to his job.

His only grandchildren, Ollie and Jere, were his heart and joy. As they would walk to and from school at Julia C. Frazier, he would always be in the round house looking out for them. He would usually add fruit to their lunches. His grandchildren called him Papa John. Therefore, he was recognized by many young people as "Papa John."

Mr. McKinney later moved to the Mill city area (Honeycutt Addition), on the corner of Collins and Charba Street. He carried on a home-loan business, where he loaned money to many people, even his relatives. He kept excellent records and was a great conversationalist. He would usually converse with people who wanted to make a loan before completing the transaction. Before retiring, he purchased land and built a house at the end of Charba Street.

Mr. McKinney was one of the first Blacks to buy graveyard space for his entire family and future generations at Lincoln Memorial Park.

Mr. McKinney enjoyed baseball and attended many games on surrounding baseball fields. He departed this life at the age of eighty-six.

The descendants of John Wesley McKinney and Mattie Rhone McKinney are: John L. McKinney, Jeremiah McKinney, Billy McKinney, Clinton McKinney (died as a child), and Mable McKinney Haden.

Their son Jeremiah McKinney married Osie Bell Jones, and their children are: Verta Mack McKinney (who died as a child); Ollie V. McKinney, who married Ulysses Smith and had one daughter, Sheryl Lynn Smith; Jere Lee McKinney, who married Richard P. Blanton and had two children, Deitra Blanton (who died as an infant) and Richard Lee Blanton, who married Shelia Anita Hicks and had a son, Rodrick Vernon, and a daughter, Jerelen Anita; and John Ray McKinney (who died as an infant).

Dr. Walter Ree McMillan Family

Family historian: Eva Partee McMillan[34]

Dr. Walter Ree McMillan was born in Quitman, Texas, October 3, 1874, to James (Jim) McMillan and Jane Regan McMillan. His paternal grandparents were Jake and Hanna who were "free people" although their own parents were slaves on the McMillan plantation in North Carolina. His mother, Jane, was the offspring of an African

---

34. Eva Partee McMillan's ancestry is explained in the story of the Isaac Barton and Chavis Lee Partee Families.—Eds.

The McMillan and Thomas families were among Dallas's most prominent Black families. Seated in this family portrait are: Herbert Thomas, Walter C. McMillan, Dr. W. R. McMillan, Tom Thomas, Marion E. McMillan, Yorktown Thomas, and Rev. Harewood. Standing are: Minnie Mae Bailey Thomas, Merriell Thomas McMillan, Beulah Thomas Harewood, Ella Thomas Patton, and Ollie Lee McMillan Mason. *Black Dallas Remembered, Inc.*

mother and an American Indian father. His paternal grandfather was Caucasian.

His sisters were Emma McMillan Brown, wife of Dr. Samuel L. Brown; Artie McMillan, whose husband was a farmer; and Lilly McMillan, a school administrator in Colorado. Julius A. McMillan, his brother, was chief surgeon and surgery instructor at Meharry Medical School for fifty years. Other brothers were: K. Willard McMillan, a Methodist minister in Fort Worth; Edgar McMillan, a railway mail clerk in Little Rock, Arkansas; Virgle, a farmer in East Texas; and Lemon, an insurance agent in Dallas.

J. L. Turner and his son, J. L. Turner Jr., are shown in their shared law office. *Courtesy of George Keaton, Jr.*

Dr. Walter Ree McMillan graduated from Meharry Medical School in 1909 with a specialization in obstetrics. He came to Dallas a year later and established an office jointly with Attorney J. L. Turner Sr. in downtown Dallas, on the corner of Commerce and Griffin Streets, the present site of the Earle Cabell Federal Court House.

Dr. McMillan married Merriell Vain Thomas in 1910. Their two sons, Walter Cartwell McMillan and Marion Ernest McMillan, enjoyed careers in education and ministry, respectively. His four children of a previous marriage, to Mrs. Aria Brinkley McMillan of Quitman, Texas, joined the McMillan family in Dallas. They were Walter Ree (Lucky) McMillan, a teacher who later became a career soldier in the US Army; Lillie May McMillan Oliver, a seamstress and wife of a minister in Newark, Ohio; Xenophon McMillan, a real estate agent and army veteran; and Ollie Lee McMillan Mason, wife of Attorney Duane B. Mason, a registered nurse and the first African American to be hired by Parkland Hospital, in 1931.

In 1921, Dr. McMillan built a hospital, the McMillan Sanitarium, on the corner of Hall and State Streets. Foreseeing the need for their services in the growing city, he encouraged young doctors to establish themselves in Dallas. Some of them were: Dr. L. G. Pinkston of Terrell, Texas; Dr. W. K. Flowers, Sulphur Springs, Texas; Dr. William Green, Kaufman, Texas; and his brother-in-law, Dr. Samuel L. Brown of Austin, Texas. These men served as doctors and surgeons at the McMillan Sanitarium before they established themselves in their own hospitals and clinics.

Greatly interested in the civic as well as medical affairs in Dallas, Dr. McMillan served his people in many areas. As a member of St. Paul Methodist Church on Routh Street, he served many years as trustee and worshipped there until his death. As a team leader in the development of the Moorland Branch of the YMCA, he was proud that his team was the most successful in fundraising contests for the

Dr. McMillan built a hospital on the corner of Hall and State Streets in 1923, the McMillan Sanitarium. *Black Dallas Remembered, Inc.*

structure, which was eventually located at Flora and Boll Streets. Dr. J. W. Anderson, Dr. Hamilton, and Mr. Willis of the Knights of Pythias Temple were some of his team members. Dr. McMillan died in Dallas in 1958 at the age of 84.

Mrs. Annie Washington Mitchell Family

Family historian: Maurine F. Bailey, with excerpts from "A Salute to Mrs. Mitchell of St. John Baptist Church" by Bernadine Robinson

Mrs. Annie Washington Mitchell was born in Atlanta, Texas, Cass County. She was the daughter of Lee Andrew and Frances Johns. Her father was a barber, and her mother a housewife.

Her grandparents Henry and Lucy (Scott) Henderson came to Texas as slaves from Kentucky and Virginia. When they were emancipated, they purchased approximately six hundred acres of land from their former slave owner, P. R. Scott in Atlanta, Cass County. A portion of this land, which was deeded to them in 1883, is still owned by their surviving descendants.

Mrs. Mitchell grew up and was educated in East Texas schools, where she began her teaching career. A descendant of a long line of educators, it was only natural that Mrs. Annie Mitchell continue the profession. She spent many years teaching in Rowlett, Garland, and Lake Dallas, Dallas County area schools.

When she came to Dallas, Mr. Andrew DuBois introduced her to the St. John Baptist Church. She cast her lot with St. John during Rev. McPherson's last year as pastor and continued to be a loyal and faithful member throughout her life.

Becoming a member of the church was not a new experience for Mrs. Mitchell. She had been a Christian since she was ten years old. She was baptized by her uncle, Rev. Calvin Jones, in Atlanta and served as organist for his church. During this time, she fondly remembered that she "wore out two organs." She was also her daughter's first piano teacher.

At St. John, she immediately became active in the two areas of the church life that she loved most dearly: music and teaching. She sang in the senior choir for seventy-five years, until her health would not permit her to continue. She taught in the Sunday School for many years and served as superintendent for one year. She was just as active in the Training Union and was one of its most ardent workers. When it was suggested that the members of St. John should spend more time in the study of Bible, it was Mrs. Mitchell, along with Rev. Perry, who set the wheels in motion to have the Sunday School lessons taught in the various homes of the members during the week. This was the birth of the St. John Sunday School extension department.

In later years, even though her health would not permit her to be as active as she would like to have been, she retained membership in the Energetic Charity Club and the Amazon Sunday School Class. She served for more than twenty years as Worthy Matron to the Shannon Rose Chapter of the order of the Eastern Star. She was a member of the Court of Calanthes and of the Daughters of Isis. She was also a member of the Phyllis Wheatley Art Club and the North Dallas Neighborhood Club.

During her teaching career, Mrs. Mitchell touched the lives of many young people of this community. Two of her students, Mrs. Birdie Anderson and the Rev. D. Edwin Johnson, became outstanding leaders in our city. For many years, young people who came to Dallas as teachers found in this Christian woman a warmth and friendliness that made her home a "home away from home."

During her late years she lived quietly with her son-in-law and daughter, Mr. and Mrs. Sterling Bailey. Her daughter, Maurine, is perhaps best known as the director of the famed Harry T. Burleigh

Choir of Lincoln High School, which now bears the name of Maurine F. Bailey Choir. Mrs. Mitchell's son, Thester Washington, who lives in Chicago, is a retired supervisor in the Illinois State Department of Revenue.

———————

Robert Thomas Moore

Family historian: Chloe Baker

Robert Thomas Moore, a native Dallas musician and the son of the late Robert Moore Sr. and Viola Cole Moore, was born October 18, 1906, at 2400 Juliette Street. The Coles, Thomas Austin Cole and Lear Nora Scott Cole, originally from Millican, a small South Texas community, moved to Dallas in the early 1900s and established residence at 2400 Juliette Street, now Munger Avenue. The residence was a three-room, shotgun-type house on a lot that was about forty-five feet wide by one hundred or more feet deep, adjacent to the east side of St. Paul United Methodist Church. It is now the property of St. Paul Church. The property was sold to the church by Mrs. Viola Cole Simmons, the Cole's youngest daughter, after the passing of all of her immediate family.

The Coles were among the pioneer families and founders of St. Paul [United] Methodist Church.[35] Each family member served in many official capacities of the church organization and gave financial support as long as he or she lived. They were active also

———————

35. The St. Paul United Methodist Church was founded in 1873, the area's first African American Methodist church. It was built in the Freedman's Town community, which had been established by formerly enslaved people soon after Emancipation, near the site of a cemetery already established by people who were enslaved in the White areas nearby. St. Paul is the only church left in what was, for more than a century, a neighborhood of numerous African American churches.

Since its founding, the area streets and neighborhoods have been changed dramatically by the creation of Central Expressway and later the Woodall Rodgers Freeway. What was once Freedman's Town is now known as Uptown. The current address of the church is 1816 Routh Street, and the area is now called the Arts District. A Texas State Historical Marker stands on the church property.—Eds.

in community and civic organizations. Both were officials in the Daughters and Knights of Pythias, a strong fraternal lodge for Blacks, [which was] organized in Philadelphia in February 1864 and grew prodigiously for many, many years.

They owned and operated one of Dallas's first grocery stores serving the North Dallas Community.[36] The Coles were proud parents of four very fine daughters, each of whom was career-oriented: Evalena, the oldest, was a devout Christian church woman; Della was a fine seamstress; Sara, a beautician, instructress, and consultant; Viola, Robert Thomas's mother, the youngest, was a nurse.

R. T., as he is affectionally called, is endowed with many musical talents and his achievements in the musical world are numerous. He is extremely modest when questioned about his career. It has taken more than two years and a lot of persuasion to finally get this story, which most will agree is commendable and worthy to be published. He is a professional piano player, band leader, composer, saxophonist, recording artist, and singer. His affectionate name for the piano is "Ole Babe."

Unfortunately, many artists, feeling that Dallas was derelict in promoting its own homegrown talent of color, left Dallas and went to other cities to gain recognition. An exception to this situation, however, was that the exceptional musical talent of R. T. could not fail to be recognized and utilized throughout the Dallas community. In 1925, while attending Booker T. Washington High School, he organized a little "Snap Band," the "Crooning Syncopators." There were seven members in the band, namely R. T., piano; Norris Wilson, trombone; Red Calhoun, saxophone; Will Wagoner, trumpet; John White, trumpet; and John R. Davis, guitar and banjo. This group was one of the first of color to play on station WRR in 1925. The station at that time was located in the ballroom at the top of the Jefferson Hotel.

---

36. What was once called North Dallas included what is now Uptown, the Arts District, and Deep Ellum. For more complete information about North Dallas, see the section on Early Settlements.—Eds.

The "Crooning Syncopaters" were kept busy with engagements in and around Dallas at such spots as Hayden's Halls in Queen City, Lincoln Manor, and Elm Thicket, as well as other surrounding areas like McKinney and Dennison. When the Hollywood Barn was built, R. T. increased the band to twelve members: R. T., Red Calhoun, Sam Mitchell, Slo Wilson, John White, Willie Wagoner, Norris Wilson, Lloyd Gish, Pretty Papa, Dan Minor, Bird Johnson, and Kag Johnson. The band name was changed to "The Texans." The Texans enjoyed many, many engagements together and very close relationships as a team.

Later, in 1931, when Louis Armstrong came to Dallas in need of more musicians, he approached R. T. about joining him. Four members of the band joined Louis: R. T., Bud Johnson, Kag Johnson, and Dan Minor went on tour with him. R. T. gave the remaining members of the band to Red Calhoun. R. T. stayed with Louis Armstrong for about five years. While in Chicago in 1936, he encountered Lionel Hampton, who was going on a tour of Europe and needed a piano player. R. T. and the band joined Lionel Hampton and went to England and France, where they toured for two years. In 1938, while on their return trip to Dallas, when the band reached Kansas City, Missouri, they were fortunate again and were able to go on the air over station WXBY, which was later changed to KXBY.

The band was the first of color to go on the air nightly. The first performance was presented at The Sunset Club on East 12th Street. From there, they would join Joe Turner with Pete Johnson's Band and jam until midnight, after which Count Basie would put the station to bed around two o'clock a.m.

Two years later, in 1940, he left Kansas City and decided to solo. He opened in Chicago at the Edgewater Beach Hotel in the Cocktail Room, playing the organ. He became known as "Bobby Moore," his stage name. He did recordings and made some records.

He remained in Chicago until 1945, and went from there to Milwaukee, Wisconsin, where he joined Lil [Hardin] Armstrong at French's. They worked together as a team for about three years.

R. T. went on to Detroit, where he spent about six months. From there he went to Minneapolis and opened at Schiek's, one of the city's most exclusive night clubs. From Schiek's club, he traveled on to New York, where he remained for about five years. [He went] from New York to Denver in 1957, and then returned to Dallas.

Upon his return to Dallas, he organized a trio, which included Milton (Bear) Thomas, Mercy Baby, and himself. The three of them went on tour in Alaska, playing first at the Oasis Club [city unknown], then on to Fairbanks, playing at the Timber-Tap Club. They went on to Juneau for about a year and from there to the Silver Dollar Club. When they returned to Dallas in 1960, R. T. said he had grown tired of the road and went into semi-retirement.

He met and married Ms. Louise Carraway, a beautician, in 1966, and together they established Louise's Beauty Salon at 1724 Hall Street. It was and still is a successful business patronized by Dallasites desirous of expert hair care.

R. T. became involved in music again. Music is in his blood. He was engaged in playing for several White clubs, such as Wynn Steak House, Tea House of the Harvest Moon, The Idle Rich, and the Aransas Club, when it was located on Forest Avenue. He decided again to retire. However, he still plays "gigs," the musician's lingo for "jobs," for those people who really enjoy music of the '50s, '60s and '70s.

He enjoys and appreciates good music but does not care too much for the loud Rock and Roll music, which he says is all right for those who like it. He says he is a musician from the "Old School," which required musicians to be able to read and play music. He feels that music is an art and should be treated as such. It is a universal form of communication, from which people benefit morally and spiritually and feel good about themselves, God, and life. It has a romantic quality, which all people can understand and [to which they can] relate.

Finally, the band played at the Old Tip Top Club located across from the old Texas and Pacific Depot. They played also at McMillan's

Cafe on Elm Street every Thursday, which was "Maid's Day Off," and later in the Old Roosevelt Club House until the wee hours of the morning. Other times they would go after hours out to the Riverside Park in Oak Cliff.

Pride in his exceptional music talents and family security were and are the unmistakable barometers of R. T.'s tremendous success. His life's musical career history, I think, is one to be told and shared.

Isaac Barton and Chavis Lee Partee Families

Family historian: Eva Partee-McMillan

Isaac Barton followed his old friends, Thomas Jefferson Sowell, Charles Henry, and Martha Ann Sowell Bryant, to Dallas from Gibson County in Tennessee around 1890. He settled in rural far North Dallas where he became a woodcutter (cutting down trees) for five dollars per month.

He married Florence Keller, daughter of extensive landowners, Henry and Mary Jane Keller. Keller Springs Road is named for Florence's father. Their [the Keller's] older daughter had already married T. J. Sowell.

Isaac and Florence Barton built a large home on Noell Road (now Montfort Drive) and farmed their large holdings. This area was called "Upper White Rock."

A son, John A. Barton, was born in 1900 and married Jessie Turner, a teacher and daughter of a prominent Dallas family. He died in 1927.

The Bartons were members of [White Rock] Christian Chapel CME Church. Isaac died on March 20, 1937. His wife died on January 27, 1939.

Barton's half-brother, Chavis Lee Partee Jr., joined him in White Rock. He came from Bradford, Tennessee, in Gibson County, on January 1, 1930. A widower, Partee and his six children lived on Valley View Lane (now the Valley View Shopping Center site), where he farmed his brother's land.

After slavery, the family had taken the name of Partee rather than Polk. The Partees were suffering persecution from the French government, as they were Huguenots. This was the reason the family—the slave owners—came to America.

When Chavis was a young man in Tennessee, the Board of Education of Gibson County decided to discontinue the colored school for a year due to the shortage of funds. Chavis, having only completed the seventh grade, volunteered and taught the students of the elementary school.

His wife, Mary Rebecca Sowell, died October 13, 1921, during childbirth. Their six remaining children were: Arlyn Clifton Partee, Cecil James Partee, Mildred Pauline Partee Taylor, Fay Partee Wells, Eva Partee McMillan, and Neva Partee.

The mother of Isaac Barton and Chavis Partee was Katharine McKinley. Isaac's father drowned a few months before his birth.

Moriah, the grandmother of Chavis Partee, was a slave in the James K. Polk household. History reports that she was sought for her fine needlework in many counties. It states also that she answered the door at the Polk residence and that she made delicious biscuits.

Moriah's son, Chavis Lee Partee, was born in 1825. He married a slave woman from the Partee Plantation. They had several children, who moved to other states after liberation. One son, Aquilla, moved to Chicago. His grandson, Cecil Partee, became a congressman who represented the Chicago District.

During the Civil War, the slaves in Tennessee hid out in the bushes whenever the Confederate Army was in the vicinity, to prevent being forced off to work for the Army. They were called "Bushmen." However, once, when the Union Army passed through, Chavis Lee and his friend Anthony Sowell showed the Army the direction of a town they were trying to locate. They learned later that the Army was marching to Shiloh, a battle ground which the Union Army took after fierce fighting.

After the death of his wife, Chavis Lee married Katharine McKinley Barton, a widow with a son, Isaac Barton. Chavis and his family bought land which they farmed outside Bradford, Tennessee.

Chavis Jr., the youngest, was born on October 4, 1875. He remained at home with his parents after the older children were gone. His mother had a sharp tongue, and there were conflicts, especially since she wanted *all* of the earnings to be donated to Mt. Zion CME Church.

In 1905, Chavis Jr. married Mary Rebecca Sowell, the granddaughter of his father's friend, Anthony Sowell.

Katharine died in 1910, at the age of seventy. Chavis Sr. died around 1918. He was in his nineties. They both lived with Chavis Jr. and his family.

Chavis Jr. died December 26, 1950, at seventy-five years of age. He was a member of the Masonic Order and Boll Street CME Church.

Chavis Lee Partee Jr. had six children. Arlyn Clifton Partee, born June 17, 1907, [was] a graduate of Lane College in Jackson, Tennessee. He taught school at Armstrong High School in Lower White Rock and at N. W. Harllee in Oak Cliff. Later he worked in politics and was one of the founders of the Dallas Progressive Voters League. He was affiliated with the Omega Psi Phi Fraternity. He died January 1956.

Cecil James Partee, born April 7, 1912, also [was] a graduate of Lane College. He taught in Royce City, Texas, [and] at Booker T. Washington, Roosevelt, Lincoln, and James Madison High Schools. He also taught at Oliver Wendell Holmes. He was a historian. He studied at Prairie View and the University of Southern California and was a member of Kappa Alpha Psi Fraternity. In 1945, he married Hazel Washington, a graduate of Bishop College in Marshall, Texas.

She received a master's degree from North Texas State University and earned a doctorate from Nova University in Fort Lauderdale, Florida. She taught in the Dallas Public School System until 1971 and has served as principal since that time. Cecil James Partee died October 31, 1974.

Their children are Glenda Partee Scott, a graduate of Mt. Holyoke College in Massachusetts, who earned a master's degree from New York City College and a doctorate at Penn State. She married Herman Scott and is presently a Superintendent of Education in Washington, DC. Her daughter is Erin Scott. Cecil Partee Jr., a graduate of Southern Methodist University in Dallas in business education, was a quarterback on the football team while a student at Roosevelt High School in Dallas and is now a businessman. He married Peggy Dodd of Dallas. Their children are Jules Partee and Cecil Partee III. Pamela Partee Lucas studied at North Texas State University in Denton, Texas. She married Joe Lucas and is presently employed at El Centro College in Dallas. Her daughter is Lotoya Lucas.

Mildred Partee Taylor, the oldest daughter of Chavis Lee and Mary Rebecca Sowell, was born August 15, 1914. She attended Texas College in Tyler, Texas. She married Harrison E. Taylor, a professor from Wichita Falls, Texas. Their two children are Sonja Taylor Neal and Harrison E. Taylor Jr. Sonja Taylor Neal married Melvin Neal of Mt. Enterprise, Texas. Their children are: Robin Neal, Sheri Lynn Neal Garrett, Melvin Neal Jr., Erick Neal, and Heather Neal. She works as a wire operator for a brokerage firm. Harrison E. Taylor Jr., a lawyer in San Jose, California, married Nancy Bray of California. Their children are: Jennifer Taylor, Stacey Taylor, Darcy Taylor, and Tani Taylor.

Faye Partee Wells of Los Angeles, California, was born on February 7, 1919. She attended Wiley College Extension in Dallas and married Harry Lee Wells Jr., grandson of George and Phyllis Jackson Wells, who came directly from Africa. They were shipped down the Trinity River to Carrollton, Texas, where they were purchased by a plantation owner in Collin County. Faye Wells's children include Leslie Wells Jackson of Los Angeles. She married Henry Jackson of Dallas. Her children are Russell Jackson, Randall Jackson, and Kimberly Jackson. Faye Wells's son is Harry Lee Wells III, an aide to Governor Cuomo of New York. He earned a bachelor's degree at the University of Southern California while a member of the football team and a master's degree in New York City. He married Carol Lamont. His children are Karl, H'Odara, and Liana. Rebecca Wells Young, a former student of Southwest Los Angeles College, married Leonard Young of Hawaii. Her daughter is Leilani Young.

Eva Partee, born May 7, 1921, an activist, married Marion E. McMillan, a minister and son of pioneer Dallas doctor W. R. McMillan. They had four children. Karen McMillan of Houston, wife of Major Robert B. Wesson of the U. S. Air Force, an engineer at NASA. Karen attended Clark College in Atlanta, Georgia and graduated in Social Studies at Bishop College in Dallas. Their children are Marcus and Nicole Wesson.

Eva and Marion's son Marion Ernest (Ernie) McMillan Jr., Director of the Fifth Ward Enrichment Program of Houston, dropped out of Morehouse College in Atlanta, Georgia, in 1964 to work in the Civil Rights Movement in Mississippi, Alabama, and Georgia. He was arrested in Selma, Alabama, for carrying a sign which read "REGISTER TO VOTE." (The organization was the Student Non-Violent Coordinating Committee—SNCC.) In 1967, while attending the University of Texas at Arlington, he organized a SNCC Chapter for this region. He immediately became the target of harassment by the Dallas Criminal Justice System. He was arrested daily for no stated reason. Eventually in 1968, he was sentenced to ten years to the Texas Department of Correction for his role in a boycott of a Dallas grocery chain, the O.K. Supermarket. Later he received a five-year sentence for his failure to appear in court on draft evasion charges, although he was in the Dallas County Jail on the date he was to appear. (The latter charge was dropped years later, when the federal courts discovered the truth.)

He served over three years in Leavenworth, Kansas, and Huntsville, Texas, systems. His children are Angela Fikes McMillan, Ohene McMillan, and Dafina McMillan.

Another daughter of Eva and Marion's, Jacqueline McMillan Hill, studied at Los Angeles City College and worked for the Dallas Legal Services. She married Charles Hill of Illinois. Her children are Anyika McMillan and Chavis Randle Hill. Presently, Jacqueline is employed by the Dallas Independent School District.

Their fourth child, Katherine McMillan Wilson, graduated from the University of Houston with a bachelor's degree in education. She earned a master's degree in psychology from Texas Southern [University]. She married David Wilson, a graduate of the University of Texas at Arlington in mathematics. He earned a master's degree and doctorate from Southern Methodist University. Their daughter is Ava Katharine Wilson.

Neva Irene Partee (twin sister of Eva Partee McMillan), of Los Angeles, worked as a laboratory supervisor at the University of Southern California Medical Center.

Minnie K. Tamplin Patton

Family historian: Mrs. Minnie K. Tamplin Patton, as interviewed by Chloe Baker and Mamie McKnight

Mrs. Minnie K. Tamplin Patton, the daughter of Mr. Henry Tamplin Sr. and Mrs. Bertha Collier Tamplin of Pittsburg, Texas, moved to Dallas with her mother and brother Willie in 1914. The family residence was established on Washington Avenue near State Street. "Minnie K.," as she was affectionately called, and Willie enrolled in in the B. F. Darrell Elementary School. Willie, age twelve, was in the fifth grade, and Minnie, age nine, was in the third grade. They lived in the

North Dallas [now Uptown] area for quite some time, after which they moved to the Booker T. [Washington] Addition.[37]

After completing their elementary education, Willie and Minnie graduated from Booker T. Washington High School. Minnie graduated in June 1925 and married Roy Patton in August 1925. Mr. Patton was the owner of Patton's Cafe and Hotel on Central Avenue. He died in the 1940s.

Roy and Minnie K. became the proud parents of three sons, all of whom grew up to be very fine young men. All three of the Patton sons—Roy Jr., Donald, and Frederick—graduated from Booker T. Washington, married, and have lovely families. The grandchildren are the pride and joy of Mrs. Patton.

Mrs. Patton is a devout Christian woman. She joined St. John Missionary Baptist Church, along with her mother and brother, shortly after they moved to Dallas. She devotes most of her time to her church, where she holds and has held numerous offices. She spends a great deal of time reaching out to others.

She is credited with having purchased and presented to the church a beautiful large Christian flag in honor of her devoted mother, Mrs. Bertha Collier. She was very gracious to those whom she held in high esteem.

A beautiful large American flag was purchased and a presentation made at St. John for her son Roy, who was also a veteran. The late Roy Patton Jr. was a photographer and a graduate of one of Dallas's prominent commercial photography schools. Additionally, he was a graduate of Prairie View A&M College.

E. Donald Patton attended Tuskegee for two years before moving to Chicago, where he graduated from the Art Institute of Chicago. He was employed by the Wrigley Gum Company, the first Black

---

37. See the full description of the creation of the Booker T. Washington Addition in the Early Settlements section of this book. The neighborhood was created in a large triangle of land between today's Central Expressway and the Katy Trail, extending from Monticello north to the SMU campus. The area is now part of the Knox/Henderson neighborhood—Eds.

employee of the company. He later moved to San Diego, California, where he pursued his career in the arts.

Fred Bert Patton attended Bishop College and became interested in a career as a police officer. He dropped out of Bishop and presently is happy and proud to be a deputy with the police department. He worked in Houston several years before joining the police department.

Mrs. Patton has received many prestigious awards and certificates. Among them is one which acclaims her as one of the world's fine Christian mothers. She organized the Dallas Chapter No. 11 of Black American War Mothers and has devoted her time and energy in making it a viable part of our Black culture.

Her scrapbook displaying her activities is most interesting and heartwarming. One very impressive picture is that of her spreading a [floral tribute] on the [memorial] of the late President John F. Kennedy. The wreath which Mrs. Patton designed and placed on the memorial of the late President John F. Kennedy was a replica of the United States Flag. The five-by-six-[foot] flag was made of red and white carnations at a cost of $65.00.

A picture of the ceremony was sent to the family of President Kennedy. They expressed their gratitude to her in the form of a citation for her very humble, humane gesture. These are but a few examples of her very fine character, her love for people, and her strong desire to help others.

The owners of Lincoln Memorial Cemetery [of Dallas] accepted a request from Mrs. Patton to designate a section of the cemetery for veterans. Afterward, she helped dedicate a veterans' monument in the cemetery.[38]

Mrs. Patton was employed by the government and served as an elevator operator for many years at the Santa Fe Building. She retired from the government after some twenty-five or

---

38. Her son Roy Patton Jr., who was born in 1926, was a veteran of World War II, and was buried in the Lincoln Memorial Cemetery in 1961.—Eds.

thirty years. Her activities have been curbed somewhat since she suffered a very serious heart attack. Besides her devoted family, St. John Missionary Baptist Church and its activities have been her life. Her very broad smile, her soft-spoken voice, and the sparkle in her eyes are evidence of her pleasing personality. One of her prized possessions is the family rocker which has rocked to sleep seven generations of babies as of 1988.

Henry and Mary Moore and Noah and Ida Penn Families

Family historians: Algernon S. Penn and Effie Penn

Henry Moore (July 5, 1840–October 26, 1922), an Irishman, owned a large farm in Grand Prairie. The Texas Power and Light Company plant and lake are now located on the farm site.

Henry married Mary Harrison (December 1844–December 31, 1909), and to that union fifteen children were born. They were Emanuel (October 19, 1863), Richard (November 12, 1865), William (January 10, 1867), Charley (November 17, 1869), Allie (September 17, 1871), Rosie (September 14, 1873, called Lula), Ida (September 12, 1875), Janey (1876), Mamy (May 1, 1880), Trudy (March 1, 1882), Jasper (April 1, 1884), Bessievive (June 12, 1886), Leon (August 18, 1888), and Arthur (August 27, 1889).[This list, which contains only fourteen children's names, is repeated exactly as provided in Volume I, p. 83.]

The family was very prosperous. Records indicate that Henry Moore donated a part of his land for a school and lodge hall in Grand Prairie.

After all the children were grown, Henry Moore retired from farming and moved to Dallas. He built a large family home on Ninth Street in Oak Cliff. All the children eventually moved to Dallas from Grand Prairie.

Noah Penn, who later married Ida Moore, came to Dallas before the Moores. He first came to Dallas with T. L. Marsalis, as his coachman. He worked with Marsalis for a year or two before leaving for Jacksonville, Texas. He worked there for a year and then returned to Dallas. Marsalis asked him to clear land for him in an area of Oak Cliff called "Jim Town." This was the beginning of Noah's very successful career as a carpenter, contractor, and landowner, especially in the Oak Cliff area.

He built a cabin for himself near Jim Town. Somehow, he made his way to Grand Prairie and met the Moore family. He married Ida Moore and brought her back to Dallas with him. The Penns had five children: Noble G., Mary Penn Starks, Maggie Penn Orman, Willie Mae Penn Jones, and Algernon S. Penn.

Noah Penn built a number of houses in Oak Cliff, with family homes at 1027 and 1031 Tenth Street. The Moore home on Ninth Street, the Penn home at 1031 Tenth, and the home Noah built for his daughter Mary and her husband, along with several others, are still standing.

Noah Penn was a very active civic worker. He was one of the founders of Greater El Bethel Baptist Church on the corner of Cliff and Ninth Streets. His name is on the cornerstone. Noah Street in Oak Cliff was named for him.

Mary Penn married Ewell Starks, one of the two sons of J. P. Starks. J. P. Starks was a renowned Dallas educator and the founder of the first Black mortuary in Dallas, Peoples' Undertakers. Mary and Ewell had two daughters, Johnetta and Thelma Marie. Maggie Penn married S. Orman, and Willie Mae Penn married Clarence Jones.

Until his retirement, the youngest child of Noah and Ida Penn, Algernon, was an outstanding teacher and principal in the Dallas Independent School District. His wife, Effie, who is from

New Orleans, is also an accomplished musician and taught private piano lessons for a number of years.

Simon Miles Pentecost

Family historian: Ellen Ruth Pentecost Larkin

Simon Miles Pentecost was born April 6, 1885, in Kilgore, Texas. He was one of sixteen children of former slaves Miles and Angelina Smith Pentecost.

Miles Pentecost came to America from the West Indies Islands. Upon arriving in the country, Miles was sold into slavery to a cotton plantation owner in Virginia whose surname was Griffin. The entire time Miles spent on the Griffin plantation he was known as Miles Griffin.

When the Emancipation Proclamation was signed and all slaves were freed, the Griffin family migrated to Kilgore, Texas. The Griffins informed Miles he was purchased in New Orleans, and they wanted to give him back his surname. They carried him back to New Orleans, searched the records, and found his surname was Pentecost.

After returning to Kilgore, the Griffins gave Miles one hundred acres of land, which remains in the family. It is known as Pentecost Addition. Miles and Angelina Smith Pentecost raised a family of sixteen children, educating them in the schools of Kilgore. Most of them furthered their education at Butler College and Texas College in Tyler, Texas, and at Bishop College in Marshall, Texas. There were teachers, principals, and successful farmers in the family.

Simon Pentecost chose Texas College to further his education. After completing his studies, he came to Dallas. He was employed for a number of years as a head waiter (maître d') in some of the finest hotels and clubs in Dallas. Among them were Park Hotel on Ervay (now known as the Ambassador Hotel), the Baker Hotel, the Adolphus Hotel, the Dallas Country Club, and the Columbian Club.

Simon married Estella Hunt of Sherman, Texas, in 1910, and they lived with the Burl Hendricks on Beaumont Street, in a neighborhood known as The Prairie. They spent many leisure hours at the park across from the Park Hotel. Today the park is known as Old City Park. To this union, four children were born: J. B., who died in infancy; Ellen Ruth; Simon Jr.; and Katie Marie.

Simon and Estella Pentecost were early settlers of Oak Cliff. They purchased a home from A. C. Pepple on October 3, 1912, at 1116 Betterton Circle. It is still owned by his daughter, Ellen Ruth Pentecost Larkin.

Simon was a natural horticulturalist and was known in the neighborhood for his abundant gardens and beautiful flowers. He supplied the neighbors with vegetables and fruits and was often called upon for advice as to planting, soil preparation, and special care of plants.

Simon lived a very fruitful and productive life. He emphasized the importance of family and education. He was accidentally killed by a hit-and-run driver at the intersection of Eleventh Street and Ewing Avenue on April 9, 1939. He is survived by his daughter, Ellen Ruth Pentecost Larkin of Dallas, Texas, and his son, Simon Miles Pentecost Jr. of Los Angeles, California.

Dr. and Mrs. L. G. Pinkston Sr.

*Family historians: Vareta Pinkston Gulley
and Stevonne Gully*

Dr. and Mrs. L. G. Pinkston and their three children, Vareta, L. G. Jr., and Vernon, arrived in Dallas from Terrell, Texas, in 1921.

Dr. Lee Gresham Pinkston was born on August 16, 1883, and lived until January 10, 1961. *Black Dallas Remembered, Inc.*

Viola Marie Shaw Pinkston was born on October 15, 1892, and lived until February 14, 1976. She married Dr. Pinkston in 1912, and they had four children, only two of whom survived to adulthood. *Black Dallas Remembered, Inc.*

Dr. Lee Gresham Pinkston, born August 16, 1883, was one of the six children of Fannie Gresham Pinkston and Ritten Pinkston. He was born in the small farming community of Forest, Mississippi, in Scott County. He attended the Meridian Academy in Forest, and subsequently graduated from Alcorn College and Meharry Medical College. Before receiving his medical degree from Meharry, he encouraged his brother, G. F. Pinkston, to join him as a student at Meharry.

Although Dr. Pinkston received licenses to practice medicine in Tennessee, Kansas, Illinois, and Texas, he chose to begin his practice in Terrell, Texas, in 1910. His brother decided to begin his medical practice in Tennessee.

Dr. Pinkston's practice as a physician flourished in Terrell and the surrounding communities. In addition to caring for his patients, Dr. Pinkston built a clinic and drugstore in Terrell. These ventures and his involvement in many civic activities kept him very busy during his eleven-year stay there.

While in Terrell, Dr. Pinkston met Miss Viola Marie Shaw. A native of Terrell, she was the daughter of Alexander and Cicily Ann Agers Shaw. Dr. Pinkston and Miss Shaw married in 1912, and to that union four children were born. One daughter died in infancy.

Dr. W. R. McMillan [of Dallas] encouraged Dr. Pinkston to move to Dallas. His first official location in Dallas as a physician was in the McMillan Sanitarium on the corner of Hall and State Streets. His association with the McMillan Sanitarium continued until he opened his own clinic in 1927. The Pinkston Clinic was located at 3305 Thomas Avenue. It provided a modern, well-equipped medical institution for Black doctors to practice and work closely with their patients.

The [Pinkston] Clinic was well known throughout the state and enjoyed an outstanding reputation. Patients and doctors were served from as far north as Denison, south to Corsicana, west to Weatherford, and east to Marshall. Patients also came to the clinic from other states, including California, Kansas, Illinois, Oklahoma, Michigan, New Jersey, Mississippi, Louisiana, and Tennessee.

Some of the doctors on the hospital staff included: Dr. J. G. Hardin, MD; Dr. M. H. McShann, MD; Dr. E. H. Browne, DDS; Dr. D. T. Cleaver, MD; and Dr. Hugh Key, DDS. The staff doctors were not only well respected for their skills in the medical profession, but also for the professional development activities they conducted each year at the clinic. Each year, fellow physicians and members of the Lone Star Medical, Dental, and Pharmaceutical Association would convene at the clinic to share the latest methods and research in the medical professions.

In 1954, Dr. Pinkston was one of the five Black physicians who were admitted to practice at St. Paul Methodist [Hospital]. This was a first for Black doctors in Dallas. The other four physicians were Dr. Joseph Williams, Dr. William Flowers Jr., Dr. Frank Jordan, and Dr. George Shelton. The county and state medical associations admitted Black doctors in 1955. In 1959, St. Paul integrated its facilities for patients.

Dr. Pinkston's activities as a community and civic leader were outstanding. His activities encompassed every area of community life. He was primarily interested in and devoted to the development of the social, business, economic, and spiritual life of the community. His concern for the youth of Dallas was best indicated by his long and unselfish service to the YMCA.

He was a charter board member of Moorland Branch YMCA and continued to serve the YMCA throughout his life. He was a member of the Metropolitan YMCA board of directors and was one of the three Dallas County members of the National Council on YMCAs. In recognition of his many years of loyal consecrated service to the programs of YMCA, the YMCA Boys Camp at Lancaster, Texas, was named in his honor by the Metropolitan Board in 1954. In 1960, he received an award for "Outstanding Service to the YMCA in Dallas."

Among his many awards for service was the President's Award from Meharry Medical College that he received in June 1959 for "50 Years of Service to Mankind."

His varied areas of service included the following: president of the Star Post Publishing Company and publisher of the *Star Post* newspaper; president of the Dallas Negro Chamber of Commerce; president of the Western Mutual Life Insurance Company; member of the board of trustees of Wiley College; member of Paul Drayton Lodge No. 9, F&AM; member of the Dallas County Selective Service Board during World War II; and an active member of St. Paul Methodist Church, serving on both the board of trustees and the board of stewards.

Mrs. Pinkston was also a very active community service volunteer. She organized and founded the Wednesday Morning Study Club on February 15, 1931. She was president of the Dallas City Federation of Colored Women's Clubs. Also, she was chairwoman of the Committee on Administration at the Maria Morgan Branch of the YWCA, served on the first board of the Hexter Memorial Lighthouse for the Blind, and was president of the Women's Auxiliary of the Lone Star Medical Association. She was chosen Woman of the Year by the Zeta Phi Beta Sorority in 1947. She participated in a number of other organizations and made notable contributions of service and funds to each.

Of the three children who came to Dallas with the family, the youngest son, Vernon, died when he was approximately twelve years of age. The daughter, Vareta, has remained in Dallas, and the son, Lee G. Jr., lived in Fort Worth a number of years before returning to Dallas.

In 1937, Vareta Pinkston married Steve Gulley from East St. Louis. They are both graduates of Wiley College, and Steve has retired from the Dallas Independent School District, where he taught in the high schools. Vareta owns the Hatcher Street Florist, which she operated for a number of years. They have two children, Lee Patrick and Stevonne. Lee Patrick has two sons, Lee Patrick II and Steven Lee. Stevonne also has two children, Derrick D. and Stevette.

Lee G. Pinkston II is married to the former Armetia Randolph. They operated the Pinkston Mortuary in Fort Worth for a number of years, until they built the Pinkston Mortuary in Dallas on Hatcher Street. They then moved to Dallas to operate the facility here. Their son, Lee III, operates the mortuary in Fort Worth.

Arthur Prestwood Sr.

Family historian: Dorothy Prestwood

Arthur Prestwood was born in 1876 to Benjamin F. and Mary E. Prestwood in the Damascus Community, Coffee County, Alabama. He was reared on a farm under subnormal conditions. He worked as a farmhand until he was seventeen years of age, at which time he began to teach school as a rural schoolteacher. He followed this profession until he was twenty-one years of age. He decided that the progress he was making was a bit too slow, as the salary ranged from twenty-five dollars to forty dollars per month.

He returned to farming and continued this career until he was twenty-three years old. He decided that there must be something in life somewhere far more profitable than teaching country schools and farming poor sandy land which he did not own.

In 1909, he hoisted his sails to explore new territory and found himself in the great Lone Star State. He traveled the state and worked at different jobs. In 1919, he was employed by the Excelsior Mutual Benefit Association, which was then operated by Henry Strickland and Silas Cofield. He worked as a leading agent in the field from 1919 to 1925, when he was promoted to manager and sent to Fort Worth, Texas, to build a district for the company.

He served as manager in Fort Worth from 1925 to 1932. He was again promoted and given the title of General Manager of the Excelsior Life Insurance Company. He served in this capacity until 1942, when Henry Strickland died. He then served as President for the unexpired term of the late Mr. Strickland.

He was elected chairman of the board of directors of the Excelsior Life Insurance Company and was president of the company at the time it was sold.

For many years he made substantial contributions to the YMCA, NAACP, Negro Chamber of Commerce, and the Progressive Voters League. He was the President of the Texas Association of Agency Officers and State Managers and served in several capacities in connection with the program of the National Negro Insurance Association and its allied organizations.

Arthur and Amy Prestwood married at the Pythian Building, 2551 Elm. As products of the insurance company, Excelsior picked up the tab. Arrayed with all the trimmings and the added luxury of an orchestra, the Prestwood's wedding set a precedent in Dallas. Amy marched down the aisle attired in the borrowed gown of Mrs. Charles Etta Jones, secretary/treasurer of the thriving insurance company. This marriage brought forth three children: Mary Catherine Prestwood Holmes of Florida, Arthur Prestwood Jr. of Florida, and Dorothy Mae Prestwood of Dallas, Texas.

Due to Prestwood's age and failing health, in 1957 he made the dreaded decision of selling the thriving and prosperous insurance company and its building located at 2600 Flora Street to Universal Life Insurance Company.

Arthur Prestwood Sr. died January 25, 1963, a victim of cancer of the pancreas. His death, like [that of] his other predecessors and business partners, was keenly felt by the community. Four months later, May 11, 1963, Amy Prestwood died. She, too, was the victim of cancer—cancer of the lungs.

Prestwood's thrust and dream for the Black community continues to be felt today. His place and the role which he played set the stage for Black achievement. He was a man who started with nothing and made something. He was a man who came from beneath the shackles of slavery to go beyond the set boundaries of opportunity. Lastly, he was a man without a formal education who learned the value of knowledge and acquired it.

Sylvester Walter and Ladora Kennedy Smith Price Family

Family historian: Ruth Price Sanders

Sylvester Walter Price married LaDora "Dovie" Kennedy Smith in about the year 1902 or 1903, in Mexia, Limestone County, Texas. Mr. Price's father, Reverend William Anderson Price, migrated from Meridian, Mississippi, and settled in Freestone County.

Their first child, Jessie Roberta, was born September 12, 1904, in Powell, Navarro County, Texas. Four other children—Essie, Luther, Oleatha, and Herman—were born to them prior to their relocating to Dallas County, Texas.

The Price family was, like many others during that period, engaged in the healthful outdoor activities of farming, hunting, fishing, riding, and such. They were people with an independent spirit. They enjoyed a pride and belief in their own worth.

While material possessions were limited, the Price family enjoyed good food, which they grew, good health, and a healthy family inter-action and were avid sports fans, especially baseball. There was an adventuresome nature manifested by the Price family's moving and relocating to many farm communities within Limestone, Freestone, and Navarro Counties from 1902 to 1927.

Finally, the move to "Big D" in 1927 represented the fulfillment of a dream held by Mr. Price for many years—to move his family to the City of Dallas, where they would have the advantages and comforts of city life and education. He could then pursue a business career in barbering and could participate in the lodge and fraternal activities which he enjoyed. Mrs. Price had not always shared her husband's dream for life in the city. She felt "the city was not the place to rear her children." But by 1927, all the children were teenage or young adult, with the exception of Ruth.

The Price family's first address in Dallas was McCoy Street, and then they moved to Allen Street. Finally, the move was made to Oak Cliff, where they remained for many years. One daughter, Mrs. Essie Craig, continues to live in Oak Cliff today.

The Price family members all became contributing citizens of Dallas—all industrious and churchgoing. They were a family of entrepreneurs and sports enthusiasts, especially the Price men.

The family owned a candy store in the North Dallas area, and Mr. Price was in charge of his own barbershops in several Oak Cliff locations, as well as North Dallas.

The family's interest in sports led to the organization of one of Dallas's all-Black baseball teams, the Dallas Wonders, in 1937. This was a professional baseball team which played baseball in many parts of Texas and, of course, in Dallas at the Old Rebel Field and Steer Stadium in Oak Cliff. The late Hank Thompson, who played with the New York Giants in the 1940s, got his start with the Dallas Wonders. Herman Price was the manager of the Dallas Wonders, as he had the fiscal and managerial ability to put the organization together. He was assisted by his father and brothers, Oleatha and Luther, and his brother-in-law, Otis Turner.

The Price brothers migrated to Los Angeles, California, in the 1940s, where Herman Price owned and operated a chain of dry-cleaning establishments until his retirement. Oleatha and Luther Price are deceased, as are Mr. and Mrs. Sylvester Walter Price.

Mrs. Jessie Clark, an active member of Munger Avenue Baptist Church for many years; Mrs. Essie Craig, a long-time member of Antioch Baptist Church and now a member of Greater El Bethel, and Mrs. Ruth P. Sanders, also active in church and civic affairs, continue to live in Dallas today. Sixteen grandchildren and twenty-four great-grandchildren have been born to the Price family.

Moran and Mattie Bell Johnson Ritchie

Family historians: Charlie Lee Ritchie and Hazel Wallace from Lillie Belle Hall

Before the end of the nineteenth century, young Moran Ritchie journeyed from the vicinity of Paris, Texas, to Dallas to become houseman to the family of Admiral Andrews. The Andrews lived on Marsalis Street in the Oak Cliff section of Dallas.

Moran was one of the three sons born to a Black woman and the young son of her master on the Ritchie plantation near Paris. These half-Black children were accepted as part of the Ritchie clan until the death of the elder statesman and the marriage of the young father. These and other problems caused the Black mother and her three sons to scatter.

The daughter of a Baptist minister who wanted a better opportunity for his daughter, the young Mattie Bell Johnson had come from Tennessee to Dallas and become the cook for the Admiral Andrews family. She and Moran Ritchie were married in the late 1800s, and on July 31, 1902, they became the proud parents of an only son, Charlie Lee Ritchie.

Charlie Lee Ritchie was born in a small frame house on Betterton Circle in the Oak Cliff area of Dallas. He remembers Mrs. Andrews, the Admiral's wife, as a beautiful grandmother-type woman with a staunch guiding interest in his upbringing. As a very small boy, he would go to work with his parents. He played and was tutored with the Andrews children until time for his afternoon nap. In the late afternoon he was given his bath, dressed in a white suit, and sent to the foot of the staircase as Mrs. Andrews descended. She would put her hand on his head and announce mealtime for the family or for guests at social functions.

By the time Charlie was school age, the family had purchased a small four-room house on Avenue A. It was located on a large lot with a big barn where they raised pigs and cows. There was also a nice garden plot. Charlie Lee attended N. W. Harllee Elementary School, and [he] recalls that he was a "pretty good scholar." He drove a one-horse wagon after school to pick up and deliver laundry for his mother, who took in washing for several families. She was said to have "a way" with white sheets.

He collected food waste from the Adolphus Hotel for their livestock and waited for his dad to get off from work, so they could go home to the delicious meal his mother would have waiting for them. He remembers a favorite stop on Commerce Street in downtown Dallas, where there was a large round water trough to rest and water the horse on the journey between Oak Cliff and Oak Lawn.

As a young man, the Ritchie offspring lived in Terrell, Paris, and Graham before returning to Dallas in 1923 following the death of his father. He worked with sporting goods firms, including the Spalding Company, A. J. Reach, Wright and Detson, and Cullum and Boren. He was married three times before he met and married Fannie Duke Martin in 1934.

Fannie Martin had lived in Dallas since 1922. She was the first of seven children born to Charles Henry and Annie Duke in 1902. She met, married, and divorced O. F. Martin of Naples, Texas. She worked in private homes in Dallas to help take care of her five brothers and little sister, who was one year and ten months old when their mother died. Fannie had her own daughter, Hazel Loyce, who was about eight years old when she met Charlie Lee Ritchie.

The new extended family lived at 1410 Compton Street, in the Trinity Heights section of Dallas, until 1937–38, when they moved to North Dallas and lived across from Booker T. Washington High School. The family moved to Irving in Dallas County in 1939.

Meanwhile, the Ritchies had gone into the grocery business in Irving. Charlie Lee worked in law enforcement and became intensely interested in politics. He led the strike to promote better school facilities for Black children in the Bear Creek section of rural Irving. This resulted in the one-room schoolhouse at Shady Grove becoming the J. O. Davis Elementary School.

He became a 33rd-degree Mason in 1946. He worked with the Dallas Democratic Party and went as a delegate to the Truman Inauguration in 1949. Also, he was invited and attended the funeral of President Harry S. Truman.

After the family moved to Fort Worth in 1959, he worked with the Tarrant County Commissioners Court and has certificates and plaques of recognition from the Child Welfare Board in 1972 and the Citizens Study Commission on Services for Children and Youth, and he [was a member of the] board of directors of Planning and Research Council Division of United Way of Metropolitan Tarrant County.

Mr. Ritchie is an elder of the Presbyterian Church and ran for State Senator from Fort Worth in 1974. When he accepted the nomination to run for State Senator in May, he had [already] planned to spend the summer in Mexico and worked [on his campaign] only after his return to Tarrant County, in mid-September. He received 38,000 votes, and his opponent won with 51,000.

Hazel Loyce Martin was born in Mt. Pleasant, Texas, in April 1922. Though reared by her mother, Fannie Duke Martin Ritchie, and stepfather, Charlie Lee Ritchie, Hazel Loyce Martin's father, Dallas photographer O. T. Martin, showed intense interest in her growth and development and assisted with her schooling during the early years.

She attended N. W. Harllee and B. F. Darrell Elementary schools and was graduated from Booker T. Washington High School in 1939. During the high school years, Hazel was active in the renowned pep squad with Ms. Viola King; the Choral Club with Mr. A. S. Jackson; Science Club with Mr. Dave and Mr. A. W. Brashear; Quill Club with Mr. J. Mason Brewer; and the Journalism Club with Mr. C. F. Wilkerson. Prior to graduation, she completed courses in shorthand, typing, and bookkeeping at Philips Business College; and later she acquired hours in cosmetology from Madame C. J. Walker School of Beauty Culture under Mrs. Hattie Horne Roark.

The family moved to Irving, Dallas County, Texas, in the fall of 1939, and Hazel became involved in 4-H Club activities under the supervision of County Extension Agent Mrs. I. O. W. Hodge.

She participated as secretary in the Extension Office at the Pythian Temple Building in Dallas, with Mrs. Hodge and Mr. C. A. Walton. She went to college on a fifty-dollar 4-H Club scholarship in 1942.

Hazel attended Prairie View State College for one year and was graduated from Lincoln University in Jefferson City, Missouri, with a bachelor of science degree in 1947. In 1948, she received the Master of Arts degree from Teachers College, Columbia University in New York City. Both major degrees are in home economics, with minors in secondary education. She has done advanced study in elementary education, home economics, and communications at North Texas State University and Texas Woman's University in Denton, Texas; the University of California at San Diego; and Texas Christian University in Fort Worth. She has engaged in numerous seminars, conferences, and workshops to advance her professional development at sites throughout the country.

In 1944, Hazel married her freshman English teacher, Mr. George W. Morton. To this union, one daughter was born in 1949, A'nelle Ritchie Morton. A'nelle completed college work at the University of Texas at Arlington and North Texas State University at Denton, with a major in clinical psychology. A'nelle works as assistant executive director for the Tejas Girl Scout Council in Dallas. A'nelle married Walter Nelms in April 1983 and gave birth to one son, Ritchie Austyn Tyler Nelms, who died in May 1989.

Hazel Loyce Morton married Clyde Wallace of Jefferson, Texas, in 1955. They are the parents of daughter Wil'Livvie Clyde Wallace, who was born in Dallas in 1959. She was an active participant in Our Little Miss Ideal Pageant, from which she won her first crown at age six. She became a Word Talent Winner and winner of the International Essay contest for Ideal Miss in 1977. Aspiring to become a concert pianist, she studied at Trinity College, London, England, where she received the Licentiate Degree and was graduated from Trinity University in San Antonio, Texas, in 1984. A serious illness in 1985, which incapacitated her for a piano career, led her to sing with the Fort Worth Opera. She is employed with the US Department of Housing and Urban Development, and she married John Calvin Strickland in August 1987.

Hazel Loyce's professional background includes work as secretary, food demonstrator, consumer affairs officer, teacher of high school and college home economics; and teacher of nursery and elementary schools. These positions were held in Texas, Louisiana, and Arkansas (1945–1947); Texas Southern University in Houston (1949–1951); Bishop College, Marshall, Texas (1951–1954); Mississippi Vocational College, Itta Bena (1954–1956); Home Management Supervisor and Teacher Trainee in Texas College, Tyler (1956–1959); and teacher of beginners and first graders with the US Department of Interior/Bureau of Indian Affairs with Navajo schools in Arizona and New Mexico (1968–1988).

Her total professional career spanned thirty-four years, including seventeen years as teacher and twenty-seven years as an employee of the federal government. The last twenty-two years were spent as Consumer Affairs Officer with the Dallas District Office of the Food and Drug Administration.

Mrs. Wallace retired from government service in September 1988 and is currently involved with "Unique Collectibles," a six-year-established business venture with tropical and marine life, exotic plants, Indian jewelry, and other collectibles, to which she has recently added imported Chilean wines.

Through the years, Hazel Loyce Wallace has remained actively involved in numerous professional, civic, social, and religious organizations. She holds membership in the American and Texas Home Economics Associations and the Texas State Nutrition Council, from which she received a plaque in February 1989 for outstanding contributions to food and nutrition. She has served on the Mayor's Committee on the Status of Women in Fort Worth and is an executive board member of the Safety Council of Fort Worth and Tarrant County. She serves on the Home Economics Advisory board of Tarleton State University in Stephenville, Texas, and is a ruling elder of the Presbyterian church. She recently completed her training to become a Stephan Minister, a lay ministry of caring which reaches out to persons in times of crisis, stress, illness, or loss.

Hazel Martin Wallace is listed in the 1971 edition of Personalities of the South and in the Volume I, 1972 edition of Who's Who of American Women, published in 1977. She received a cash award in 1978 in recognition of a field model design adopted throughout the country for ad hoc professional meetings for the commissioner of the Food and Drug Administration. She was awarded quality salary increases in 1981 and 1985, and [she] received a certificate commemorating twenty years of government service. In 1986 she received a Commendable Service Award for exemplary services to the Public Health Services, Federal Drug Administration.

The widowed mother of two adult daughters, Mrs. Wallace lives in Fort Worth next door to [her stepfather], the eighty-seven-year-old Charlie Lee Ritchie. [Her mother], Mrs. Fannie Duke Martin Ritchie, died in 1986 and is buried in Lincoln Memorial Park in Dallas.

D. Rowen Family

Family historians: Dr. Robert L. Prince Jr.
and Morita Rowen Prince

D. (Doc) Rowen was born in the year 1860 in Jerusalem. He came to America as a young man and worked as a kitchen helper on a ship. The ship that brought him here debarked in South Carolina. He migrated to Alabama and made his home there for several years.[39]

---

39. After *First African American Families of Dallas* (Volume 1) was published in 1987, further research conducted by Remembering Black Dallas members revealed that Doc Rowen's life story was not as he had long portrayed it. In unpublished material, he was said to have been born into slavery in 1854, in Newbern, Hale County, Alabama. He remained in Newbern, Alabama, throughout his childhood. He grew up working with others in the cotton fields, and following Emancipation, he remained in Alabama until migrating to Dallas in 1880. He later explained that he had made up the Jerusalem story to divert attention away from his humble beginnings as a slave.—Eds.

Doc Rowen was born into slavery in 1854 in Alabama. He migrated to Dallas in 1880, and he lived until October 14, 1932. *Remembering Black Dallas, Inc.*

He came to Dallas, Texas, and was joined in holy matrimony to Nannie Terry in October 1880. To this union were born eight children: Leoma Rowen, born August 15, 1881; Fred Rowen, July 4, 1882; Roy Rowen, July 22, 1885; Oscar Rowen, November 25, 1886; Mozella Rowen, March 26, 1889; Angel Rowen, September 14, 1893; Jerome Rowen, February 15, 1895; and Dee Rowen in 1901.

Doc Rowen was known as a capitalist and was a very prominent merchant, real estate owner, and promoter of business enterprises in Dallas. His oldest daughter, Leoma, was also business oriented. She established a millinery shop featuring handmade designer hats, which was located at 2616 Juliette Street (now known as Munger Avenue). It was quite a lucrative business.

During Doc Rowen's life, he displayed his ability by owning and operating a dry goods store, which was located on Elm Street between what is now Central Expressway and Good Street in the downtown area. He built a two-story brick building at 2618 Juliette in 1910 and out of it operated a first-class grocery known as Rowen's Grocery, with daily delivery service. This store served the Black sector of North Dallas.

Doc Rowen made many contributions to Dallas as a citizen. He was one of the first stockholders in the State Fair of Texas. On April 12, 1879, he was made a trustee for one of the first graveyards for Blacks, Freedman's Cemetery, which was located on Hall Street (near Central Expressway) and West Street. This was recorded in City records in Volume 566, page 475. Doc retired from the grocery store "No. 3" in 1928 after amassing a small fortune in rental property in many sections of Dallas. A street was named after him in Dallas. Also, he was the first Black man to own an automobile—a 1915 Cole 8.

Doc Rowen died October 14, 1932. His living descendants are grandchildren and great-grandchildren. Among those descendants are Morita Williams Prince, daughter of Leoma Rowen Williams, and her children; Dr. Robert L. Prince, a gynecologist/obstetrician in Dallas; and Dr. Jeanette Elaine Prince Lockley, mathematics teacher at Mountain View College in Dallas. All of these descendants currently live in Dallas.

A. J. and Lena Sherman

Family historian: Callie Spencer,
as interviewed by L. B. Hall

Lena Sherman was born in 1878 in Dallas, Texas. Her husband, A. J. Sherman, was born in Hope, Arkansas. To this union two children were born: Callie and William.

Mr. Sherman worked at Trinity Cotton Oil Company in Dallas, and Mrs. Sherman was a housewife. They lived in what was known as Queen City. Their daughter, Callie, attended Wheatley School one year. She completed her elementary work at Starks School and graduated from Booker T. Washington High School in 1926. She then attended Philips Business College and Wiley Extension College.

William attended Queen City School. After finishing Queen City, he attended the Dallas Colored High School.

Callie vividly remembers some of the teachers who had an impact on her life while she was in school. They were: Mrs. Lillian Hardee, Mrs. Fannie Gipson, Mrs. Edna E. Ezell, Mrs. Lela Wilkins, and Mrs. Priscilla Tyler. Her Latin teacher for four years was Ms. Julia C. Frazier.

Allen C. and Beulah Smart Family

Family historian: Doris Baker Jones

Allen Smart came to Dallas in the early 1890s from Oxford, Alabama. He was accompanied by his brother, John Smart. They both found jobs as farmhands at the Brownlee farm, which was

Beulah Cunningham Smart married her childhood sweetheart,
Allen Smart, and they had five children, three of whom survived to
adulthood. *Black Dallas Remembered, Inc.*

on Beckley just south of what is now Kiest. They worked hard, saved their money, and returned to Oxford, Alabama, to marry their childhood sweethearts.

Allen and John married cousins Beulah and Linnie Cunningham, respectively, and brought them back to Dallas. They bought some land in the 1300 block of East Tenth Street and built two homes there. They continued to work as farmhands for the Brownlees as well as the Freeman families.

Around the turn of the century, Allen and Beulah Smart, both Methodists, donated land for the establishment of Elizabeth Chapel Colored Methodist Episcopal Church. This church was first located at 1300 East Tenth Street. John Smart was ordained there as a minister, and he and his family moved to Mount Pleasant, Texas, where he was assigned pastor.

Elizabeth Chapel Colored Methodist Episcopal Church.
Preservation Dallas.

Allen and Beulah had five children: Alvin, Robert, Maggie, Norman, and Clarence. The first two were born on East Tenth Street. Around 1902, Allen leased part of the Brownlee farm, which is now A. Maceo Smith High School, and started farming for himself. His last three children were born at this spot. Allen and Beulah worked hard, saved their money, and purchased thirteen acres of land at Five Miles, where Ripple Street is now located. They continued to lease the Brownlee farm and were the only Black family "out on Beckley."

Sometime in the early 1920s, Allen Smart tried to buy the Brownlee farm. In fact, he signed a contract to buy this land. This did not work out. Some unknown group of Whites objected to the purchase, and the deal was called off. He was eventually compensated for the broken contract and used this money to attend Texas College. He banked at the Mercantile Bank and became good friends with the banker who assisted him in getting compensated for the broken contract on the farm.

Allen's two oldest sons died, but the youngest two, Norman and Clarence, stayed with him and assisted with the farm chores. Meanwhile, Maggie Smart graduated from Booker T. Washington High and Texas College, with an AB degree in English. While in college, she met Chilton Baker, and they were married in 1925.

Allen Smart died in 1932. His wife, Beulah, continued to lease the Brownlee farm until 1934, and then she moved to 1302 East Tenth Street.

Chilton and Maggie Baker started buying a newly built house located at 2407 Dathe Street in Queen City but gave this up during the Depression. Maggie got a job teaching in Oklahoma, since she could not teach in Dallas. Married women were not allowed to teach in Dallas during this period. Chilton and their only child, Doris (born March 19, 1927), moved in with Beulah, [his mother-in-law], on East Tenth Street. Chilton was employed as a Pullman porter, a very prestigious job at the time.

Maggie, Chilton Baker, and Doris moved to 1206 East Tenth Street in another house owned by her mother, Beulah, in 1938. Their daughter, Doris, attended N. W. Harllee and Lincoln High School. She finished Lincoln High in 1943 and went to Prairie View College. She graduated from Prairie View in 1947, married a week later, and moved to Marshall, Texas.

Maggie and Chilton Baker continued to stay at 1206 East Tenth. Norman Smart and his wife, Erma Smart, stayed at 1300 East Tenth. Beulah Smart died in 1956. Maggie Baker died in 1975, and Chilton Baker died in 1977. Norman and Clarence Smart are also dead, and they had no children.

Doris Baker Jones, the granddaughter of Beulah and Allen Smart and the daughter of Maggie and Chilton Smart, is a member of Elizabeth Chapel CME Church and is presently living at 3435 Navajo Court. She is employed at Texas Employment Commission. She is active in the Washington Lincoln Alumni Association. She received a master's degree in counseling from Louisiana Tech, Ruston, Louisiana. She is proud to be a Dallasite with such a rich heritage.

Additional facts about the family include: Allen Smart was a farmer and member of the Masonic Lodge—a 32nd-degree Mason. He was also a founder and donor of land for Elizabeth Chapel Church and a friend of the late R. L. Thornton Sr., a prominent Dallas resident. Beulah Smart was a member of the Eastern Star Lodge, and she was known as "Othermania" to her granddaughter, Doris, and other children in the neighborhood of Tenth Street. Maggie Smart Baker taught in Crandall, Texas, and in Oklahoma and was dean of women for two years at Leland College in Louisiana. Chilton Baker was a bass singer with many choirs in Dallas, and he also sang in the Dallas Summer Musical, *Showboat*, in 1963. He was a Pullman porter and a US Postal worker in Dallas, and he was principal of the Klondike, Texas, Black School in the 1920s.

Paul and Sallie Smith

Family historian: Vallie Jo Smith Estell

Paul and Sallie Smith came to Dallas before the turn of the [twentieth] century. They were prominent pioneers and real assets to their community. They bought the land and built their home in the Booker T. Washington Addition—a neighborhood of Negro homeowners. Some of the families rented their houses from the Anglos in [what later became] Highland Park, but they lived independently in the Booker T. Community.

Paul and Sallie Smith owned the first and only grocery store in that community. It provided food and staples, some they sold and some they gave to the needy families in the community.

Paul was well known in the Highland Park Community. As he drove through the community in his horse-drawn wagon, Anglos would give him clothes for his children and money for his moving services. Thus, his children Joe, Audrie, and Clarence seldom wanted for anything.

Paul Smith, a 33rd-degree Mason, was highly respected by his brothers. Mr. Dave Garner and others said, "Paul Smith was a loyal brother who would recite the ritual from memory when opening their meetings and knew everything to be known about their order. He was a smart and respected man."

Paul and Sallie Smith were members of Trinity Methodist Church, where he was a trustee. Mrs. Smith was a soloist in the choir, an ardent worker, and a teacher in the Sunday School and participated in many other facets of the church life.

Their son, Joe Ambrous Smith, a fifty-year employee of the Dallas Times Herald Newspaper Company, was loved and highly respected by the president and employees of the company. He earned the position of supervisor of the employees, a position not given to many Negro employees at that time. Joe A. Smith married Sereptha Mitchell, the daughter of William Wallace and Melvina Mitchell.

Mr. William Wallace Mitchell, a teacher in Nacogdoches, Texas, married Mrs. Melvina Thorn Mitchell. To this union were born Diuette, Mortimer, Audrey, Terie, Theodore, Sereptha, and Lloyd Mitchell.

Melvina Thorn Mitchell was the daughter of freed slaves Delia and William Thorn. William Wallace Mitchell was known as Professor Mitchell in Nacogdoches and was admired and respected by the students and adults in and around that city.

Mr. Mitchell passed away, and Mrs. Melvina later married Mr. Battle. They moved to Dallas in the 1900s, bringing with them the Mitchell and Battle children: Knox, Ida Mae, B. K., and others.

Theodore, a soloist in the New Hope Baptist Church Choir, was also a 33rd-degree Mason and a famous actor. He performed in many plays at Theatre Three of Dallas and made several movies in Hollywood, California. He played the role of Pearlie in *Pearlie Victorious*.

He married Mrs. Enola Flowers Mitchell, a teacher at the Wheatley School for many years. She was also a choir member, Sunday School teacher, and ardent worker in the New Hope Baptist Church. She was an avid reader and was often invited to do book reviews in the church and community. She was also a very active member and two-term Basileus of Zeta Phi Beta Sorority. They were parents of one daughter, Geraldine.

The Smiths and Mitchells were prominent citizens of Dallas. Joe was a long-time employee of the Dallas Times Herald. Lloyd was a long-time employee and mail handler at Union Station Post Office in Dallas.

To the union of Sereptha and Joe Smith were born Vallie Jo, Theodore, and Paul Wallace. To the union of Lloyd Everett Mitchell and Ida Mae Mitchell were born Valentine, Meredith, Lorraine, Delores, and Mamye Lois Mitchell. Lorraine is a teacher in the Dallas school system. Lorraine and Leroy Jones are parents of twin daughters.

Vallie Jo is married to Roscoe Estell Sr. Their daughter, Charlotte, and her husband, Dwain Murry Govan, are teachers in the Dallas Independent School District. Charlotte and Dwain are the proud parents of Charlento Joy, Charissa Marie, and Dwain Murry Govan Jr. Roscoe C. Estell Jr. is in the electronics field and is employed at the Dallas–Fort Worth Airport.

Vallie Jo and Charlotte Jo are active members of St. John Missionary Baptist Church. They are musicians, choir members, and leaders of children's fellowship. They are also members of Delta Sigma Theta Sorority, Inc.

These children, grandchildren, and great-grandchildren gained a rich heritage from their parents, grandparents, and great-grandparents: Joe Ambrous and Sereptha Winona Smith.

Charles M. and Lula E. Moore Swann Family

Family historian: Muriel Swann Smith

Charles M. Swann was born in Weatherford, Texas, circa 1870s. In 1890 he married Lula E. Moore, daughter of the late Henry Moore, for whom Moore Street in Oak Cliff was named.

The Swanns moved to Grand Prairie, Texas, where Charles M. Swann built their first home and reared all six Swann children.

In later years, the Swann family moved to Dallas, Texas, and settled in the Oak Cliff area. It is there that Charles M. Swann, with the help of his sons, built the family dwelling located at 1120 East Ninth Street in Oak Cliff. The house still stands in its original location. Mr. Charles M. Swann also built rental property on Ninth, Noah, and Dale Streets.

One of the sons, Crystal Swann, was a tailor by trade. He owned and operated his tailor shop on Tenth Street in Oak Cliff. He is the father of one of the surviving members of the family, Muriel Swann Smith.

Lula and Charles Swann celebrated their fiftieth wedding anniversary on the wedding day of one of their nieces. *Black Dallas Remembered, Inc.*

Still surviving of the Swann Moore family are: Ella Maye Swann, wife of the late Allen L. Swann and a retired Dallas Teacher; Mrs. Sarah Moore, wife of the late Arthur D. Moore, brother of Lula Moore Swann; and the only surviving granddaughter, Muriel Swann Smith.

Taylor Anderson and Mary Jane Coit Tarpley Family

Family historian: Eunice H. Gray Dotson

One hundred and twenty-two years ago, a young Black man was born in Wylie, Texas. His name was Taylor Anderson Tarpley (August 1, 1865–October 21, 1938).

The Tarpley family is shown in 1914, with Taylor and Mary Jane seated in the middle. Standing, from left, are: Mamie, her son Joe Tennyson, Laura, James Franklin, Willie Mae, Zollie Scott, Flemmie, and Pearl. Seated, from left, are: John; Vassie; Taylor; Mary Jane, holding one-month-old Edgar Taylor; Hallie Lillian; and DeArville. *Courtesy of George Keaton, Jr.*

He and his mother, Anne Turner, moved to Northwest Dallas County and settled in [what is now] Addison, Texas. His mother purchased a large farm on Dooley Road, now Midway and Keller Springs Road. Taylor met, courted, and fell in love with Mary Jane Coit.

Mary Jane's mother was Harriet Coit. She was reared by the slave owners of her parents, the Captain Henry Coit family. Mary Jane's mother, Harriet, owned a tract of land on the corner of Alpha and Preston Roads.

Taylor and Mary Jane were married January 7, 1886. They lived with his mother to work her extensive cotton farm. They were very prosperous cotton farmers. By 1918, they had fifteen children:

Sammie Tarpley, died at two months; James Franklin Tarpley (now one hundred years of age); Mamie (Mrs. Roy Simpson), deceased 1945; Laura (Mrs. Wallace Patterson), deceased 1986; Willie Mae (Mrs. Albert Sowell); Zollie Scott Tarpley (deceased 1965); Jessie Tarpley (died in infancy); John Allie Tarpley; Pearl (Mrs. Samuell Powell); Flemmie (Mrs. James Ripley Gray), deceased 1982; DeArville (Mrs. Jack W. Kelley), deceased 1983; Hattie Lillian (Mrs. Alfred Love); Vassie (Mrs. Clarence Henry); a baby who was stillborn (no name available); Edgar Taylor Tarpley, deceased 1981.

Ambitious and anxious to rear his children in his home and on land he could call his own, the young, enterprising father bought a one hundred and six–acre farm of sloping terrain. It had a branch [of a creek] starting at [what is now] Keller Springs Road and extending the length of the farm. A trickling stream of water ran through the branch from a spring on the southwest corner of Keller Springs Road. Each side of the branch was lined with large hackberry, persimmon, and bois d'arc trees. These trees were interspersed throughout the farm.

Taylor and Mary Jane were hardworking people and proud of their family. They instilled in their children early in life the values of responsibility, ambition, and family pride. The family had plenty of chores to do, such as feeding the animals, tending the fruit trees, and preparing the meals. As chores were meted out rotationally, each child knew what his job was. Thus, they learned the value of responsibility and cooperation. This was quite evident when the Tarpley family was recognized as one of the largest cotton farmers in the area.

The parents insisted on their children getting an education. Most of them began their early training in a one-room schoolhouse (grades one through seven), located at Keller Springs Road and Noell Road [now called Montfort Road]. Because schools were not integrated, the Tarpley children traveled to Dallas to do their high school work. They attended Oak Lawn Elementary and Junior High, Darrell High School, and Booker T. Washington High

School. Some of the children boarded in private homes or lived with relatives because daily transportation from Addison to Dallas was impossible.

If any of the children indicated they wanted to go to college, their father provided them the opportunity to go to Wiley College in Marshall, Texas. John Allie received his bachelor of science degree from Wiley College and obtained a master's and PhD at Ohio State University. He taught at Bennett College, Greensboro, North Carolina, and later he became supervisor of Colored Schools there. He continued in the same position when the schools became integrated. Widely known as an educational leader, he traveled in his professional work all over the United States, Canada, and fourteen foreign countries. His wife, Lucille Sanford Tarpley, attended Wiley also and taught at Bennett College. Both are now retired and reside in Greensboro. A stadium for sports activities was named and dedicated in his honor by Dudley High School, Greensboro, NC, in December 1981.

Pearl Tarpley Powell received a four-year certificate in English at Wiley College and taught in Mansfield, Louisiana.

Edgar Taylor Tarpley received his bachelor's and master's degrees from the Agricultural and Technical College of North Carolina in Greensboro. His wife, Frances Marks Tarpley, graduated from Bennett College. They both taught school in Charlotte, North Carolina. Both are now deceased.

James Franklin Tarpley, a veteran of World War I, became a skilled carpenter. His fine work was sought by anyone building a new home in the Addison and Carrollton, Texas, area. His wife, Ada Fontno Curtis Tarpley, passed in 1966. James Franklin lives with his daughter and son-in-law, Addie and Jimmy Leonard, in Fort Worth, Texas. He was born December 25, 1887.

Zollie, a veteran of World War I, was a skilled pottery craftsman and retired from a pottery company on Maple Avenue in Dallas, Texas. His wives were Stella Whitehead, Lola Williams, and Ethel Anderson.

Having learned the basics of sewing and designing from their mother and Mamie, Vassie Henry, DeArville Kelley, Pearl Powell, and Flemmie Gray worked for Nardis of Dallas for many years. Vassie also attended Prairie View Extension College.

Willie Mae Sowell was a licensed beautician and dress designer. For many years she conducted classes in home canning for the District Home Demonstration Club. Hattie Lillian worked for the Vance K. Miller family, owner of Vance K. Miller Office Supply in Dallas. Laura Ann Patterson, who attended school in Oklahoma, also worked for the Vance K. Millers until retirement.

The home life Taylor and Mary Jane provided for their children was filled with love, humor, fun, and religious training. Since Taylor was one of the original organizers of the White Rock Christian Methodist Episcopal Church, the entire family attended services there on Sundays. Most family members are still affiliated with the CME church.

For entertainment, there were frequent church picnics. At least once a year, Taylor would give a big free barbeque, inviting the entire community. He would kill a hog or calf and barbeque it. It was like a big family "Potluck Reunion" when the community gathered on the Tarpley farm to share food and tid-bits of gossip. The children would play ball games.

The love, trust, respect, and sharing the parents imparted contributed to a very close-knit family. The early training that the family must "Stick Together" resulted in a legacy and heritage that members of succeeding generations are still carrying on.

The tradition of education, training, and accomplishment continue into the third, fourth, and fifth generations of Taylor Anderson and Mary Jane Tarpley.

The following are offspring of the second generation:

- Mamie Tarpley Simpson: Joe Tenneyson Simpson; R. C. Simpson; Raymond Simpson; and Christa Bell Simpson Sims
- Zollie Scott Tarpley: James Tarpley and Joan Ruth Tarpley Winn

- DeArville Tarpley Kelley: Marie S. Kelley Ross
- Flemmie O. Tarpley Gray: Loda Bell Gray Simmons; Lodine Gray Gooden; James R. Gray (Rollerson) Watson; Gilbert Taylor Gray; Eunice H. Gray (Simmons) Dotson; and Opal Gray Conner
- Laura Ann Tarpley Patterson: Eunice Patterson and Allie Mae Patterson Pipkins
- Willie Mae Tarpley (Wiggington) Sowell: Flavious Wiggington and Albert T. Sowell Jr.
- Hattie L. Tarpley (Miller) Love: Leroy Miller Jr.
- James Franklin Tarpley: Addie Allen Leonard

The following are offspring of the third generation:

- Raymond Simpson: Donna Simpson; Denise Simpson; Raymond Simpson, Jr.; and Laura Ann Simpson
- R. C. Simpson: Sharon Ann Simpson
- Christa Bell Simpson Sims: Carolyn Sims Anderson and Cynthia Sims
- Flavious Wiggington: Irby Don Wiggington
- Gilbert Taylor Gray: Gilbert T. Gray Jr.; Brenda Gray Wedgeworth; Denise Gray Dorsey; Renay Gray Felder; and Jill Gray Aimes
- Opal L. Gray Conner: Lawrence Conner Jr.; Harold L. Conner; and Phillip L. Conner
- James Tarpley: James Keith Tarpley and Debbie Tarpley Lafitty
- Loda Bell Gray Robinson Simmons: Mary Jo Robinson Deal
- Lodine Gray Gooden: Lorraine Gooden Grover and Oliver Gooden, Jr.
- Eunice Gray (Simmons) Dotson: Cheryl A. (Simmons) Dotson Floyd; Patrice Dotson (Channel) Carter; and Traci L. Dotson
- Joan R. Tarpley (Winn): Ikoyi Winn
- James R. Gray (Rollerson) Watson: Jessie Rollerson; Revoydia Rollerson; Richard Rollerson; andVicki Lyn Rollerson
- Leroy Miller Jr.: Ronnie Miller and Frieda Miller

Taylor Anderson Tarpley and Mary Jane Coit Tarpley were married for fifty-one years before death took Mary Jane away in September 1937. Taylor lived only thirteen months after her death, and he passed away in October 1938. Along with many of the other deceased members of the family, they were laid to rest at White Rock Cemetery Garden of Memories, [accessible at that time] on Celestial Road. The majority of this large family has remained in the Dallas area. A few are in North Carolina and California.

Finis Sr. and Legurtha McCain Tatum Family

Family historian: Dorothy Tatum Prestwood

Finis Tatum Sr. was born in Lancaster, Texas, in 1885, to the parentage of D. W. Tatum and Eliza Brown Tatum. Finis's two brothers were Autry and Eugene Tatum.

In 1924, Finis met and married Legurtha McCain of Avinger, Marion County, Texas. The couple was wed in the Dallas home of Legurtha's first cousin and her spouse, Mr. and Mrs. Samuel Hudson Sr., who lived in the Booker T. Washington Addition. Finis and Legurtha left Dallas immediately for Oklahoma City to live with Legurtha's brother and his wife, Arthur and Louella McCain. After a short stay in Oklahoma, the Tatums returned to Dallas and purchased a home in the Oak Cliff (Trinity Heights) area on Childs Street, later renamed Crete Street. Three children were born to this marriage: Finis Jr., Dorothy Lee, and Bobbie Jean, in this sequence. All three children still reside in Dallas.

In 1927, the Finis Tatums united with the Elizabeth Chapel CME Church on Tenth Street in the Oak Cliff area. The present site of the church is 3419 Michigan Street, near South Oak Cliff High School.

Finis Jr. and his wife, Ella Ruth White Tatum, became parents of two children: Finis (Indianapolis, Indiana), and Michael, a member of the Armed Forces who is now deceased.

Dorothy Lee Tatum Prestwood is the mother of three sons— Dwight Body, Keith, and Kirk Prestwood—and three grandchildren— Dadrian, Jacklyn, and Jessica. Kirk is married to Brenda Parker.

Bobbie Jean Anglin is the mother of two children: Steven Smith and Karen Camille Ingram. Camille is married to Darrell Ingram and has a two-year-old daughter, Candiz.

Yorktown Thomas Family

By Eva Partee-McMillan

In 1883, at the age of two years, Merriell Vain Thomas arrived in Dallas with her family from Bedford, Tennessee. She was the youngest member of the family. The family lived on Flora Street at the present site of Booker T. Washington Arts Magnet.

Merriell was a graduate of Paul Quinn College, and in 1910 she married Walter Ree McMillan, a 1909 graduate of Meharry Medical School in obstetrics. Dr. McMillan built a hospital, the McMillan Sanitarium, in 1921, on the corner of Hall and State Streets. Together they became two of the most prominent and respected members of the community. Merriell Thomas McMillan worked with her husband for a while, managing the drug store located adjacent to the McMillan Sanitarium at Hall and State Streets. The couple had two sons, Walter Cartwright McMillan and Marion Ernest McMillan.

Mrs. McMillan was one of the founders of the Business and Professional Women's Club of Dallas and the Women's Auxiliary of the Medical Society. She joined Bethel AME Church on Leonard Street in 1899. She was a class leader for twenty-seven years and a member of the Senior Choir and the Missionary Society Board. She was also a member of the Moorland Branch YMCA.

Her father, Yorktown Thomas, a Tennessean, was proud to have served in the Civil War and to have had the privilege of viewing President Lincoln's body as it lay in state in Washington, DC, in 1865.

Mrs. McMillan's sisters were: Annie Thomas Ricks of Omaha, Nebraska; Beulah Thomas Harewood, a seamstress and wife of Reverend Harewood of Barbados; and Ella Thomas Patton, mother of Dallas educator Dr. J. Leslie Patton. Her brothers were: Tom Thomas, a journeyman; Herbert (Hub) Thomas, co-owner of The Pride of Dallas Taxicab Company with Charlie Weems; and Walter Thomas, who delivered ice and wood.

Mrs. McMillan died at the age of eighty-six, on September 30, 1967.

The McMillan's son Walter Cartwright McMillan, a retiree from the Dallas Independent School District, married Kathleen Durham, a retired educator. His children are Ammon Frances McMillan Parks, an educator in Syracuse, New York, and wife of an Army officer, Donald Parks; and Michael McMillan, a teacher in Fort Worth.

Marion Ernest McMillan, a minister, married Eva Partee. Their children are Karen Wesson, M. Ernie McMillan, Jacqueline Hill, and Katherine Wilson.

John J. and Lurena Alzira Tyiska Thompson

Family historians: Lillian Evelyn Thompson; James J. Tyiska Thompson, M.D.; Finis Thompson Fonsworth Stewart; and Shirley Thompson Loving

Josh and Celia Tyiska were born in Oklahoma City, Oklahoma, and were brought to Henderson, Texas, as slaves by the Smith family, their owners. They were members of the Cherokee tribe, and Celia's mother was of Dutch descent. After gaining freedom from slavery, the couple, along with Josh's six brothers, reclaimed their family name of Tyiska, which came from their Cherokee Indian heritage.

The children of Mr. and Mrs. Tyiska were: Sudie Tyiska Reddic; Lurena Tyiska Thompson (1866–1956); Annie Tyiska Jackson (1880–1928); Hannah Tyiska Thomas; Diana Tyiska Thomas; Cora Tyiska; Jeff Tyiska; and John Tyiska.

Square and Lucy Ann Thompson were born in Henderson and farmed one hundred acres of land. All of their children were born on the farm, which remains in the hands of the heirs today.

Their children were: Mary Thompson Tyiska, Nelson Thompson, Lugan Thompson, Erwin Thompson, Cleveland Thompson, John J. Thompson (d. 1933), Johnson Thompson, and Jesse Thompson.

Lurena Alzira Tyiska married John J. Thompson after slavery, and they became parents of thirteen children. Ten were born in Henderson. Linnie, the first child, died at birth, and another son, Bennie, lived only two weeks. The surviving children were Arthur E. Thompson, Lillian Evelyn Thompson, Lewis Ross Thompson, Earl Edward Thompson, Lucy Ann Thompson Glasper, Cora Thompson Pyrin, John J. Thompson, Joseph Thompson, Celia Mae Thompson, Johnson Thompson, and Finis Thompson Fonsworth Stewart.

Before coming to Dallas in 1911, the family moved to Marlin and then to Fort Worth for two years. In North Dallas, they lived on Fairmount Street and Thompson Street. They later lived on Burford Street (now Routh Street) next door to St. Paul Methodist Church and across from No. 2 School. Booker T. Washington [later] was built on this site.

This pioneer Dallas family joined the Evening Chapel CME Church the year they arrived in Dallas, 1911. The church was later renamed Boll Street CME and is presently named Cedar Crest CME Cathedral.

The four younger children, James, Lillian, Earl, and Finis, attended Primary Department, No. 2 School and B. F. Darrell School. In 1919, the family moved to Oak Cliff, where the children attended Ninth Ward School—now N. W. Harllee School.

Arthur E. went to Meharry Medical College for four years, completing his medical degree in 1915. He returned to the family home in North Dallas on Thompson Street. He opened his Thompson's Maternity Clinic in Oak Cliff in 1916. He used the one-seated surrey to drive to his office every day.

Arthur married Evelyn E. Stewart of McKinney, Texas, and two children were born to the couple. Arthur left Dallas and opened his practice in Bryan, Texas, where he was associated with Doctors Flint, Carter, and Hammond. He drove the one-seated surrey to Bryan, Texas. He was the high school football coach at the Bryan High School in Bryan, Texas. He also coached football at Prairie View College. He died in 1936 at Prairie View Hospital after a brief illness.

Lucy Ann married Arthur Glasper and owned a dress shop on Cochran Street for several years. Her two children died in infancy, and Lucy died in 1972.

Cora Thompson Pybrin owned a cafe on Hall Street, and her husband was employed at the cotton gin company. Cora died in 1917.

Johnson Thompson was employed at the Adolphus Hotel for many years and acted as official family chauffeur of their two-seated surrey. He moved to Kansas City, Kansas, where he died in 1925.

Celia Mae Thompson attended Dallas Colored High School at Hall and Cochran Streets and earned a bachelor's degree at Wiley College in Marshall, Texas, in 1923. She taught in Denton and Dallas school districts and owned a beauty shop on Eleventh Street in Oak Cliff. She specialized in marcel waving. [Marcelling was a popular hair style for both Blacks and Whites during the 1920s, similar to finger waves, but done by a different method.] Celia Mae died in 1940.

Lewis Ross Thompson (1890–1972) completed his education in Henderson, Texas, Rusk County. For nearly a quarter of a century, he was employed by the Columbian Club, Dallas, as residence manager. He also worked at the Baker Hotel, Adolphus Hotel, Dallas Country Club, and Golden Pheasant Restaurant. He also worked on the railroads between Dallas and California for several years. He was married to Oneida Powell Thompson. Their children were Allene, Lewis Jr., J. C., John, and Shirley.

Edward Earl was born August 20, 1909, and he was a graduate of Booker T. Washington High School. He owned barber shops at Hall Street and Thomas Avenue in North Dallas and on Tenth Street in Oak Cliff. Earl passed the State Board of Barbers. He moved to Los Angeles and later to Detroit, where he continued in his career as a barber. He married Nettie Mae Shelton. They had one daughter, who died at birth. Edward Earl died in 1965.

John J. graduated from Ninth Ward, now N. W. Harllee, and from Booker T. Washington High School. He attended Wiley College one year. He earned a bachelor of science degree from Clark University. He served in the United States Army Medical Division and afterwards received a medical degree at the College of Physicians and Surgeons in Boston. He married Ann Durham of Boston, Massachusetts, who died in 1984. He received a certificate of appreciation for forty years of service to Omega Psi Phi Fraternity, Inc. on December 17, 1977.

Lillian Evelyn Thompson graduated from Ninth Ward School and from Booker T. Washington High School. She earned a Bachelor of Arts Degree at Wiley College in 1929, and she studied further at Colorado State Teachers College and Prairie View A&M University. She was presented as a 1930 debutante in Dallas by the Idlewild and Dunbar Social Clubs during the fall and spring seasons. Lillian began her career in 1930, and she retired from the Dallas schools in 1977. She has been honored by numerous civic, social, and community organizations for outstanding service. Among the awards she received were a Centennial Award celebrating her service of seventy-two years at Cedar Crest CME Cathedral and a Delta Sigma Theta Sorority Award for fifty years of affiliation.

Finis Thompson Fonsworth Stewart was born in Marlin, Texas. She attended Wiley College. In 1930, she married Clifford Fonsworth of Houston, and to that union one son, Clifton Jr., was born. Her husband died in 1944. In 1947, she married Robert E. Stewart of Dallas. They became the parents of a daughter, Lillian Stewart Rogers. Finis has three grandchildren: Earnest Todd, Veronica Lynn, and Carren Elizabeth Rogers. Finis was employed by the *Houston Informer* for twenty-eight years, serving in various capacities of the newspaper. She is a member of the AKA Sorority.

The Thompson-Tyiska family members have made outstanding contributions to all areas they have touched.

Ned and Elizabeth Miller Welch

Family historian: Ruth Welch Edwards, daughter of Dr. John Welch, with Deborah Bedford Fridia

Ned Welch came to Dallas County from Kentucky in the 1800s. Ned and Elizabeth Welch were the parents of thirteen children: Richard, Harrison, Gilbert, Edward, Amos, Ben, Arthur, Isom, Charles, John, Tom, and Mattie.[40]

[The two youngest,] Mattie and Tom remained on the farm throughout their lives. Tom had no children, but Mattie married twice and had a total of ten children, two of whom died as infants. Her first husband [whose name may have been Loving] died in 1910. She then married Gip Jackson.

Her offspring, including the Loving children, were the following: Esther Ruth Loving Williams was a nurse by profession. Orland,

---

40. Only twelve children were named in the original story, however recent research found that a thirteenth child, Emma, lived only until age nine, when she died of measles.—Eds.

who moved his family to Los Angeles, California. Tyree was a charter member of the Regular Fellows Social Club, and his wife, Shirley, and son, Tyree Jr., still live in Dallas. Charles and his family moved to San Francisco, California. Charles was the father of two sons, Charles W. and James. Charles W. Jr. is a chef by profession. James was the father of Karen, Kim, Kip Errand, and Kamela.

Mattie's children by her second husband were the following: Lillie Belle Jackson Francis lives in San Francisco, California. Alene Jackson Walker lived in Chicago. Eunice Jackson Epps was a vital member of her church, Sims Chapel AME in Carrollton. Mary Lee Jackson Mapps was the mother of Lillie Marie McKenzie Glenn and Gwendolyn McKenzie Turner. The two sisters were teachers in the Dallas Independent School District.

Harrison Welch was a realtor and notary public, and he moved his family to Wichita Falls, Texas. He and Maud were the parents of three children: Elaine, Toussaint, and Inez. Inez, the youngest, had one daughter, Annie Mary Knighton Hall. Annie Mary is currently employed in the Seattle Public School System.

Edward Welch and his wife Ella lived at 3002 Flora Street. He was the owner of a furniture store in the early 1900s.

John Welch graduated from Dallas Colored High School in 1902. He attended Howard University, received his medical degree, and returned to Dallas about 1910. He had an office in the early years above the Penny Savings Bank at 2415 Elm Street. Later he had an office at the Pythian Temple. He married a local high school teacher, Miss Pender Eva Rodgers. Dr. and Mrs. Welch were the parents of three children born in Dallas: Elizabeth, Ruth, and John. John died very young. Elizabeth became a nurse. Ruth Welch Edwards is the mother of Brenda Edwards de Luz. Ruth was a teacher in the San Francisco School System for over thirty years and is now retired.

Charles Welch was a plumber. He and his family lived in South Dallas on Akard Street. The family moved to Chicago during World War II.

George and Phyllis Jackson Wells Family

Family historians: Waymon Wells and Odie Lee Wells Sims

George Wells and Phyllis Jackson Wells came to Dallas from Collin County after they were freed from slavery. They settled in Frankford in far North Dallas near the Collin County line.

Years earlier, the couple, along with Phyllis's four brothers, was shipped into Texas directly from Africa and sold down the Trinity River between Carrollton and Farmers Branch. They were purchased by the Wells family, slave owners of Collin County. Foreign slave trade was outlawed in America in 1808. It is evident that slaves were smuggled into this country as "contraband goods," a common practice at the time.

Two of Phyllis's brothers chose to return to Africa after they were freed. The other two, Lias and Mose, came to Dallas County with George and Phyllis in order to be able to own land. Ownership of land was forbidden to Blacks in Collin County.

Once settled in Frankford, they worked hard, saved their earnings, and purchased land. George and Phyllis's land and homestead were located in Upper White Rock between [today's] Midway Road and Inwood Road.

The Wellses and Jacksons were among the families who organized St. Paul African Methodist Episcopal Church, the oldest AME Church in the Dallas District. It was originally located on Forest and Hillcrest Lanes. Presently, it stands on Coit Road next to a more modern building which is used for worship services. The area was called Lower White Rock.

Many other ex-slaves bought land and farmed in far North Dallas. Some of the present locations which they settled were: Marsh Lane, Keller Springs Road, Midway Road, Alpha Road, Montfort Drive,

Spring Valley, McShann Road, Forest Lane, Noel Road, Hillcrest Lane, Abrams Road, Belt Line Road, Valley View Lane, Inwood Road, Royal Lane, Preston Road, and Coit Road. This area was predominantly Black-owned until the 1940s and 1950s.

Four of the Wells' twelve children were born in Collin County: Kate, Mary, Ella, and George Jr. Those born in Dallas County were: James (Jim), Jonas, Laura Bell, Fannie, Sallie Ann, Junie, Angie, and Harry Lee.

The three oldest sons—George Jr., Jim, and Jonas—paid for their own land before they married. They built homes and farmed land in Upper White Rock, in the area now bounded by Montfort and Inwood and which extended beyond Spring Valley. Their additional holdings were in Carrollton, Lewisville, and on Hillcrest Lane.

George Jr. graduated from Prairie View College and taught in schools in Van Alstyne, Sheppton, and Addison. He married Beulah Mitchell, a Dallas teacher, and continued farming while enjoying his teaching career.

Jim married Bertha Henson, daughter of Rev. George W. Henson, pastor of St. Paul AME Church. A son, Waymon A. Wells, was born. Bertha died, and later Jim married Levie Mosley, daughter of Calvin and Charlotte Mosley, who owned land on Preston Road near Spring Valley, and who had migrated from Tennessee. The four daughters of Levie and Jim are Imogene Mills, Odie Lee Sims, Laura Bell Dewitty, and Helen Wells.

Waymon graduated as valedictorian at Booker T. Washington High School and with high honors at Bishop College in Marshall, Texas. He earned a bachelor's degree in science from Bishop and did further studies at Southern Methodist University and the University of California at Berkeley. He taught mathematics and science at Vickery High School, Julia C. Frazier, and Booker T. Washington. He served as assistant principal at Pearl C. Anderson Junior High School and Lincoln High School. He ended his career in education as principal of Fannie C. Harris and N. W. Harllee Elementary Schools.

Laura Bell Wells married Tommy Coit, who owned land on Spring Valley Road. Their children were Jim, Edna, Jonas, Tommy, Wallene, Marvin, Ola Mae, and Ruth.

Jonas Wells married Clara Holmes. His children were Earnest, DeLaurence, Clarice (Epps), and Isaac Barton Wells, pastor of St. Paul AME church in Pleasant Grove.

Harry Lee Wells married Myrtle Keller. Two children, Theresa (Poole) and Beatrice (Perry), were born to this union. Later he married Gertrude Gray of Elm Thicket. Ten children were born to them: Lauretta (Page), Harry Lee Jr., Ella Faye (Jenkins), Maurice, Ethel (Steele), Birdie Mae (Pearson), Margaret (Nelson), Dorice (Thomas), Doris (Falls), and Franklin.

George and Phyllis made many contributions to their community. Their children, grandchildren, and great-grandchildren continue the legacy left by their foreparents.

William Jackson (Black Jack), the oldest son of Phyllis's brother, Mose Jackson, was an educator in the Dallas Public Schools for many years. He served as teacher and principal at B. F. Darrell and Phyllis Wheatley schools.

Robert Lee Dewitty Jr., son of Laura Bell Dewitty, is a transplant surgeon at Howard University Hospital, where he has served for many years.

T. J. Coit, the grandson of Tom and Laura Bell Coit, is a retired electrical engineer at Hunters Point Shipyard in San Francisco. At present he serves as special consultant at the shipyard.

Mary Heads Carter, granddaughter of Mose Jackson and grandniece of Phyllis Wells, taught for many years in the Dallas School District and was principal at Crispus Attucks Elementary in Upper White Rock.

Konstantz O. Sims, daughter of Odie Lee Sims, received a bachelor of psychology degree at the University of Texas at Arlington and a master's degree in counseling at North Texas State University. She served as counselor at Bishop Dunne High School in Dallas and at Notre Dame High School in Wichita Falls, Texas. She organized the counseling program at Notre Dame High School. Presently she is employed by the federal government.

George and Phyllis instilled many sound values into their twelve children. These values are continuously being passed on to each new generation. One lesson that received priority from their son, Jim, was a lesson in thrift: "If you earn a penny, go ahead and spend it. If you earn a nickel, save at least one penny."

William Wilkerson Family

Family historian: Floyd F. Wilkerson

The Wilkerson family had its roots in the White Rock area out Preston Road in northern Dallas County. William Wilkerson, taking his name from the White Wilborn family on West Alpha, was unschooled. During his early life, following his birth about 1825, he recognized his name as Willcason. After reaching adulthood, he reluctantly took as his mate an Anglo woman on the Wilborn Plantation.

To this union were born several children, as the Bible page attests. The writer never saw his grandfather, William Wilkerson, but he did have the pleasure of knowing his aunts, Sara Ann and Elvira, and his uncles, George, John, and Henry. The writer's father, Calvin, was the youngest of the Wilkerson children.

On the same lane where the Wilborns, as they were called in those days, lived, there lived another family by the same name. So, William decided to change their name to Willcason, and then to Wilkerson. Large families were the vogue then, because the children furnished a pool of free labor for harvesting crops.

The soil in the White Rock area was stubborn and yielded sparse crops of stunted cotton plants; therefore, the yield per acre was small. The Wilkersons struggled to make a living off the land from Emancipation until 1888, when word reached them that cotton grew as "tall as a man" in Forney, Kaufman County, Texas. William, accompanied by his wife, children, and their families, gave up their land and donated some acreage to Mount Pisgah Baptist Church in 1888. A deed from the Dallas County Courthouse validates this voluntary transaction. The land is located on Preston Road near Valley View Lane. The church recently disposed of the land and purchased another edifice on Webb Chapel Road.

The Wilkersons remained in Forney from 1888 until about 1900, when they moved to the City of Dallas and settled in the Freedman's Town area of North Dallas near the Booker T. Washington High School location. They remained there until about 1905, when the patriarch died.

Sara and family moved to Booker T. Washington Addition near Highland Park. Elvira remained in Forney with her family. Calvin and Henry followed Sara to Booker T. Washington Addition in Dallas. John remained in North Dallas. George moved to Ennis, Texas, with his daughter and son-in-law.

Survivors include Elvira's daughters, Sarah Ann and Emma Lee. Calvin's son, Floyd, has two children, Daryl Freeland and Dalarie Almeta. Daryl's two sons, Daryan and Darian, are the youngest survivors. John Wilkerson's grandchildren, Lorenzo and Marjorie Bonner Paris, are his living descendants.

Charley and Charlotte Wesley Young

Family historian: Lavora Young Allen

Just across the Trinity River west of Dallas in a small community lived the family of Charley and Charlotte Wesley Young. They were the parents of two children, James D. Young and Annie Levora Young Allen. Annie Levora Young Allen is the only surviving member of the family.

Before settling in West Dallas, Charley had been a wandering laborer for the Texas and Pacific Railroad. During his working tenure with the T&P Railroad, he wandered from Hattiesburg, Mississippi, his birthplace, to Hawkins, Texas. There, he met Charlotte. His work brought him to Dallas, Texas, where he became a section foreman for the railroad. Later, Charlotte joined him in West Dallas.

They were humble working people. Their family was the first in the immediate community to own a Model T Ford. They were very happy. They could ride to church, which primarily encompassed all of their social life. They were members of Jackson Temple Christian Methodist Episcopal Church. Charley took James and Annie to Sunday School, while Charlotte stayed at home and prepared dinner before going to the eleven o'clock service. She sang in the choir. Their church activities were many, such as Saturday night fish frys, Heaven and Hell parties, summer revivals, and traveling magicians.

Charlotte was very emphatic in assigning and supervising household chores. Most of all, when the children became school age, she was very concerned about their receiving a formal education. When Annie was five years old and James was six, they were enrolled in Saint Peters Academy in North Dallas [now Uptown]. They attended Saint Peters Academy for three years. The untimely death of Charlotte in 1928 made it inconvenient for Charley to keep the children in Saint Peters Academy. Therefore, he enrolled them in Fred Douglass Elementary School in West Dallas to complete their elementary education. They completed their high school education at Booker T. Washington in about 1937 and 1938.

James entered the Civilian Conservation Corp and Annie entered Texas College in Tyler, Texas. She graduated from Texas College with honors and taught in Mineola, Texas, for seven years. She completed her teaching career with the Dallas Independent School District after nineteen years of service. She has been enjoying retirement for seven years at home in Dallas.

Other First Families

This section has been included to provide available information on other pioneer families that we have received through donations to the Black Dallas Remembered Collection, personal interviews, and other sources.

John Wesley and Pearl C. Anderson

Born in Missouri in 1861, John Wesley Anderson began his medical practice in Dallas in 1888. As a physician, dentist, and businessman, he acquired great wealth. He married Pearl C. Anderson in 1920, and together they made outstanding contributions toward the development of organizations and institutions in Dallas and throughout the country. Dr. Anderson died in 1947. Mrs. Anderson remains active in community activities.

Anthony Boswell

Anthony Boswell was born a slave in Alabama and bought his freedom before coming to Texas. He settled in the Oak Cliff area, acquired a large tract of land, and became a successful merchant as co-owner of a grocery store. Elizabeth Chapel CME Church was named for his wife, Elizabeth.

John O. and Ethelyn Chisum

Dr. John O. Chisum and Ethelyn Mildred Taylor, both native Dallasites, were married September 12, 1923. Ethelyn was the daughter of William Henry and Virgie Collins Taylor. Dr. Chisum, an oculist, and Ethelyn, a teacher and counselor, were both very active in professional and civic organizations. Ethelyn was the first Black counselor/dean in the Dallas Independent School District at the Booker T. Washington High School.

Marcellus Clayton Cooper

Born in Dallas on the [William Barr] Caruth farm, Marcellus Clayton Cooper (1863–1929) became the first Black dentist in Texas. After working on the farm and attending grade school in the White Rock area, Cooper completed high school in Springfield, Missouri. He moved there to live with his father. After high school he returned to Dallas to work at Sanger Brothers Department Store. He left Dallas in 1891 to attend Meharry Medical School in Nashville, Tennessee. He returned to Dallas in 1896 and began his dental practice. He was a very active participant in the development of the community. The M. C. Cooper Dental Society in Dallas is named for the early pioneer.

Three of his six children still reside in Dallas. They are Mrs. Marzell Hill, Mrs. Doris Marie Anderson, and Mrs. Dorothy Rhone. Marcellus Cooper lives in San Antonio, and William J. Cooper lives in San Antonio.

Ollie Durham

Ollie Durham was born March 13, 1889, to Tom and Laura Williams Durham in Waelder (Gonzales County), Texas. His parents journeyed from Oklahoma to Waelder in the mid-1850s. Mr. Durham had five brothers and five sisters.

Mr. Durham built over five hundred houses from Gonzales County to Dallas. He also worked as a cattle brander and cook on the LBJ Ranch, and built barracks at Kelly Air Force Base in San Antonio during World War I. He built a number of houses in the Oak Cliff and West Dallas areas. Several churches were built by Mr. Durham and his employees. He is still an active member of Smith Chapel AME Church.

Elston/Lang Families

Russell James Elston (1898–1949), the son of Griff Elston, married Verne Grace Jefferson, the daughter of John Jefferson. Their daughter, Bobbie Elston, married Harold Wendell Lang Sr. (May 13, 1926–

February 14, 1980). Dr. Lang was the son of the late Hulen L. Lang and Mrs. Annie L. Lang.

Both Dr. and Mrs. Lang attended Lincoln High School. Bobbie grew up in East Dallas and Harold in Wheatley. Both taught in the Dallas Independent School District. Harold held several positions in DISD, including principal of Lincoln and N. W. Harllee Schools.

Dr. Richard T. Hamilton

Dr. Richard T. Hamilton came to Dallas from Montgomery, Alabama, before the turn of the [twentieth] century. He was a very active community leader and was instrumental in helping finance many building projects, including the Moorland Branch YMCA that opened in 1926. Due to illness, he retired in the 1930s and returned to Montgomery.

Dennis Wallace Harding Sr.

Dennis Wallace Harding came to Dallas from Scottsville in East Texas. He married Ida King, who grew up near the old J. P. Starks (No. 4) School. They purchased a home on Flora Street and later moved to 3603 Roseland Street.

Their children were Harold Marion, Dennis Wallace Jr., Sybil Marie, William Alexander, Wildy, Allene, Emily, and Hilda. The family acquired a great deal of property in the North Dallas area. All of the children attended Bishop College.

Norman Washington Harllee

Norman Washington Harllee, the son of Evan and Luisa Harllee, was born in North Carolina in 1852. He came to Dallas around 1886, after receiving a bachelor's degree from Biddle College in North Carolina and a master's degree from the University of Chicago.

He was principal of five schools in Dallas and was the first superintendent of the "Colored Division" of the State Fair of Texas.

He married Florence Belle Coleman in 1891, and they had one daughter, Florence Harllee Phelps. She is a retired teacher and social worker and lives in Dallas with her husband, John C. Phelps. They have two daughters, former City Councilwoman Lucy Patterson and Norma Barrett.

Samuel Hudson Jr.

Samuel Hudson Jr., a native Dallasite from a pioneer family, married Ella Lois from Houston, Texas. Samuel Jr. worked with federal housing, and his wife was a music teacher in the Dallas Independent School District.

Their five children are: Mary Lois Hudson Sweatt, Dallas; Estrellita, Los Angeles; Camellia, Los Angeles; Sam III, Dallas; and Clifford, Houston.

Mary Lois is married to Dr. James Sweatt of Dallas and is the founder and owner of Mary Lois School of Dance. Estrellita is an artist, and Camellia skated with Ice Capades before her marriage. Sam III is a State Representative and local attorney.

Mrs. Ophelia Kerl

Mrs. Ophelia Kerl sang in all four productions of *Showboat* at the Music Hall in Dallas, beginning in 1936. Her husband also sang in several of the productions and with other vocal groups. Mrs. Kerl has two daughters, Billie Roberts and Beverly Mitchell.

Dr. Mansell McShann

Dr. Mansell McShann was born on a large farm in North Dallas that his family acquired in the 1870s. Dr. McShann returned to Dallas to practice after receiving his medical degree from Howard University. He and his wife, Frances, were very actively involved in civic and professional activities in Dallas.

Part of the McShann farm became an all-Black residential street, McShann Road, between Preston Road and Montfort Drive.

Turia Dell Marshall

Turia Dell Marshall was born in the 1890s in Millican, Brazos County. He grew up in Dallas and received degrees from Wiley College and Prairie View A&M College. T. D. Marshall began his teaching career in Dallas early in the 1900s. He was a very active church and civic leader. He became the first principal of Lincoln High School, when it opened in 1939. He and his wife had one daughter who died after graduating from college at a very early age.

The Miller Families

Three Black families came with William Brown Miller to Dallas in 1847. They were Clayton and Betty Miller, Archie and Charlotte Miller, and John and Lucy Miller.

They cleared the land and began constructing one of the largest plantations in Dallas. The thirteen hundred acres of land were part of the L. Van Cleave Survey. After a cabin was built, Miller returned and brought his family and farm and building implements.

One of the descendants, Henry Hines, owned and operated the Miller Switch Ferry that crossed the Trinity River near the present site of the US Highway 75 bridge. Historia Miller Jones, granddaughter of Archie and Charlotte Miller, was a lifelong resident of Oak Cliff.

The old Millermore House was moved to Old City Park when Good Street Baptist Church was built on Bonnie View. The family holds a big reunion every year. Donald Payton is the family historian.

Dr. J. Leslie Patton

A native Dallasite, John Leslie Patton (1905–1971) was not only an outstanding teacher and principal, but an orator, historian, writer, and researcher. He was principal of Booker T. Washington High School for thirty years. He also served as deputy superintendent in the Dallas Independent School District.

He and his wife were both very active in civic, church, and professional organizations in Dallas. Their daughter, Dr. Bobbie Franklin Wells, resides in Dallas. She donated his extensive collection of memorabilia to Black Dallas Remembered.

Nathaniel Penn Sr.

Mr. and Mrs. Nathaniel Penn Sr. were early residents of North Dallas on State Street. Mr. Penn moved to Dallas from Waxahachie, Texas. They had three children: Nathaniel Jr., Anne, and Ethel. Nathaniel Jr. (July 12, 1916–November 26, 1985) worked on the *Dallas Express* newspaper for a number of years. He later worked with the US Postal Service for twenty-seven years, from which he retired.

Before moving to California, Anne was librarian of the only library for Blacks, which was located in North Dallas.

Dr. Lee G. Pinkston

Dr. Lee G. Pinkston (1883–1961) came to Dallas in 1921 from Terrell, Texas, where he continued his practice in the McMillan Sanitarium.

Born in Forest, Mississippi, he attended school there and after high school graduation completed degrees at Alcorn College and Meharry Medical College. Pinkston Clinic, which he opened in 1927, was the third Black-owned hospital in the history of Dallas. Dr. and Mrs. Pinkston were both very active participants in the community.

Their two children live in Dallas and are both business owners. Vereta Pinkston Gulley is the owner of Hatcher Street Florist. Lee G. Pinkston Jr. owns Pinkston Mortuary.

Dr. Phillip M. Sunday

Dr. Phillip M. Sunday (1870–1946) came to Dallas in 1908 and began his practice. He was born in Pensacola, Florida, attended Fisk University, and received his medical degree from Meharry Medical School.

He and his wife, Margaret Goulsby Sunday, were civic leaders in Dallas. Mrs. Sunday is still active in Dallas organizations.

Dr. Edgar E. Ward

Dr. Edgar E. Ward was born in Dallas and graduated from the Dallas Colored High School in 1911. He began his medical career in Dallas following his graduation from Meharry Medical College in 1915.

Edgar Ward Place in West Dallas is named in his honor. Dr. Ward was medical director for the Excelsior Life Insurance Company. He was elected Bronze Mayor of Dallas in 1937. He and his wife Pauline were very active in the community.

Other Family Story Contributors

Pettie Abernathy Johnson; June White Birdsong; Alma Brown; A. A. Braswell; Mable Jackson Chandler; Ruby Hunt Cook; Ina and Nina Daniels; Deborah Bedford Fridia; Vareta Pinkston Gulley; Helen Hurd; Elinor Sedberry Jackson; Ophelia Kerl; Bobbie Elston Lang; Marie Loud; Dr. Hazel Partee; Donald Payton; Ella Muriel Penn; Almita Pinkston; John Archie Bramblett Sanders; Emily Harding Simmons; C. C. Tedford; Dr. Bobbie Franklin Wells; and Dr. Joseph Williams.

Part IV
Oral History Transcripts

Marzelle Cooper Hill
Interviewed by Deborah Bedford Fridia
September 28, 1988

My mother was Genevie Turley Cooper, a schoolteacher, and my father was Marcellus Clayton Cooper [1863–1929], a dentist. I was born in a little three-room shotgun house at 1491 Villars Street. My father moved the house over on the lot and built a five-room bungalow at 1521 Villars Street.

My next-door neighbors when I was a little girl were John and Emma Richardson. Christabel Higginbotham and her family lived next door to us at one time, before they bought their home on Roseland Avenue. Christabel was a playmate. The Norwells had boys that I played with.

Down on Villars Street, we always had plumbing and water. I remember when I was small and the toilet was out in the back. It had running water. It was used by people in our house and those in the little rent house in the back where the Richardsons lived. Eventually, we had gas in the house.

My mother died at an early age, and my father remarried. His wife was Willie Beals Sparks Cooper. My mother had two children. My brother died when he was seven.

I attended Bethel AME Church located on Leonard Street. It was a one-story brick church with an annex on the south end. It was located on Leonard and Cochran Streets. Rev. Abington was the pastor when I married. My friends at church were Lucille Williams Anderson and George Terrell. We went to Sunday School together.

I attended school at the Dallas Colored School and the Dallas Colored High School at Hall and Cochran. They were both at the same location. The principals were Mr. Williams and Mr. B. F. Darrell. Cecil Robinson, Mrs. Rutherford, Edna Ezell, and Mrs. Hall were some of the teachers. There were not many children in school during that time.

I walked to school from Villars to Hall Street. When I first started going there, the sidewalks were not paved. We held on to people's picket fences to keep from getting in the mud.

We did not have a car. We had horses and buggies. My father had two. He had a single buggy and a surrey. He had two horses and called them both Nellie. The surrey was used on Sunday because the whole family could ride in it. He used the single buggy when he went to his office during the week.

His office was first located in the Bluitt Building. Dr. Bluitt had a sanitarium down on the corner of Commerce and South Pearl. He had a cleaning establishment in the basement that his nephew ran. On the next floor was Dr. Bluitt's office, Lawyer Mason's office, and my father's dental office. On the upper floor was Dr. Bluitt's Sanitarium, where his patients were. Dr. Bluitt's Sanitarium was the only one where Black doctors could practice. Blacks later on could go to the basement of St. Paul Hospital and be treated.

I attended the Dallas Colored High School. At first there was the old red building, and then they built another building. In high school I studied chemistry, physics, domestic science, sewing, and cooking. Also, Julia Caldwell Frazier taught Latin; Priscilla Tyler taught English; Professor Fox taught history; and Professor Newhouse taught science. The principals were Professor Williams and Professor Darrell.

We had oratorical contests. Kids from my school would compete with kids from Terrell and other towns close to Dallas. I took piano music from Mrs. Hamilton, my godmother, and Miss Hammerstein, a White music teacher. Mrs. Hammerstein would come to the house. The lessons cost twenty-five cents and fifty cents.

On Cochran Street, across from the high school, there was a movie house. Eventually there was a movie house down near the track on Elm Street near Hawkins Street. There was another one on Central Avenue near Swiss Avenue, called Black Jack's movie house. Another one across the street was called the Ella B. Moore Theatre. She had live shows, with dancing girls who would come to Dallas. In my late teens, when Ella B. Moore brought live shows, I was able to go.

Blacks lived on Villars and San Jacinto. Just a few Blacks—about five or six families—lived in the 1500 block. Harold Harden built a four-family apartment house on one lot. Around the corner, there was one old man we called Brother Jones—on San Jacinto Street between Villars Street and McCoy Street. He lived in a shotgun house. He used to do laundry work for White families. Those were the only Negroes in that neighborhood.

The next nearest Black neighborhood was in the vicinity of Roseland and Washington Avenues. They lived on Hall going north toward San Jacinto, up toward Thomas Avenue and State Street. I lived in the same area until I was an adult. There were other pockets of Blacks. One friend by the name of Grace Weems lived in East Dallas on Carroll Street. I did not have friends on The Prairie, but a lot of Negroes lived there. Friends came from Oak Cliff to Dallas Colored High School on the Samson Streetcar.

My father was born in Dallas County in what they called the White Rock Community.[41] His mother was a slave, and his father was a White man. His mother's name was Sallie Lively. His grandfather's name was Marcellus Cooper. My grandmother on my mother's side was Kate Turley. Her mother was brought over from Africa as a little slave girl. She lived in the "big house" and never did live in the quarters

---

41. Several sources say that M. C. Cooper was born on the William Barr Caruth farm, near today's NorthPark Center. His mother Sally Lively was enslaved by John Caruth, the father of William Barr Caruth, and lived on the Caruth Plantation when M. C. Cooper was born.—Eds.

with the other "niggers," as they called them then. My grandmother's father was a brother to the people in the "big house." They never did let my grandmother go down and play in the quarters on the plantation. She had to live with her mother in the big house. Sometimes she would go down and play in the quarters because there was nobody in the big house to play with. Her mistress in the big house would pinch her when she returned. She never would spank her for going down there. She would slip off and go down there because she was lonely. My grandmother would tell me these stories.

The White woman had a horse that she would ride on Sundays going to church. She would let grandmother ride with her. When they got to this White church, my grandmother Turley could not go in. She would have to sit on the steps outside the church.

The only services the Negroes would have on this plantation was when they would slip off at night and go way down—that's where we get the Jubilee songs—singing way down in the plantation fields.

Grandma Turley could read the Bible just a little. She could not read much. She could just sign her name, Kate Turley. She had no opportunity for school—no education.

My father's father, the White man, moved from Dallas to Springfield—either Springfield, Illinois, or Springfield, Missouri. He took my father up there, and my father went to school there. He came back to Dallas later. His father gave him the opportunity for an education.

My father attended public school in Springfield, and then he came back to Dallas. He worked in the wholesale department at Sanger Bros. Department Store. He worked there eleven years, to go to Meharry Medical school to take dentistry. At that time, you didn't have to have a high school diploma to go to Meharry. He received his dental degree at Meharry Medical College and returned home after he finished a three-year course.

My mother attended Fisk University for seven years. Grandma Turley worked as a domestic servant and had three sons and one daughter. She took my mother out to Grand Prairie to live with a brother of hers. She was a Normal School graduate. They did not get degrees. That meant that she went to Fisk through high school and then went to Normal School. Grandmother did not have help in sending her daughter to school. She did it all herself.

When they built the Knights of Pythias Temple, officed there were Dr. Hamilton, Dr. Edgar Ward, Dr. Cooper, Dr. A. H. Dyson, and Dr. White. My mother taught in Dallas County a very short time before she married. She taught in [Irving] in a Negro community called Bear Creek. She taught all grades. She was the only teacher there at one point.

I attended Wiley College in Marshall, Texas. Dr. N. W. Dogan was president. After finishing Wiley, I went to George R. Smith College, a Methodist college in Sedalia, Missouri. I taught there two years and then came back to Dallas and began teaching at Booker T. Washington High School. I taught English at George R. Smith College and Ancient and Medieval History at Booker T. Washington.

The principal at Booker T. Washington was J. J. Rhoads. Some of the faculty members were: T. W. Pratt, Melvin Banks, S. H. Davis, Virgil Sheppard, Lillian Hardee, Kathryn Robinson, Lawrence Grimes, Portia Washington Pittman, Alexander Jackson, and Marjorie Humber Jackson. I taught four years. When I married, I had to stop teaching. I went to Denver, Colorado and lived there two and a half or three years.

I married David B. Hill, a Dallasite. His parents were Napoleon Hill and Bertha Hill. They lived on Cochran Street. They had three children, two boys and one girl: N. B., David, and Francetta. David was the oldest, and Francetta was the second child. David's father was a chief cook and worked at a bank downtown: American and then First National. It was on Elm Street.

After returning to Dallas, I did not work immediately because married women could not teach in Dallas. Later on, I worked at the Community Chest Employment Office. Frances was born in 1931, so I worked there about 1932 or 1933. I was the only Black employee. We had a segregated office. I only dealt with Black clients. I had to answer the phone when people called and wanted help. I would try to help them apply and check their references. There weren't many jobs in Dallas then during the Depression. My salary then was $12.50 or $15.00 per week. This was considered a good job. About 1931, we bought our first car, a used Ford.

When Frances was about six years old, I began work again. It was during the Depression, and Mrs. Halaria Morgan had worked with someone at the City Hall helping to get food for Negroes. They moved this White woman that Mrs. Morgan worked with down to the [Dallas] County [offices]. Halaria Morgan was moved down there with her, as a part-time employee. Mrs. Morgan was not considered a probation officer. However, when they arrested little colored boys, they would put them downtown next door. Mrs. Morgan would go out in her car and tell the parents where they were or take them home. They just had a small section for them. They did not arrest the little Negro girls, just the Negro boys. They did not keep them down there very long.

Mrs. Morgan died; she had pneumonia. I knew the kind of work she was doing. Mr. Morgan, the insurance man, would take her down to the County somewhere, and she would be home by noon. So, I said to my husband, "I wonder what she did down there, because I would like to have a part-time job like that, so I could be home with Frances." I mentioned it to Dr. Hamilton, who was my godfather and a very influential Negro citizen then. He mentioned it to Lawyer Turner, who had connections and practiced law down there. They mentioned it, and a year later, Mr. Parker called me and told me I had the job.

When I went down there, nobody paid me any attention. Finally, one of the White juvenile officers came over and showed me where the registration book was and where I could find out whether there were any little Negro boys in jail. If there were, I could get the address and go and tell the parents where they were.

Mr. Gray, the White man, really wanted to come on to me. But I was too intelligent. He did not know how to approach me. He was very nice because I was completely ignored by the others. No one ever showed me anything, except in one or two instances. I worked over in one corner of this office on the sixth floor of the [Dallas] County Records Building.

I would see one White woman working with women who would come in out of the community. She would give them a check or something. I wondered what that check was for, and I finally found out. If those White mothers needed a little bit of money, they would give them some. We had no agency looking out or furnishing money or groceries for welfare then. So, I finally found out what it was all about.

I was finally sent out on a case where the neighbors had complained about a little boy. I went out there. He was a retarded child, and the neighbors had been keeping him. The mother had to quit work and keep him. She needed groceries because she could not work. I took her in my car down to the Records Building and told her to go over in the corner and talk with Mrs. White about her problem. That was the first time a Negro had received a check. They gave her five dollars every two weeks for about two months. By that time, she had been able to make some other plans to take care of this child.

Mr. Parker told me, anything I wanted to know, to ask Mrs. Wiley. Mrs. Wiley was one of the women who worked up there. I went to her one morning to ask her something, and she raised her voice at me. She said, "Well, you will just have to wait." You see, when I would go down there, and no Negro children were in jail, I could go back home, and nobody bothered me. I did not have to keep any specific hours one way or another.

Anyway, when Mrs. Wiley told me I would just have to wait, I left. When I came back two or three days later, she apologized to me. I told her, "We are two grown women, and when you raise your voice at me, I am inclined to raise mine, even though that's not appropriate under the conditions in which I am working here." Her attitude changed toward me completely.

Finally, she said to Mr. Parker, who was our chief officer, "I don't see why Marzelle can't have a desk over here like everybody else."

There was one dark corner in the southwest corner of the big office on that floor. It was over near a window that had an exit to the fire escape. We were on the fifth floor of that building. They put an extension cord with a bulb and a desk over there. Nobody bothered me. I could go down there when I wanted to and come back when I wanted to.

Finally, Mr. Parker called me one day and told me he had bad news for me. He was the one that had to give it to me. My services were no longer needed. He said, "Marzelle,"—nobody called me anything but Marzelle, nobody called me Mrs. Hill—"You need not rush down in the morning to clear your desk." Since he had never bothered me about keeping hours, I said, "Mr. Parker, I'll come down as usual because I would like to go down early to see if I need to make any home calls, and such."

I told my godfather, Mr. Hamilton, what happened. He contacted Charlie Brackins, a very prominent Black real estate man in Dallas; Rev. Jackson, pastor of New Hope; and W. H. Pace, who was with the *Dallas Express* newspaper at that time. They went down and talked with Mr. Parker. Mr. Parker told them he did not have anything to do with my being dismissed from service. They went to the Juvenile Board, which was composed of all the District Judges. The District Judges made up the Juvenile Board that controlled the Juvenile Department.

Finally, they ended up with the County Judge, Judge Ben Fly. He told them, "Yes, he let me go because he had too many complaints from his constituents in the County about having a Negro woman down there with a desk."

Maynard Jackson told him if they would give us a Negro probation officer, because we needed one, they would arrange space for her.[42] Maynard Jackson did that, and I had an office in the educational Building of the New Hope Baptist Church. The church was on the corner of San Jacinto and Central Avenue at that time. Then I had an

---

42. Maynard Jackson was the son of Rev. A. C. Jackson of New Hope Baptist Church in Dallas, and he was the father of Maynard Jackson Jr., who later became the first Black mayor of Atlanta, Georgia.—Eds.

office in the Leach Building on San Jacinto Street. Finally, my office was in the Henry Ford Building on Allen Street.

The work had progressed so that by this time I was doing delinquent children, dependent and neglected children, adoption investigations, and anything else that was referred to the County related to Negro children.

Then the County hired Kathryn McDade as a part-time secretary for me. It cost lots of money to pay rent for me as an individual probation officer and for a part-time secretary. In the main office they only had three stenographers for nine or ten officers, including the chief probation officer.

Finally, they built the building out on Harry Hines Boulevard for the Juvenile Department. I talked with the man in charge and told him the Negro community had begun to ask me if I was going to have an office out there in that building. He showed me the blueprints of the office out there on Harry Hines, and where my office was going to be. It was down the hall to the back and to the right, and it was the last office room on that floor. It was across the hall from the two restrooms for Negro men and women. But I was permitted to move out there in the new building.

Mr. Santee, a photographer, was on the first floor of Pythian Temple on Elm Street. Mr. Galloway had no permanent location and would carry his photographic equipment on his shoulder. Women were fine dressmakers. Some only sewed for Whites. Mrs. Guest was one. I think she lived on State Street. There was a dress shop called Flora Ma'i. It was owned by Florence Watson, Marie Burke, and Ruby Reed. That dress shop was located in the McMillan Building on State and Hall Streets. It was the McMillan Sanitarium. The Sanitarium and his office were upstairs. Mrs. McMillan ran the drugstore for him. Other businesses in the building were a beauty shop and a barber shop.

Myrtle B. Anderson on Hall Street had a printing shop and a cleaning/pressing shop. There was a restaurant on Jackson Street called Richardson's Cafe. There was another restaurant on Allen and

Juliette (later called Munger) called the McMillan Cafe. Those were all Negro-owned.

Dr. Frank Jordan

Interviewed by Deborah Bedford Fridia

October 16, 1988

I was born in Clarksville, Texas, Red River County, on January 19, 1906. My parents were Frank Jordan and Louvinia Crenshaw Jordan. I stayed in Clarksville until I was about seven years old. Then my mother moved to Dallas. I attended Dallas Colored High School on Hall Street. That was the elementary and the high school. One of my teachers was Mrs. Barnes. Some of my friends were the Harden children, Joe Starks and his family, the Brashears—A. W., Bernice, and Maurice—and the Salads. One of my high school classmates was Blanche Johnson Davis. Mrs. Julia Caldwell Frazier was my high school principal. Mr. Williams taught mathematics and science.

I have been a member of the New Hope Baptist Church since I was about nine years old. The church was on San Jacinto Street and Central Railroad. A. S. Jackson was pastor. My favorite church activities were BYPU and Starlight Band. We read the Bible and learned Bible verses. Mrs. Callie Hicks was in charge of the Starlight Band. Joe Starks was my church friend.

As a teenager, I played marbles in the street. I lived at 1308 Roseland Avenue. The Hardens and Will Joneses were my neighbors. My house was the usual shotgun house with no indoor facilities. We moved across the street with Mrs. Will Jones when my father died.

Mrs. Frazier would have Halloween parties at her house. She would make you have a good time. If you did not dance, she would make you dance or get somebody to teach you how to dance. We bobbed apples in a tub with all kinds of prizes. She made you have fun. She was so stern in school nobody wanted to go to her parties. She was very lively at home and a lot of fun. We would get home about nine p.m.

I did my pre-med work first at Howard University in Washington, DC. Then I went to Meharry College in Nashville, Tennessee. When I graduated from Meharry, I went to St. Louis City Hospital for an internship. The internship was one year.

When I was going through college, I worked at the hotels in Atlantic City and at summer resorts and racetracks. I waited tables, bellhopped, assisted in the kitchen fixing potatoes and peeling apples.

After medical school, I went to St. Louis and did my internship. I came back to Dallas in 1936 and opened my office in North Dallas in the Green Building on Thomas Avenue.

We (Black doctors) were not allowed to practice in the hospitals. I had to do work in my office or the Black hospitals—Pinkston Clinic and McMillan Sanitarium.

When other hospitals opened, our only problem was the lack of training to take over jobs assigned to us. We had to go back and get further training. The first hospital to open to Blacks was St. Paul. We used the restrooms and all facilities at St. Paul, and you did everything you could do.

[The] San Jacinto Streetcar line was the main line to North Dallas. The San Jacinto line came out Ross Avenue to San Jacinto Street and Washington Avenue. For a while they had jitneys. They would carry you for a ride for a dime from your neighborhood to downtown. They were operated by Blacks. The street cars were segregated. I did not have a car when I first started practicing. Sometimes Dr. Green would let me use his car. I charged about three dollars for a home visit. My first car was a Chevrolet, I think. I lived with my mother on South Central Avenue. It was a brick home. She owned that house.

I belonged to the Dunbar Club. Most affairs were at the Pythian Temple. Some were at the North Dallas Club. There was a club in Oak Cliff, too.

Blacks owned general stores and merchandise stores. Mr. Lewis owned a dry goods store down on Elm Street. There were barbecue stands, liquor stores, and a bakery shop on Hall Street owned by Mr. Rice's father. There was a produce market next to him, but I don't know who owned it. These were Dago stores.[43] There was a candy manufacturer and ice cream parlor.

I owned a candy manufacturing company for a while. I worked for Atlanta Life as a doctor and examined people who were applying for a policy.

Other doctors in Dallas were: [Drs.] Harding, McShann, Green, McMillan, Lewis, Trotter, Key (dentist), and Billups. Dr. Brown, Dr. Williams, and I were in our building at 3808 Thomas Avenue.

Dr. Lucille Williams Lane
Interviewed by Deborah Bedford Fridia
July 25, 1988

I, Lucille Marian Williams Lane, was born in Julaski County, Tennessee, on March 9, 1890. My mother and father met and lived in Birmingham. My mother was from Marietta, Georgia. She was the oldest of three children. When my parents met in Birmingham, my mother was teaching, and my father was a letter carrier. Our family home was in Marietta, Georgia, twenty miles north of Atlanta. My grandmother was born in October of 1842. My father died in January of 1895, just after my fourth birthday.

---

43. "Dago" was a widely used derisive term referring to Italians.—Eds.

I came to Dallas with my mother, Minnie P. Lyman Groves, after my fourth birthday. We went to Dallas from Marietta, Georgia. In Dallas, we bought a home at 3707 State Street.

My mother married again when I was five years old. Her husband, Mr. Groves, was by profession a broom-maker. It so happened that Mr. Hughley decided to move his broom-making business to Los Angeles. Mr. Groves went along with him. Mama did not go at that time but somehow she had the thought that one day she would go after he was settled in Los Angeles. But that time didn't arrive until 1921. She then went to California and liked it very much.

My mother taught at the Darrell School. She was the first-grade teacher. In fact, she taught at several schools. She taught the first grade in three schools where she was assigned from time to time. She taught twenty-nine years. Her retirement came in 1921, and it was at that time that we decided to move to California.

One of her principals was N. W. Harllee, who lived next door. Another one was the husband of her best friend. His name was Charles Rice. One of the finest of primary teachers was Julia Caldwell of Columbus, Georgia. They said she was one of the finest primary teachers they ever had in the state. She began teaching in high school and became the Latin teacher.

I attended the Booker T. Washington School, which was No. 2 School. I attended the Frederick Douglass School, which was No. 4 School. At [Frederick] Douglass School, John W. Ray was my principal. At No. 4, I had John P. Starks for principal. For high school, I went away to Knoxville College and stayed in the Little Girls' Dormitory. I was in Knoxville four years. After I finished Knoxville, I went to Tuskegee, where I specialized in dressmaking and ladies' tailoring. I finished from Tuskegee in the class of 1912.

One of my classmates in elementary school was Frederica Chase. I was two years older than Freddie. She grew up and finished Howard University. Ruby Wiley was one of my friends. Martha Morrow was one of my childhood friends. Alluria Len was one of my best friends. The Rices—there were three of them: Ella, John, and Robert—and the

Rowens were friends I played with. Georgia Slaughter, Alice Slaughter, Ethelyn Taylor—she married John Chism—were friends. Lena Shropshire and her sister, Edna, were playmates when we were little girls around five and six.

I lived at 3707 State Street until I left Dallas to teach in Paris, Texas. I stayed in Paris three years and then moved back to Dallas. I had my state certificate and three years' experience in Paris. I applied to teach in Dallas and was elected. I taught the second grade, first at No. 2 [School]. Then I decided that I would transfer to another school because I had done some work in home economics. I applied for a job in home economics.

The home economics teacher before me resigned, and I took over the home economics department. I opened the first lunchroom. The children were bringing cold lunches, so I told Dr. Kimball that I would like to open a lunchroom so we could give the children hot lunches at a low price. I was elected, and we took over the work. The boys and girls in the seventh grade did the cooking. The lunches cost fifteen cents.

We had soup on Monday and hash on Tuesday. I remember those two very well, but I don't remember the other days. It was a hot lunch. The parents would come after lunch to see if there was anything left.

Mr. Kimball was the superintendent of schools. B. F. Darrell was the principal. Did I have an easy time getting the program started? I just did it. The parents cooperated. Ha! They came every day to see if there was anything left. If there was, they would buy it.

Mrs. Clemmons made the pies for me. Mrs. Clemmons was one of my neighbors, and she made sweet potato pies about the size of a bread-and-butter plate. I sold those for fifteen cents apiece. A grand time? Oh, we did! Parents loved for the girls to take home economics. I taught them housekeeping, how to keep the house clean. I had a little class that I taught a little sewing. I taught them how to mend, how to darn socks, and so on.

Oh, we had the Book Lovers Study Club. That was a club of twelve of us, and we met in the homes once a month and studied. The Priscilla

Art Club had a lot of assignments. We made a lot of pretty things, embroidery, fancy work, etc. Some of the members of the book club were: Minnie Dupree, Christine Gipson, Beatrice Mecoff, Ethelyn Taylor, and Virginia Stewart. Ann Jackson Ewing, Beatrice Gotleib Taylor, and Allistar Barnett Hooper were Priscillas.

The clubs we belonged to had the dances. They were held at the North Dallas Club. That was a fine club. We did not have too many teas.

My house at 3707 State Street was a cottage with two large bedrooms and a sunroom. There was a living room, dining room, kitchen, laundry room, and a nice big porch on front and back. The porch on the front went across the front of the house and around one side. The house was white with a gray trim. It had a picket fence, and it was on a cement foundation that stood about twelve inches high. On one side, I had a lawn, and we played croquet. We kept the grass cut short. We had lemons—a lemon tree that bore very heavily. We had a lemon tree in California, but we had a lemon tree in Texas, [too]. We had peaches. We never bothered with vegetables because there was always a store across the street.

My family attended the Congregationalist Church because it did not go in for separatism. One was organized in my house (in Berkeley). In Dallas we went to the Congregationalist Church on Harrison Street in downtown Dallas. We were not the only Black family in the congregation. There was a Negro couple there.

The George Mitchells were my next-door neighbors. The Tylers, Priscilla and Maggie, were on the other side. I heard from Priscilla for a long time. My first car was a LaSalle made by the Cadillac people. That was their small car. It was a beige two-door. My father gave it to me in 1919. We were always on the highway going to Fort Worth—always. Gas was fifteen cents a gallon. I don't think too many Blacks owned cars.

Dr. J. W. Anderson was my doctor. He was a friend of my father's in Meharry. His wife belonged to the Congregationalist Church. His office was downtown. Her name was Drucilla.

Mother taught with Virgil William's mother. I knew the Pattons—they were younger.

Interviewer's note: Mrs. Lucille Williams Lane was interviewed in the Haven Nursing Home, Oakland, California on July 25, 1988. Mrs. Lane expired June 13, 1989.

Thomas Tolbert
Interviewed by Deborah Bedford Fridia
October 1988

My name is Thomas Tolbert. My people during those days did not realize that I might need a middle name, so I never had one. I have gotten along very well with that name.

I was born January 31, 1909, on Lawrence Street in a community called The Prairie. Now, The Prairie, as some of you have probably heard, was south of Commerce Street, going out toward the Fair Park, during those early days. I might add that during those days there wasn't a paved street south of Commerce Street. So that neighborhood didn't have any paved streets—no running water, no electric lights, and no gas. But we lived on The Prairie.

My time there was just one year because my grandfather built a house out on Spring Avenue, which was referred to as out at "Plum Nellie, plum out of the city and nellie in the country," as they would teasingly say to us. He built this house out on Spring Avenue. It is still standing and is now known as the Lone Star Funeral Home. It was run by the late Mr. Joe Bookman and his wife, who is still there.

I was one year of age when we moved out on Spring Avenue, and I heard—I don't know because I was quite young—that people would drive out there to see that house because it was painted. During those days, I don't think there were over four or five houses on The Prairie that were painted. As I recall, the Beals lived in a two-story, white painted house—that was Dorothy Rhone, Marie Anderson, and Marzelle Hill's grandmother. They lived not too far from us. It was a showplace, too, of course.

Anyway, we lived there on Spring Avenue in a big white house with three rooms on one side. There was a hall that extended from the front porch all the way through the house to the back porch. And then, on the other side of the hall, there were two big bedrooms. As I recall, our rooms were very large. The thing that I think of now, with regret, my people had—it wasn't a baby grand—a flat, box-like piano that had been in the family for many, many years. Out of a need for space, they almost gave it away, because they sold it for eight dollars.

We lived there in this house, and we were quite comfortable. My step-grandmother was a very charming lady. She was my grand-father's third wife. My grandfather was the late J. R. Perkins, who was one of the first businessmen in charge of doing transportation. He always had teams and wagons. They were big moving vans. They were used to move people in the city. They had an office down on Bryan Street and St. Paul—where the Post Office is standing today. It was a small office downtown. He had a telephone, which was used by many of the White people who had businesses in the block. It was a neighborhood convenience.

During my early days, which were interesting days, our house was nicely furnished. I still have some pieces out of that Perkins house in my house at the present time—especially in my library, and one or two pieces are in my living room.

We lived quite comfortably. We had plenty of chickens. We had hogs and dogs in addition to mules, horses, and cows. As I grew older, I did not admire the things so much because I was responsible for cutting the grass for the horses, drawing the water for the stock, and staking the cows. It grew to be quite a job; however, my grandfather didn't think it was much of a job, and he persisted with it, almost till the day he passed away.

We enjoyed a good life there because Dallas was beginning to unfold as a city. We used to enjoy Sunday evenings when people would go riding. They were beginning to buy cars, and, of course, Blacks used to drive the Cadillac car that they bought, I am sure, secondhand. They would drive down Second Avenue and make a left-hand turn and come down Spring Avenue for a block and stop by our house to get some water and to eat whatever was offered them. We enjoyed these people. I remember the Davis family that lived on Cochran Street. They had a son named Herman Davis. They used to come by quite often. And then, of course, there were other people—Dr. John Dodd's parents would drive out to see us. They had a piece of property on the opposite side of the road. They later built the house for his parents to live out there.

Those were the good old days. You did not hear too much about crime. There wasn't but one telephone in our block, and that was the Perkins' [his grandparents] telephone. Of course, I was glad for other folks to be able to afford a telephone because they didn't mind saying, "Go down there, Boy, get so-and-so, and tell them to come to the telephone." They would hold the telephone up until he would come. I would bring them on in, and they would use the telephone, and they would say, "Thank you, Mr. Perkins," and then get along. I would be standing there. I received no courtesies, tips, or nothing. It was just a courtesy of the neighborhood.

Anyway, the time passed, and I began to think in terms of going to school. They sent me to a school over in what was called the Honeycutt Addition. Now, Honeycutt is a little neighborhood that started at the beginning of—well, down below Lagow Street. That's where the Ambassador's Church is standing on the corner of Baldwin Street. And that church was down in the block where the house that was occupied by Mrs. Nona Littleton Bell stands. They built a home there after someone burned the church down. But I am ahead of my story now.

The school was presided over by Professor Charles W. Asberry, whose residence is next-door to my place where I am living now.

He was my first teacher, and when school opened that first day, he had about thirty-five or forty children from the beginners on up through the sixth or seventh grade. And we had school.

One night someone came along, as the result of a disagreement in the church, and burned the schoolhouse down. That year we didn't have any more school until they could find some place for us to go. They moved us over to another church house over on Hamilton Street—right back of the one in the Honeycutt Addition. There was a little, one-room church there. So, we started school, and a lady by the name of Mrs. Rosie Rainwater Weisner was the teacher. She kept the school going several years and did a good job of it, so far as we were able to see. We had big days during those times. We would have a Christmas tree, and we would have an Easter program.

And then, we would have the school closing. Everybody was on the program for school closing. They would borrow some sheets from the neighbors and pin them together, and then they would get boards and make a stage across the front of the schoolroom. Some of the young men in the neighborhood would draw the curtains. We would assemble there and have our program. Everybody had to be on the program with a speech, a dialogue, or singing a song. They had to be seen.

I shall never forget this. The first time I ever heard "Lift Every Voice and Sing" was from a copy that Mrs. Rosie had placed upon the blackboard. We learned to sing this song at every program we had in the community. They referred to it as the Negro National Anthem. And White people said, "Well, why is it the Negro National Anthem? You've got one anthem, and we don't need but one." "Well," we said, "we need ours, too." Sometimes that would be rather questionable, but we would go right on.

Miss Rosie became impaired because of her health, and she gave up the schoolwork. A man came out to be in charge by the name of Mr. Smith. He lived up on McKenzie Avenue. Now, McKenzie was quite a nice street that ran off Haskell Avenue.

It was down there by Professor Jackson's house, where Professor Smith lived. He came and started school in a house. We had never had a schoolhouse before this time. He was a very fine man. He would come to school riding his horse. And then there was a teacher that worked up there with him by the name of Miss Beatrice Martin. She belonged to New Hope Baptist Church. Then, she became Mrs. Beatrice King. She has a daughter who taught here, Jewell Snare. I believe she is retired now. A very splendid lady. She sang beautifully. She had a heavenly voice.

Then there was Miss Dean, Naomi Dean Favors, who was my other teacher. We were getting to be big-timers then. And I might remind you that we still brought our lunch to school in a five-pound lard bucket, and we would have biscuits, syrup, and bacon. We would have a big dinner. Sometimes we would have a dime, and, of course, you would be surprised—in those days you could get a dime's worth of cheese and crackers and maybe a little bit of baloney and have a spread. Those were big days when you had a dime to spend for your lunch.

That was a [Dallas] County school. The County paid for it, and they would come up once or twice a year to see how we were getting along having school. They finally built us a building on Collins Avenue. It was a white building with two big rooms. That building is still standing. I think it is used as a CME Church. It was about that time in the next year or so that Professor J. H. Warner became the principal. He was a very fine man. Mrs. Martin was still out there, and so was Miss Dean. They had about three or four teachers and had gone to five or six rooms. But it was still a rural school—no lights, a pump for water, no sewage, of course, but that was school. We were getting along very well. And they decided some of us ought to go to high school.

The first person I knew to go to high school from that community was a lady by the name of Miss Ruth Jackson. She had a brother by the name of Clifford Jackson, later the Reverend Clifford Jackson, who is still here in the community, in Grand Prairie, I believe it is.

So, Ruth went to high school and did very nicely. On the last day of school, she would come by the school to show the teachers her card and that she had passed her work. Then the next semester, her brother Clifford went over to Booker T. Washington High School. They would accept us as students there. I did not realize that once you went over there, they would put you back to the seventh grade, which they did. Miss Frazier had charge of that then, and I had heard so much about Miss Frazier. I know many of you have too.

I shall never forget when we walked in, Miss Frazier said, "Where are you going, boy?" I said, "I am going in the principal's office to see about enrolling." She said, "The principal ain't got time to enroll you. Come on into my room." I went on in there, and she asked, "Where are you from?" and I told her. It was getting a little warm, so I told her there were a couple of other people out there from the Fairground School. She said, "Go out there and get them." So, I went out there and got these people.

She carried us down to the principal and he said to her, "Miss Frazier, you just go ahead and adjust them where they ought to be." So, she adjusted us—by putting us back to the seventh grade. The principal at that time was Professor Joseph J. Rhoads. That was his first year in Dallas as a principal. He followed the principalship of Professor C. F. Carr.

So, Mr. Rhoads took Miss Frazier's word for it, and they put us in the seventh grade. They had three rooms for the seventh grade. It was during that time that I enjoyed a very good educational experience because we had three teachers who were distinguished as great teachers—Mrs. A. V. West, Mrs. Lagon Tucker Lewis, and Mrs. Syrus E. White. They were truly great teachers. When we left the seventh grade, we stood our own, because we were promoted to the low ninth. We started our high school from there. I am being too detailed, I guess.

By the second year at Booker T. Washington High School, they decided to allow Black students to attend the International YMCA Conference at Helsinki, Finland. Of course, that did not mean too much to me because I had never heard of Helsinki and had no idea about going. But when they got through sifting around on the ones they thought were capable, I was elected to be the delegate from the Southwest to go to the International YMCA Conference at Helsinki, Finland.

That was an interesting experience. It took thirteen days for us to make the trip across the Atlantic. In that party were some of the most distinguished Black people in America: Dr. John Hope Franklin, who had been for many years the president of Morehouse College; Dr. Johnny Astra Myers, who was the senior secretary of the Colored Work Department of the YMCA of America; and there were several other men whose names I don't recall right off the reel.

Money was a problem, but we found out, as we have found out about our people, we always find money to do whatever we want to do. Under the sponsorship of Dr. Rhoads, they started raising money for this delegate. May I mention that at this time there had only been three Negroes in Dallas who had been to Europe.

The first Negro to go to Europe from Dallas was Dr. A. S. Jackson, pastor of New Hope Baptist Church; then Dr. C. W. Abington, pastor of St. James AME Church; and Rev. E. Ellington Roseland, pastor of Macedonia Baptist Church. Now this was prior to 1926—[they were] the only Blacks who had been across the Atlantic.

Getting back to where I am now, they started raising money in the churches. They said, "How much do you need?" You need at least fourteen or fifteen hundred dollars because it is expensive. They were going on a cabin-class ship. Cabin-class is rated as first-class. You had a private room. It was going to be expensive because they had to go to New York. I remember fare to New York then was ninety-nine dollars. Then, of course, you had your hotel expenses there, prior to shipping out. Well, they got that, and gave me eleven hundred and fifty dollars, as I recall, for my expenses and the ticket and that kind of thing.

We went on to the YMCA Conference. It was a great occasion. I was selected to be the boys' speaker for Black boys of the world at the great conference there. They didn't train me for my speech [before I went] because they did not know I was going to speak until I got there. So, I had a nice paragraph. I usurped most of it from a speech that was made by Dr. Channing Tobias.[44]

Anyway, we stayed in Helsinki for eight or nine days, and we lived in a school there in town. People there had never seen a Black man before, and they would walk up and ask you if they could touch your hand to see if the color would come off and that kind of thing. And we would let them go ahead and do that. It was quite an experience.

There were fourteen Blacks [in our group]. There were four Black youth. One of the distinguished young men there, C. C. Spaulding Jr.—distinguished because of his father, C. C. Spaulding, who had been one of the founders of the North Carolina Mutual Insurance Company—when he returned to America, he went to Clark University in Worchester, Massachusetts. We used to correspond occasionally.

When we left Helsinki, we toured Europe. We toured the thirteen countries in Europe, which was a wonderful experience—France, Germany, Switzerland, and others. When we came back to America, there were people waiting at the ship to greet us. We had become quite distinguished. We were highly congratulated for our behavior and our contribution to this world conference. So, about that time, I was ready to come home. I came home and had to ride the train because airplane riding was not in vogue in those days.

When I came home to New York, my friend was there, A. V. Smith from Fort Worth, Texas. We rode back to Texas together on the train. We had very comfortable accommodations. We had no Pullman. In those days Black people could not ride the Pullman cars, but we had some pillows they let us use to sleep on at night. It took us three days to come from New York to Dallas, Texas, during those days. We made it all right.

---

44. Dr. Channing B. Tobias (1882–1961) was a well-known religious and civic leader, sometimes referred to as the Booker T. Washington of his day. He was most well known for his work with the YMCA. His papers are housed in the libraries of the University of Minnesota, including the speech he gave at the meeting in Helsinki, Finland (https://archives.lib.umn.edu)—Eds.

We came back to Dallas and Booker T. Washington High School. I was given a very nice reception. At a date they had established, they had an assembly, and I was the speaker for the occasion. There were cheers and that kind of thing. I was made to feel that I had been a very good representative.

The next year I graduated from Booker T. Washington High School and made plans to go to college. In those days there was not too much talk about going to school out of the state, because most folk weren't able to go to college in the state. But there were some that went to Howard, Fisk, Wilberforce, Lincoln, and other big-time schools—those were big-time schools in those days. Now, Miss Frazier was a graduate of Howard University, and she encouraged one of our students to go to Howard. Her name was Helen Wilson Johnson. She passed away not too long ago. A brilliant student! And there were others. I don't want to create any feeling of animosity, because I don't have a record here, but there were several others.

There was a college down in Austin named Samuel Huston College.[45] I was asked to accept a scholarship there, which I did. I enrolled and was there four years. I had a very wonderful experience as a college student. I was active in the activities on the campus. I became a member of the Alpha Phi Alpha Fraternity. I went to some of the student conferences at the different colleges in Texas. At that time, they would let us walk across the campus of the University of Texas and attend, occasionally, some student meetings in some of the big buildings there on campus. There was no thought of our going to school there, of course, but they let us walk across the campus. I used to go over there to the University Co-op, where I would buy my books. I could rent a book for the weekend for a dime. If I had a dime, I would go over on a Friday afternoon and rent a book. Quite often, I would sit

---

45. Samuel Huston College was a private coeducational school for African American students which grew out of an 1876 plan created by the Methodist Episcopal Conference. In 1952, it merged with another historical institution called Tillotson College, which had been chartered in 1877, and today it is called Huston-Tillotson University (https://htu.edu)—Eds.

in my room and read Friday and Saturday nights, so that I could take my book back on Monday.

I had some wonderful experiences. I remember reading some books by Jessie Vossett, one of the first Black fiction writers I had ever heard of. I read several of her books. Sometimes I would share with another person, and they could sit up and read all night. It was all right. So, I did my reading very consistently. I would read the *New York Times*. I am still doing it until this day. I learned to read the *Book Review* section of the *New York Times*. I was also completely fascinated by what was happening at the stock market on the financial page. That newspaper isn't bought very much in downtown Dallas now. I like the *New York Times*.

But one of my greatest experiences I had when I was in college, in addition to my regular class work, was reading Negro periodicals we were exposed to then. There was a newspaper called the *Chicago Defender*, another called the *Pittsburgh Courier*, another called the *Kansas City Call*, [and] another later on called the *Amsterdam News* out of New York City.

These newspapers particularly, the *Chicago Defender* and the *Pittsburgh Courier*, stimulated much racial pride and ambition on the part of young Negroes in America. Dr. Robert S. Abbott, the owner and editor-in-chief of the *Chicago Defender*, was from Georgia, but he went to Chicago and developed this Black newspaper. Every week there would be in great big letters across the headlines "Segregation Must Go! Segregation Must Go!" Then there would always be on that front page, I regret to remind you, a list and a story about the most recent lynchings that had taken place that week and where they were. It's a sad story. This was between 1928 and 1932 that this was going on.

Then, of course, there were many Negroes who were becoming distinguished as great singers. I recall that we rode from Austin in a truck to San Antonio, which was eighty-five miles, to hear the greatest tenor of his day—a Black man by the name of Roland Hayes. Roland Hayes was a great singer. They let us sit in the upper balcony at the

Music Hall in San Antonio, Texas. I recall very well when Mr. Hayes and his accompanist stepped out on the stage. Of course, later on, there were other great singers: Florence Cole Talbert would come through Austin and sing. And they had some great shows from New York; *Broadway Rastus* was one of them.

There was a Negro woman by the name of Mrs. Ella B. Moore who, with the help of her White friend, bought a building—a theatre building—down on the Central Track. It was not a street. The Central [Railroad] Track was our main thoroughfare then, going from Commerce Street all the way up the Central Track to Hall Street. On Saturday and Sunday evenings, we would be out there by the hundreds dressed up in our Sunday go-to-meeting clothes, up on the Track.

This lady (Mrs. Moore) would bring Black shows down to Dallas. One of the greatest shows she presented was called *Broadway Rastus*. It had a great effect. Even Whites were coming over to see what was taking place in "dark town."

I don't want you to think that we were just having a good time. Intellectual thought was developing. There were people who had come out of harbor at that time. Mrs. Frazier was in her prime, and she was facing retirement. There were some other distinguished people. There was a lady by the name of Mrs. Frederick Chase Dodd, who was the second Black social worker employed by the City of Dallas. Mrs. Halaria Hagan Morgan was the first Black lady who served as a social worker. They were nice to her. She had a desk out in the hall in the City Hall. And that was considered quite an advancement. Mrs. Morgan was doing that work to help those who needed welfare assistance.

That went on and Dallas began to grow. We had great Black men here by that time: Dr. Joseph J. Rhoads, Dr. R. T. Hamilton, Mr. Charles T. Brackins, Mr. W. S. Willis, Mr. E. J. Crawford, Dr. A. H. Dyson, Dr. Bluitt, and many others. I don't want to make any hard feelings, but I can't think of everyone right off. One of our most progressive men was the late Professor J. P. Starks. Then, we had Professor

N. W. Harllee, Mr. B. G. Darrell, and others. They were community leaders, and they got things done.

The men I mentioned were largely businessmen, and they were professionals. Dr. R. T. Hamilton was a doctor. Then there was a lawyer, A. S. Wells. There was an Attorney Griggs here in Dallas. We only had three attorneys in Dallas during the time I was beginning my professional work as a teacher.

I came back home in 1932. I had graduated from Samuel Huston College and got a job the first year. The times were very hard. People did not have work. You could see people lined up two or three blocks to get food. I got a job that first year working as a caseworker. There were about eighteen or twenty of us employed by Mrs. Dodd.

Dr. Frank Jordan was a caseworker, and Sam Hudson, J. K. Miller— I can't think of all of them. We went into the homes and checked the iceboxes and closets, to see if they had any food. If they didn't have any food, we would give them a ticket to go downtown and get six dollars' worth of groceries. The six dollars' worth of groceries would feed a family of two people for about two weeks. Times were hard during those days.

After a year of doing that social work, as we called it—all of us did our social work on foot, we walked. Now, we could ride out to the community. They had streetcars during those days, but after that we would go from house to house, and word would get out—"Here comes the man." We were known as "the man" who would write you up or write you down. It was always more helpful to write them up.

After that time, I got a job teaching out at Carrollton, Texas. That was quite a successful experience because I was to be the principal—I was the only teacher. I think I had about forty-five students, from the beginners through the seventh grade. I taught in this one-teacher school in a building that was brought there from somewhere else. We had a wood stove and a pump out in the yard. We didn't need any electric lights because we left school in time to get home before dark.

I roomed on an adjoining farm with a lady by the name of Mrs. Henrietta Bush. She was a member of the Turner family over at White Rock. They were all related. It was quite a nice experience. We had a big fireplace to keep warm by, but I didn't have any fire in my room. I would go in there early and go to bed. I stayed there one year.

I came into Dallas to work at Lincoln Manor School. It is now H. S. Thompson School. Mr. J. B. Ritchie saw me down at the Board of Education, and I was waiting to see the man to ask for a job. Mr. Ritchie said, "Tommy, what do you want down here?" I said, "Mr. Ritchie, I want a job." He said, "Go on home, I'll get you a job." So, I got up and went on home, as he told me. He called Mr. C. F. Carr. In those days Mr. Carr was the Black spokesman for folks getting jobs in the schools. In two or three days, Mr. Carr passed my house and said, "Well, you got your job. Just be quiet, and you'll get a letter in a few days."

Of course, I did get a letter, and I started teaching school with Mr. Ritchie. I worked there a year and a half, and then I was transferred over to Booker T. at my request. I wanted to do high school work. That must have been about 1934. I worked at Booker T. until 1939. In 1939, they had completed the Lincoln High School out here on Oakland, and I was assigned to work there under the leadership of Mr. T. D. Marshall. We opened that school in January 1939.

We went in for the faculty meeting the morning we opened. While we were in faculty meeting, the sheriff came out there and locked the door—locked us up in the school because they [Whites in the neighborhood] had filed an injunction on our having the school. And we were in there looking out, and the children were all around the building looking in. So, they got into action on the telephone, and by twelve o'clock, another policeman came out and unlocked the building, and then we started having school.

We had the bombings in South Dallas at that time. They bombed up Myrtle Street, as far as Eugene Street. I beg your pardon, as far as Romine Street. People were afraid. To my knowledge there was no bombing at school. There were threats of bombings. We weren't molested going and coming from school. We were never attacked or anything like that. This was being done by immature [White] men and women. They wanted to take the school since they were living in the neighborhood. So, they were down to business. Since they couldn't move the school, the Whites moved out. That's how we began to settle that neighborhood.

Of course, I was there for several years. I went to Europe again for World War II in 1942 and stayed away three years. They announced I wouldn't hardly get back because I was overseas fighting. But to my pleasure and their surprise, I walked in one day and said, "I want my job back." And I got it.

I worked for Mr. Marshall for sixteen years, without ever missing a day or being tardy. Of course, my students were never tardy coming to my class. They had a hard time if they missed a day because they had to bring their mother or bring me a note. In those days we had school.

I became a principal in 1955, the same year that Mr. Marshall retired. I was principal for one year at the N. W. Harllee School in Oak Cliff. Then, at that time, they [Dallas Independent School District] were negotiating about what they were going to do at Forest Avenue High School. They voted that it was going to be turned over to Negroes in South Dallas, and they changed the name from Forest Avenue High School to James Madison High School. At an opportune time, at the close of the school year, it was announced that I was to be the acting principal. I wasn't elected principal that year—I was acting principal.

We went on out and started having school. There was considerable talk and some controversial experience there. The Whites did not want to give up the old Forest Avenue High School. But I went on and started having school.

Every day, every morning, there would be announcements over the radio. TV wasn't very [prominent] in those days. But they announced that Principal Tolbert was going to have school, and everybody should come on to school. They [White people] would stand across the street to see what was going to happen. I don't think I had sense enough to get scared. I was having school. I had a fine staff of people on the faculty, courageous people who never thought about their lives. They just thought about opening the James Madison High School, which they did.

That first year, it was pretty unpredictable as to what would happen. But no one was ever hurt, no one was ever hurt. I stayed at the Madison High School for four years, and then I was transferred over to the L. G. Pinkston High School, which they built and named after Dr. L. G. Pinkston.

If I may go back just a little bit, the Madison High School began to boom as an educational institution. We projected our educational concepts through a book that I wrote called *The James Madison High School Teacher's Handbook*. It became quite a popular production. It announced a five-year educational plan at the James Madison High School. The Assistant Superintendent of Schools said that he had never heard of a school having a five-year plan. That was Dr. Frank Williams. But at the end of the five years, he came back and said, "Well, you did it. This has been a very wonderful experience. You have made it, and you are to be commended."

That was quite an experience, as far as student performance was concerned. I went to Mrs. Charlesetta Jones's house and asked her for a gift to the school. She said, "Well, what do you want?" I said, "I want an organ to place in the auditorium of James Madison High School in your mother's honor." She said, "How much is it going to cost?" I said, "About $6,000." She said, "Well, go on and pick out what you want." I went to a big-name firm downtown and picked out this organ which is still in the James Madison High School.

That was quite an interesting occasion, and we had beautiful commencement exercises and fine musical programs. It was referred to as the "silk stocking" Black school of Dallas. Blacks were getting Forest Avenue; they were getting South Boulevard; they were getting all the streets nearby. Whites were leaving. The street I tried to recall a minute ago was Park Row. There was never any trouble getting the neighborhood. They [White residents] just moved. And we had some very representative students. Some fine young people, who were proud of James Madison. They dressed well and [presented themselves] well. We got along very nicely.

Then they built this school in West Dallas, the L. G. Pinkston High School. It was a very beautiful school, a very large school. We had no confusion there, as we had with James Madison. I enjoyed the challenge of opening another high school. Of course, I was privileged to pick many of my faculty members. I picked some very choice people I thought could hold up to the job, and they did. It went well. We got along all right. I was very happy with the way things looked.

Mrs. Pinkston came out one day to see the school that was named in her husband's honor. I said, "Mrs. Pinkston, we have not completed this school." And she said, "I know, you want an organ, don't you?" I said, "Yes, ma'am." She said, "I know. Go down and get what you want."

So, when I went down to this music store (Ha!), the man said, "Now, Mr. Tolbert, how many organs are you going to buy?" I said, "I think this is the last one because I am about to run out of buildings." So, we had this wonderful organ in the L. G. Pinkston High School. At that time, I don't think there was an organ in West Dallas. It made history. People came from all different parts of West Dallas to see and hear the organ.

The people in West Dallas had been, and still are to a certain extent, victims of malicious, ugly reports. We had less trouble opening the L. G. Pinkston High School than [we] did the James Madison High School. We received better cooperation. There was a feeling of appreciation for the school being in West Dallas. Now, there was the crowd that didn't go to school—that carried on like the crowd in South Dallas. But they did not bother us. I was never insulted by anyone in West Dallas during the six or seven years I was there.

Then, we carried on. They added new buildings and additions to the school. We received very good grants for equipment: televisions, and all that type of thing. So, it became an institution that was very much needed in that area. The people in West Dallas had been denied the opportunity for making money for nice homes. Not many people in West Dallas had gone to college, and they appreciated those who had gone, who came out there to serve. We had beautiful programs. Mr. Roy Hicks was the teacher of music, and he always had a very fine organ program. We had school talent shows, an awards night, of course—we had an awards night at Pinkston—people were lined up all the way back to Singleton Avenue in cars.

The streets were paved, we had lights, we had air conditioning, and many special service rooms. All in all, it turned out to be a very encouraging experience. This was about 1965. I stayed there about five years, and I began to get tired. As a matter of fact, I did get tired. I decided to retire. I had worked forty years. I had grown weary, so I decided I would quit. I retired in 1970.

People in Dallas think they are enjoying the golden years now. In my thinking, we enjoyed the golden years when I was in high school and college, and when I began my professional career as a teacher.

There weren't as many opportunities, and there weren't as many open doors for job advancement as we have now. But we had men and women in this town who, during those days, went to the front to see that young men and women got jobs and would quietly be placed in positions of respect. We had Black men in the community who went to the front—there was no need to go to the government, because the government wasn't going to do anything. There was no need to go to the city council because I don't think we had one. We had a commissioners' form of government for Dallas. But these men would go down in committees, and that's how we got our streets paved, how we got our electric lights, how we began to put in bathrooms. I remember there weren't over six families that had bathrooms, very prominent people.

Then, we had men who became nationally known for their endeavors in civic affairs, fraternal affairs, educational affairs, and business affairs. For instance, we organized in Dallas in those days one of the first Negro Chambers of Commerce. Dr. R. T. Hamilton and others were very active. A man came here by the name of A. Maceo Smith, who was very active in the affairs of the Dallas Chamber of Commerce. Then, we had men who opened and represented business. For instance, you had the late Professor J P. Starks, who in addition to being principal of what was then known as No. 4 School (later named J. P. Starks School) ... There is a new building out in Oak Cliff now named the J. P. Starks School. Starks was a businessman.

He was a very progressive man, and under his sponsorship and leadership, his neighbor, Will Ewing, was projected and moved into a position of having a Black funeral home. At that time, Negroes were being buried by a White funeral home downtown. So, they opened this funeral home there on Elm and Pearl Street. I remember very well when the first funeral home and the first Black undertaker took charge. Then, they began to open other funeral homes. Mr. E. Crawford opened the Crawford Building as an undertaking place. And, of course, there was Wren Funeral Home and others.

Professor Starks was interested in another outlet that Negroes needed. That was a newspaper. So, they organized the company that sponsored the *Dallas Express*. And the first man who was editor of the *Dallas Express* was the late Dr. W. E. King. Dr. King started the *Dallas Express*, and it was published once a week. He passed on, and the man who succeeded him as editor was Professor John W. Rice, editor for a number of years.

The Brotherhood Eyes [an independent newspaper] existed, to everybody's awareness. It was an eye. It saw everything that was going on. It reported a lot of things people did not want known was going on. It reported it anyway. This man sold this paper, and people were sometimes afraid to go and get *The Eye*, because *The Eye* may have gotten them. But they had *The Brotherhood Eyes*, and then they had another gazette here, the name I don't recall.

The man [who published *The Brotherhood Eyes*] came here, I think, from Denison, Texas.

Then the national newspapers began coming into Dallas. Then, we had newsstands, barber shops, and drugstores. You could always pick up the Black papers at the drugstore on the corner of Hall Street and Thomas Avenue and other places, such as the Pythian Temple.

The National Pythians of Texas built their headquarters here, which is still standing down on the corner of Good and Elm Street. It is the Union Banker's Building now. It was a fine building in that day downtown on Elm Street. It was built by a Black architect by the name of W. Sidney Pittman. W. Sidney Pittman was married to Portia Washington Pittman, who was the daughter of the late Dr. Booker T. Washington. They lived here in Dallas for a number of years.

[It was] The Grand Lodge of the Knights of Pythias, who would meet here and bring people from all over the state and throughout the nation. Everybody would look forward, when I was a boy, to those meetings. They would have the great public meeting and a national orator. The greatest orator of that day was a Black man by the name of Roscoe Complin Simmons. Mr. Simmons's speech would be heralded and written up and talked about throughout the city and throughout the state. Those were the days.

We had Negro ministers and businessmen who began to have stores in the different neighborhoods. The Negro businessman always had a pretty keen competitor, because there was always the Italian merchant. I don't mean any harm by saying it, but they were referred to as the "Dago" stores. And, in every well-situated neighborhood you would find an Italian store—the Dago store. They were pretty alert in business. They would have their store in the front, and they always lived in the back. You could buy on credit, you could buy all day and all night, every day in the week. They would write you down. You would pick up your bread, and he would jot it down. Then you would come back on Saturday and pay on your bill.

There were other businesses. There were the Beals who had a store. They had a wood business there, too. They were very prosperous people.

There were some others that I can't recall right now. Well, there was a man by the name of Mr. Page. Mr. Page lived down on Allen Street right off of Thomas Street. He had a daughter named Lucille, who became a teacher here in Dallas. I think she is a Mrs. Williams now living in California. Mr. Page was an iceman. I am sure there were others. My grandfather had this transfer company. There was another Negro firm located further downtown, called the Big Four Transfer Company, owned by a Mr. Salad. The Salad family was very much alert and had a fine business there.

Then Negroes were builders. You had some Negroes who were contractors. Professor A. S. Penn's father was a contractor. He was a well-known contractor, and he did good work. There were painters and paper hangers. Some had learned as apprentices how to do plumbing work. Dallas began to unfold. Blacks began to buy homes and paint their houses and get bathrooms. I recall we had two Negroes living in brick houses. There was a Dr. Bluitt, who had a brick house up on the corner of Pearl and Allen Streets. There was a Dr. Bryant, who had a brick house down on Bryan Street. If I am not mistaken, there was another brick house, but I don't remember exactly who owned it. Then there were some palatial homes. Attorney and Mrs. A. S. Wells had a big, two-story house on Bryan Street. There was a Negro who had a grocery store and had accumulated considerable wealth, the Rowen family. They occupied a very nice place there on the corner of Boll and Juliette Streets. They owned that property there. Mrs. Robert A. Prince is one of the descendants. They held it there until the Expressway development came through and bought their property. There were other Negroes who were doing well.

They were going off to the schools in the North. Madame Pratt went to the Conservatory of Music to study there. Then there were others who went to Fisk.[46] Madame Pratt was the daughter

---

46. Fisk University, a private, historically Black school, was founded by the American Missionary Association in 1866 in Nashville, Tennessee, as the Fisk Freed Colored School. In 1930, it was the first African American educational institution to be accredited by the Southern Association of Colleges and Schools. Its forty-acre campus is listed on the National Register of Historic Places.—Eds.

of Professor Charles Rice, for whom Charles Rice School was named. She was the sister to Professor John W. Rice and Reverend Robert Rice. That was the Rice family. Incidentally, her parents were among the first graduates of Atlanta University. Professor Rice and Mrs. Sally (as she was called) were among the early graduates of Atlanta University in Atlanta, Georgia.[47]

I don't know if I have anything else to add. Except, we had a great society in Dallas in those days. I can recall, later on, the first group of Negroes that I remember being demonstrated in *Life Magazine*. They were on three or four pages, under the title of "Life Goes to a Party." They showed the picture of these beautiful young Black girls making their debut to Dallas society. I was one of the escorts at that time. It was a very beautiful occasion and was at the Pythian Temple Ballroom. They came that night in their high hats and beautiful gowns, in limousines and cars that they had rented. It made social history for Dallas. After that, Dallas began to unfold as quite a social center.

We had Red Riders here. There is one man that I think ought to be remembered as one of the early advocates of social justice, Mr. Charles R. Graggs, who was a member of New Hope Baptist Church. He had a daughter who was buried not too long ago, Mrs. Ouida Graggs Chambers. Mr. Graggs was a very courageous man. We had another man who was courageous that they threw—took him up bodily and threw him—out of the courthouse on that hard sidewalk—a man by the name of Professor G. F. Porter, who responded to being asked to come and serve on a jury. When he went down to report to serve on the jury, they said, "No, we didn't send for you." He said, "Oh, yes you did. I am supposed to serve on this jury." They said, "Oh, no, you are not going to serve here."

---

47. Atlanta University was founded in 1865 by two formerly enslaved men, James Tate and Grandison Daniels. In 1988, it merged with Clark College, which was founded in 1869, to become Clark Atlanta University, a historically Black doctoral research university (https://www.cau.edu).—Eds.

And, of course, they had quite an argument, and they picked him up and threw him physically out of the courthouse. When I got down there that morning, he was sitting in the back of the cloakroom, and his hands were bruised. He had soiled his clothes. But that was one of the early steps toward this thing of civil rights coming to the front.

From then on, we began to talk about civil rights. We had the NAACP to come to the front. Then the NAACP took an active part in encouraging the Black vote. Go out and vote, and we did. It had to do with better job opportunities. The NAACP and Urban League worked together for better housing for people. That's how we began to get these big housing projects throughout the city.

[When I was coming up] Dallas was an interesting town. Oak Cliff was another town, and we had many representative Black people living in Oak Cliff. There were professional people who had distinguished families: the Penn families, the Moores, the Boswells. These people I am calling still have descendants here in Dallas. There was the Jack Clark [family] and many others. Pardon me if I don't call all the families.

Then, Blacks began to move up into North Dallas. The first neighborhood in North Dallas I can recall was up near the end of McKinney Avenue, which came to be known as Frogtown. Some of our prominent professional people lived in Frogtown.

As the Mexicans began to come in and move into that area, it was referred to as Little Mexico. They gradually began to push Blacks out, and Blacks began to live on Ross Avenue. My grandmother lived on Ross Avenue in one of the big old mansions there that Whites had given up. She took charge of it and lived there many years. And up Ross Avenue, as far as Ervay Street, we had Negroes during that day. Then back of Sacred Heart Cathedral, which is now called [Our] Lady of Guadalupe, Blacks lived back there on those streets: Cochran, Flora, etc. Some of them held on to that property. I know a lady who sold some property there a few years ago and became a millionaire. They had some very distinguished people living in that area, including Attorney and Mrs. Mason, Attorney and Mrs. Chase Dodd, Mr. and Mrs. Beau Thomas. Mr. Beau Thomas had a cab line. In those days your cabs were Cadillacs. It was called a service car, and they would drive you back and forth to town for two or three dollars. Most of his customers were Black. You would drive around and look very distinguished in the taxicab. They would drive you in funerals and weddings and that kind of thing.

Then Blacks began to move on up further. One of the early families that I knew up in North Dallas was the Harding family. Miss Allene Harding, Harold Harding—they lived one block off Ross Avenue in the Roseland/McCoy area. They had a lovely home there. There was the Chambers family up there. There was a Reverend "Blindman" Burke. He used to visit churches and give ladies beautiful bouquets of flowers. It was quite a neighborhood. The community was gradually moving on over toward Haskell Avenue. Then there were these new churches in our area, but they were a long time developing. Then Blacks began to move up Central Track.

All in all, it has been an interesting experience for me. I have lived here all my life. I was born in Dallas. I spend much of my time now in my library, which people say is one of the finest in Dallas. I have collected the writings of many Black people who have inspired Blacks in Dallas, those who have visited my home, and those who live in different parts of these United States.

We have nice streets, we have cars, we have beautiful churches, we have wonderful ministers and church congregations. I do think that we have reached a very high level of accomplishment, even though there is still much to be done. I am glad we have done so well. And when we get there to the other land, let us be able to say, "we did our best."

Alvernon King Tripp

Interviewed by Samuel Wicks

1988

The first quarter of the twentieth century's Dallas history and the first twenty years in the life of Alvernon King Tripp were nearly parallel occurrences. Born January 3, 1898, two years before the turn of the century, Alvernon King was a young, astute witness to the events that took place over the first quarter of the twentieth century in Dallas.

What was it like as a Black growing up in Dallas during that period? This is how the remarkably active, ninety-one-year-old Alvernon King Tripp responded to that question for Black Dallas Remembered: "I can think of some 'bad' things, but we didn't think they were 'bad' at the time."

Some of the bad things Mrs. Tripp spoke of were having to walk three to five miles daily to the nearest school and being segregated or denied access to public facilities because of her race. She also recalls the horrible incident of the lynching of two Blacks in downtown Dallas.

Alvernon was born in Joppy, Texas south of Dallas, the first of four children of Ben and Mary King. Her father later became successful in wood and dairy business ventures. The Kings moved to Spence and Cooper Streets in 1900. A few years later, Alvernon entered Colored School No. 4, Frederick Douglass, on The Prairie, and had to walk three miles to school. When she entered Colored High School in 1911, she was forced to walk five miles to North Dallas.

Mrs. Tripp recalls almost no legal challenges to or protests against the racial evils of that period. There were some individual heroics, she recalls. The National Association for the Advancement of Colored People was founded in New York City in 1909, by sixty Black and White citizens. Ten years later, ads in the *Dallas Express* in 1919 announced efforts to form a local chapter of the NAACP in meetings held at the New Hope Baptist Church.

Mrs. Tripp has fond memories of her pastor at New Hope, the Reverend A. S. Jackson: "He was just as smart as Dr. G. W. Truett, the pastor of First Baptist Church," she says with proud reflection.

A streetcar scene involving (starring) Rev. Jackson is embedded in Mrs. Tripp's mind, as a stark reminder of the segregated days of her youth. The fair-skinned Rev. Jackson was standing in the rear of the car chatting with a seated group of young ladies, including Alvernon Tripp. The trolley conductor (White, of course), thinking Rev. Jackson was White, stalked to the back and insisted that Rev. Jackson move to the "White" side of the movable racial signs.[48] Rev. Jackson bravely resisted the conductor's demands. He stood there and kept talking to the girls.

Mrs. Tripp says race signs were indeed the symbolic signs of the time—rigid racial segregation.

City Park, located on Gano Street near Colored School No. 4, was an attraction to Alvernon and many of her schoolmates. A city ordinance, however, forbade them from entering the park because of their race. "I was crazy about the band stand. I would often stand across the street and listen," she reminisces. "And we would sometimes go to the park and play." Only threats of whippings by her dad, not the racist ordinance, curtailed her visits to City Park.

One of the saddest chapters in the annals of Dallas history occurred on March 3, 1910. A Black man was lynched downtown, having been accused of raping a White child. Mrs. Tripp said this outrageous act took place at midnight, [carried out] by a group of Klan-like Whites. She recalls the Black being forcefully taken from the "Red Courthouse" downtown [he was thrown from a second-floor

---

48. The "racial signs" or "race signs" were printed cardboard signs placed in the aisle on a seatback. One side was printed with "White" and the other side with "Colored." The signs were moved at the discretion of the conductor, depending on how many "Whites" got on the car. The more "Whites," the further back the signs were placed, often limiting the number of African Americans who were permitted to ride on that car.—Eds.

window] and dragged to Main and Akard. There the White mob hanged him from an arch that had been constructed for a huge Elks Convention being held in Dallas.[49] "After the Elks left town, city officials ordered the arch torn down," said Mrs. Tripp.

Some of the more pleasant events experienced by the youthful Alvernon King included attending the State Fair [of Texas] on Negro Day and watching some renowned stage acts performed at downtown Black theatres.

That one day at the State Fair was eagerly anticipated, she said. Among the national notables making appearances at the Fair were Booker T. Washington and Dr. George Washington Carver. It was during that period that Prairie View College began to have exhibits at the State Fair, recalls Mrs. Tripp.

Making annual appearances at "Fat Jack's Theatre" on Elm Street was the famed vaudeville troupe "The Lafayette Players." She also recalls seeing Ethel Waters perform at the Star Theatre on Elm Street near Central Avenue.

House parties were the big social events in Black Dallas during that period. Mrs. Tripp remembers a South Dallas neighbor who hosted some of the more lavish parties in the city. That neighbor was Attorney Joseph Wiley, who had moved to Dallas from Boston, Massachusetts, in the early 1900s. According to Mrs. Tripp, Attorney Wiley amassed a lot of property and successfully encouraged Dallas Black citizens to buy homes. Attorney Wiley frequently hosted dance parties at his home at Lenway Street and Colonial Avenue. His sister played waltz tunes on the piano. The guests would dance late into the night.

Reflecting on a racist city ordinance of that period, Mrs. Tripp tells of the time Attorney Wiley, whose home faced Colonial Avenue, was forced to move the house around the corner so it would face Lenway Street. The reason: "The city forbade Blacks and Whites from living on the same block ... that was the law," she recalls with a laugh.

---

49. See Footnote 29 for recent commemorations of the life of Allen Brooks, the man referred to in this horrifying memory.—Eds.

White neighbors made several unsuccessful attempts to force Mrs. Tripp's father to move cattle from the family-owned dairy at Spence and Cooper Streets. Ben King went to court several times to resolve the problem.

After high school, in 1915 it was off to Prairie View College for Alvernon King. Following graduation and a one-year teaching stint in Gilmer, she returned to Dallas, where she taught at Booker T. Washington and an elementary school.

Alvernon King was secretly married to Charles Evans. Married women could not teach in Dallas at that time. In 1926, the young couple decided to live in the far west and moved to Salt Lake City, Utah. She returned to her native Dallas in 1970.

At age ninety-one, Alvernon King Tripp harbors no grand illusions about witnessing a second turn of a century in the year 2000. "I live my life day by day, and if it's the Master's will, then I'll be around," says the remarkable lady who remains an alert and astute witness to the events of the twentieth century.

In Closing

In understanding the history of African Americans here in Dallas, as in all segments and sectors of American society, one must acknowledge and accept the fact that their moment-by-moment experiences continue to include a struggle against racism and denied opportunity. A deep and sensitive understanding of this fact raises one to a level at which he or she can only marvel at the undiminished pursuit by African Americans for dignity and justice.

—Dr. Mamie McKnight, Volume II, p. 55

Index

Note: individuals are listed alphabetically by surname, not necessarily by family.—Eds.